4450
80E

RETAIN PER CDO

D0710758

EERL Withdrawn
Surplus/Duplicate

COLLECTED ECONOMIC ESSAYS

Volume 5

FURTHER ESSAYS ON ECONOMIC THEORY

COLLECTED ECONOMIC ESSAYS
by Nicholas Kaldor

FURTHER ESSAYS ON ECONOMIC THEORY

NICHOLAS KALDOR

HOLMES & MEIER PUBLISHERS, INC.
New York

HB
171
K29
1978

RASMUSON LIBRARY
UNIVERSITY OF ALASKA-FAIRBANKS

First published in the United States of America 1978 by
HOLMES & MEIER PUBLISHERS, INC.
30 Irving Place, New York, N.Y. 10003

Copyright © 1978 by Nicholas Kaldor

ALL RIGHTS RESERVED

Library of Congress Cataloging in Publication Data
Kaldor, Nicholas, 1908–
    Further essays on economic theory.
    (His Collected economic essays; v. 5)
    Includes index.
    1. Economics—Addresses, essays, lectures.
I. Title. II. Series.
HB171.K29 1978   330'.08   78-15676
ISBN 0-8419-0294-1

Printed in Great Britain

CONTENTS

INTRODUCTION

The present volume contains a collection of papers in the field of macro-economic growth and distribution theory subsequent to those included in the first two volumes of my Collected Essays published in 1960.[1] The purpose of this Introduction is mainly to explain how these papers came to be written and how, in the course of writing them, my ideas underwent continual change so that each new formulation produced the need for a further reformulation.

The period following the Second World War was in some ways a period of "counter-reformation" of economics. Coming after the stirring 1930s, when the whole traditional theory came under attack (partly on account of the theories of imperfect or mono-polistic competition and partly as a result of Keynesian macro-economics) the "mainstream" effort of the post-war era was to resuscitate traditional theory and to isolate (if not eliminate) the effects of the intellectual revolution of the thirties. The new cognition concerning the existence of "imperfect" markets and oligopolies proved particularly difficult to digest within the traditional framework: the result of the difficulty was that these doctrines were gradually ignored and forgotten and the later formulations of the theory of general economic equilibrium assumed away their existence. Equally Keynes' main proposition that the general level of production in an economy is (normally) demand-constrained and not resource-constrained was side-tracked by assuming the existence of a government or a monetary authority which secures continuous full employment through the successful use of appropriate policy instruments and thereby validates the traditional "laws" of allocation economics.

I found this "synthesis" of Keynesian macro-economics with Walrasian (or Marshallian) micro-economics intellectually barren

---

[1] *Essays on Value and Distribution* and *Essays on Economic Stability and Growth.*

and irrelevant. I felt instinctively and intuitively that the validity of the main propositions of traditional value theory are confined within the narrowly defined framework of static economics with perfect markets, perfect competition, perfect foresight, the universal rule of constant returns to scale, and so on, and hence that it is hopeless to build on them or to marry them with the tools of macro-economics which operate with empirically measurable concepts and aim at the formulation of testable hypotheses—not in an imaginary world, but in the world actually observed.

However, as I gradually learnt, I could get away from the traditional way of looking at things only in a succession of steps. These entailed finding the crucial changes in assumptions needed to escape from the rigidity of the traditional models and introduce a better insight of how the world really works; and advances came to me sporadically, in the course of writing and lecturing on the same broad subject through several decades.

In retrospect, two major changes in my viewpoint stand out. The first and most important was the perception of the fact that an economy is not "resource-constrained" merely because it is at "full employment". The second was that theoretical analysis, to be fruitful, must be closely related to, and firmly based on, empirically derived "laws" or regularities. It was as a result of the recognition of these two factors that I became aware that economic growth cannot be properly analysed until one takes account of the crucial differences, in terms of behaviourial assumptions, between the primary, secondary and tertiary sectors of the economy.

The first fruit of the search for an integrated macro-theory was the "Keynesian" theory of distribution formulated in a paper written in 1955 and reproduced at the end of the first volume of my Essays.[1]

This put forward a macro-economic theory of the share of profits in the value of output which was distinct both from the classical notion of profits being the surplus remaining after remunerating labour at subsistence wages, and from the neoclassical notion of its being the payment for the use of capital as a "factor of production", determined by its specific contribution to

[1] "Alternative Theories of Distribution", in *Essays on Value and Distribution*, pp. 228–36.

output as measured by marginal productivity. Instead it showed profits as being generated by entrepreneurial expenditures on investment, the specific function of profits being the provision of the savings (at least the great bulk of the savings) for the finance of investment. As both Ricardo and Marx emphasised, it is in the very nature of profits (in contrast to other types of income, whether rent or wages) that they should largely be devoted by its recipients to accumulation, and not to consumption.[1]

These ideas (in combination with others described below) were developed more systematically (with the mathematical help of D. G. Champernowne) in the framework of a fully fledged growth model which was published in the December 1957 issue of the *Economic Journal* and reproduced in the second volume of my Essays.[2]

The purpose of the model was to show how three basic relations (a savings function, an investment function and a technical progress function) can determine the conditions of "a steady state" equilibrium of constant growth. Apart from an investment function based on adaptive expectations concerning future sales and profit rates, and of the "classical" type savings function already described, the main innovation of the model was the "technical progress function" which made *realised* technical progress dependent on the rate of increase of capital per worker. In a world in which technology is embodied in capital equipment and where both the improvement of knowledge and the production of new capital goods are continuous, it is impossible to isolate the productivity growth which is due to capital accumulation *as such* from the productivity growth which is due to improvements in technical knowledge. There is no such thing as a "set of

---

[1] I called this theory the "Keynesian" theory of distribution, largely on account of a famous footnote on the "widow's cruse" in Vol. I of the *Treatise on Money* (1930); though I found no traces of it in the *General Theory* (published 1936). I must have been influenced however (without knowing it at the time) by Keynes' wartime pamphlet, *How to Pay for the War*, which gives a far more explicit account of the role of profits in the provision of savings.

[2] "A Model of Economic Growth", *Essays on Economic Stability and Growth* (1960), pp. 259–300. Both this paper and the earlier one on distribution theory owed a great deal to the pioneering work of Sir Roy Harrod (*An Essay in Dynamic Economics*, 1948, which was an expansion of ideas first put forward in "Essay on Dynamic Theory", *Economic Journal*, April 1939 pp. 14–33) and to numerous discussions in Cambridge with Joan Robinson in the early 1950s.

blueprints" which reflect a "given state of knowledge"—the knowledge required for the making of, say, the Concorde is only evolved in the process of designing or developing the aeroplane; the costs of obtaining the necessary new knowledge is causally indistinguishable from the other elements of investment. The recognition that the effects of improvement in "knowledge" cannot be isolated means that one cannot distinguish movements along a "production function" from "shifts" in that function, and that the whole notion of a given "production function", whether of a macro-economic kind (the "surrogate production function" of Samuelson) or of the micro-kind with a separate function applying to each firm or industry, falls to the ground; and with it all theories which "explain" the prices of the factors of production or of distributive shares on the basis of the "marginal productivity" principle.

This model was subject to a number of important limitations, and the subsequent papers reproduced in this volume can be best characterised as attempts to overcome these limitations.

The first of these, "Capital Accumulation and Economic Growth", originally given as a lecture to a conference of economists in Corfu in 1958, had as its main purpose to show how a "neo-Keynesian" growth model relates to the "classical" models of Ricardo and Marx (which, as I show, are essentially the same as the famous mathematical model of von Neumann) on the one hand, and to the neo-classical models on the other hand. It served two other purposes as well—one of which was to develop at much greater length[1] my criticism of the "production function" approach and the impossibility of assigning specific "marginal productivities" to the "factors of production" (whether these are broadly or narrowly defined) once we leave a world endowed with a given number of (linear) production processes (unchanged through time) and allow for technical progress as a continuous process in time. (I could equally have said, "once one allows for non-linearities, and in particular for increasing returns to scale", which has exactly the same destructive effect on neo-classical

---

[1] See pp. 31–58 below.

growth models—or for that matter on the neo-classical theories of
general equilibrium—as the introduction of technical progress.)[1, 2]

The other purpose was to put forward a new specification for
the "investment function" which is less open to criticism on
account of the possibility of instability arising out of the assumption that the amount of investment per unit of output capacity
is likely to be larger the higher the rate of return (so that a rise in
profit, by leading to a rise in investment, leads to a further rise in
profits, and so on). The investment function of the 1957 model
assumed in effect (in the manner of Harrod) that investment
decisions are mainly governed by the rate of growth of output,
but that the higher the expected rate of profit, the more compensation there is for the risks assumed in making an investment, and
the more worthwhile it is for the entrepreneurs to adopt a more
labour-saving technique, requiring a higher amount of investment
per unit of output capacity.[3]

In fact, the assumptions of the 1957 model were sufficient to
produce a stable solution to the equations; these assumptions,
however, were themselves highly restrictive in that the stability of
the model required the supposition that the responsiveness of
investment to changes in the rate of profit was below a certain
critical level[4] which in turn was shown to depend on the differ-

---

[1] In "Increasing Returns and Technical Progress. A Comment on Professor Hicks'
Article" (*Oxford Economic Papers* February 1961, p.1.), which is not reproduced in this
collection, I have argued, that since there is no way in which the one can be empirically distinguished from the other "it is meaningless to say that the phenomena oh
served are to be explained by 'returns to scale' *rather than* by technical progress, or the
other way round" (p. 3).
[2] The same strictures equally apply to the von Neumann model which is of course
wholly dependent on the assumption of a *given* number of known *linear* processes of
production, which remain unchanged over time, thus excluding both increasing returns and technical progress.
[3] This is in apparent contradiction to the neo-classical view according to which
there is an inverse relationship between the chosen capital/output ratio and the rate of
interest. However the neo-classical view (*inter alia*) abstracts from risks and uncertainty;
whereas in reality the effect of uncertainty is to cause economies in capital investment
by shortening the period of time during which the investment is to be recouped out of
profits. See also p. xiv below.
[4] Cf. the inequality shown in *op. cit.* vol. 2, p. 279. This condition was ignored by a
number of critics (cf. K. Kubota, "A Re-examination of the Existence and Stability
Propositions in Kaldor's Growth Models", *Review of Economic Studies*, July 1968, pp.
353–9, and McCallum, B. T., "The Instability of Kaldorian Models", *Oxford
Economic Papers*, March 1969, pp. 56–65) and one of the critics admitted this explicitly
in a comment on my Note (see my note, "Some Fallacies in the Interpretation of
Kaldor", *Review of Economic Studies*, January, 1970, pp. 1–8, and K. Kubota, "A Comment on Kaldor's Note", *ibid.* p. 9). But the precise implications of the assumptions

ences in savings propensities between wages and profit incomes respectively.

The change in assumptions in my Corfu (1958) model take more explicitly into account what was implicit in the 1957 model, i.e., that the scale of operation of the typical firm grows more or less *pari passu* with the growth of the economy[1] and such firms expand their output capacity so as to maintain it in a more or less constant relation to their sales. In this case it is legitimate to assume that increasing risks are not associated with an expansion of capacity as such. There are no greater risks involved in producing a larger output out of a correspondingly larger capacity. On the contrary, a firm with a large turnover and capital is considered less risky than a small one. But additional risk is involved in the adoption of more mechanised, and hence more labour-saving, methods of production if that requires an increase in investment *per unit* of output capacity. Moreover, while on the broad facts of experience there is a strong trend component in sales (since apart from short term variations the volume of sales of the typical or "representative" firm is constantly growing with the growth in the size of the market) there is no such trend in the share of profit on turnover or in the rate of profit on capital. It is legitimate therefore to assume with Keynes that "the facts of the existing situation enter, in a sense disproportionately, into the formation of long term expectations"[2] as far as future *sales* are concerned (so that current investment decisions are based on the *recent* rate of growth of sales, in accordance with Harrod's principle) but that

---

required for stability were fully cleared up only in D. G. Champernowne's paper, "The Stability of Kaldor's 1957 Model", *Review of Economic Studies*, January 1971, pp. 47–62.

[1] Historically, with the growth of manufacturing industry the number of "firms" tended, if anything, to be reduced and not increased: over the last hundred years or so there was a tendency towards an increased concentration of production in the hands of large corporations—a movement which has appeared to have operated with accelerated force during the last twenty-five years. In contrast to this all neo-classical theories assume, in effect, that the output of the individual firm remains more or less constant irrespective of the growth of the industry; and any increase in output involves a corresponding increase in the number of firms producing it (except in so far as the "optimum size" of the firm changes as a result of a change in technology; in that case however the change would have occurred irrespective of the change in aggregate output or in demand). Under these assumptions there is no room for an "investment function" of the Keynesian type or for the operation of the acceleration principle as a determinant of the rate of investment.

[2] *General Theory*, ch. 12, p. 148.

in regard to the expected margins of profit on turnover, and the expected rates of profit on capital, what is projected into the future is not the currently prevailing rate, but the average of rates which prevailed over a considerable period in the past. In other words, decisions to change the capacity to produce are far more responsive to recent events than are decisions to change the "capital intensity" of investment (i.e., in the investment required per unit of output) since decisions of the latter type reflect profit rates prevailing over a whole range of past periods, of which the current profit rate is only one of a number of components.

In the paper on "Capital Accumulation and Economic Growth" I used the existing output/capacity ratio as a proxy for the *average* profit rates over a whole series of past periods. In a later paper, Champernowne has shown[1] that it would be quite easy to incorporate this assumption in a more explicit form in the framework of the 1957 model by assuming that the component of investment dependent on the rate of profit reflects not the current rate of profit, but the average rates of profit which obtained over a series of past periods. The longer this period is the wider is the range over which the investment function will be consistent with a stable solution.

The next essay reproduced here, "A New Model of Economic Growth", written in collaboration with J. A. Mirrlees, is a considerable advance on the earlier models in that it takes full account of the fact (which was implicit in the earlier models) that technical progress is infused into the economic system through investment, and it thus becomes "embodied" in the plant and machinery created in any given period. The model thus captures the phenomenon of technological obsolescence by assuming that once technology has been "embodied" in plant and machinery, the production flowing from that equipment (for any given amount of labour used in conjunction with it) remains constant over time; its profitability however will diminish owing to the competition of technologically superior equipment installed at subsequent dates. Hence at any given time production is undertaken

---

[1] "The Stability of Kaldor's 1957 Model", *op. cit.*, pp. 55 ff.

with the aid of a whole series of "technologies" because long before any *new* technology completely displaces an old one, it itself becomes "obsolete" in relation to even newer technologies. The fact that such obsolescence is broadly anticipated, leads to the adoption of new criteria of profitability (or "viability") for undertaking investment, generally measured in terms of a "pay-off period" (or cost-recoupment period) though it still remains subject to the expectation of a satisfactory rate of return (calculated on the basis of the anticipated stream of profits over the expected operative lifetime of the newly created equipment). The model thus shows that with a limited number of parameters—i.e. the required pay-off period (measured in years) the rate of physical depreciation (assumed to be of a radio-active character, with a constant fraction of equipment disappearing each year due to accidents, etc.) and the factors determining the "natural" growth rate (i.e. population growth and the productivity growth resulting from technical progress, when the rate of growth of capital and output are the same) together with the savings propensity out of profits (and wages) the equilibrium values of all the important variables can be uniquely determined—i.e. the amount of profits generated by the system and the share of profits in output (which is also the sum of all the quasi-rents earned on equipment of different vintages), the operative lifetime of the equipment, the investment/output ratio and the share of the labour force transferred to new equipment each year. The fact that the numerical solutions to the equations, for realistic values of the parameters, produce sensible results gave some confidence in the basic hypotheses underlying the model for explaining the inter-relationships of an industrial economy such as the United States.[1]

The next paper reprinted in this series, "Marginal Productivity and the Macroeconomic Theories of Distribution" (published in 1966) served a dual purpose. It was partly intended as an attack on the neo-classical methods of reasoning employed by Professors Samuelson and Modigliani in support of their view that it is the

[1] See pp. 72–7 below. Unbeknown to me at the time, virtually the same model had been put forward many years earlier by a German economist, Professor H. J. Rüstow (*Theorie der Vollbeschäftigung in der freien Marktwirtschaft*, Tübingen, 1951; *Akkumulation und Krisen*, a doctoral dissertation in the University of Heidelberg, 1926.)

"marginal product" of capital which determines the share of profits in income, and not some macro-economic factor, such as the relationship of investment to output, given the savings propensities out of profits and wages. But its more important purpose was to clarify the reasons why the savings propensity out of profits must be very considerably greater than the savings propensity out of wages and salaries, or of "household incomes" in general. The distribution formulae originally given in "Alternative Theories of Distribution", published ten years earlier, led to a reformulation by Dr. Pasinetti[1] which involved a rather different interpretation of my theory from the one I had in mind. Dr. Pasinetti showed that if society is divided into two classes, "capitalists" and "workers", and that if the "capitalists" save more of their income than do the workers (presumably because they are richer) and the workers save the same fraction of their income, whether it comes in the form of wages or dividends, then as workers' incomes increase as a result of the accumulation of savings, the system will tend to a long-run equilibrium situation in which the extra consumption out of the workers' dividend-income will precisely offset their savings out of wages, so that the rate of profit will depend only on the rate of growth and the proportion of *profits* saved, s_p, irrespective of the workers' savings propensity, s_w or of anything else (such as the form of the production function). Samuelson and Modigliani (and Meade and Hahn before them[2]) were concerned to show that this result is subject to the inequality (which was the original postulate of my "Keynesian" distribution theory)

$$s_w < \frac{I}{Y} < s_p$$

and they went on to suggest that this inequality may cease to hold when, as a result of the workers getting a sufficiently large share of the ownership of capital and hence of total dividend

[1] "The Rate of Profit and Income Distribution in Relation to the Rate of Economic Growth", *Review of Economic Studies*, vol. 29 (1962) pp. 267–79.
[2] Cf. J. E. Meade, "The Rate of Profit in a Growing Economy", *Economic Journal*, December 1963, together with subsequent Replies, Notes and Rejoinders by J. E. Meade, F. H. Hahn and L. L. Pasinetti in the *Economic Journal*, June 1964, June 1965 and March 1966.

income, the rate of profit rises (presumably because of the consequential fall in the savings ratio) which in turn causes the capital/output ratio to fall (in accordance with a "well-behaved" neoclassical production function) and hence at any given growth rate, I/Y may go on falling until it no longer exceeds s_w.

There are several snags in this argument, the most fundamental being that it does not explain how business enterprises (as a group) can operate at a profit when their capital expenditures are insufficient (or only just sufficient) to offset workers' savings (*i.e.* the leakage between income paid out by entrepreneurs and the expenditures generated by that income). A capitalist system can only function so long as the receipts of entrepreneurs exceed their outlays; in a closed system, and ignoring Government loan expenditure, this will only be the case if entrepreneurial expenditure exceeds workers' savings. Unless one treats the consumption expenditure of entrepreneurs as an exogenous variable, given independently of profits, it is only the "Kaldor-Pasinetti inequality" (i.e. the excess of business investment over non-business savings) which can ensure the existence of profits.[1]

My second main objection to the Samuelson-Modigliani critique is that they treat finance which is externally provided on exactly the same footing as internal finance through ploughed-back profits—a firm is assumed to choose one or the other according to which happens to be the cheaper method of obtaining finance. In a world of uncertainty however the biblical principle "unto every one that hath shall be given" dominates the scene. Finance raised externally—whether in the form of loans or of equity capital—is complementary to, not a substitute for, retained profits; and it can never provide more than a proportion of a firm's financial requirements.[2] Moreover, since the individual enterprise—for reasons first perceived by Marx—must go on expanding so as to keep its share in the market (and to improve on

---

[1] This point received the clearest emphasis in H. J. Rüstow's writings, cf. note p. xiv above. It is also implicit in Keynes' whole analysis in the *Treatise on Money*.

[2] This is the reason why 80–90 per cent of *gross* business investment (including depreciation) is invariably financed out of retained profits in all countries, irrespective of how developed the "capital market" which they possess. The percentages are not as large in terms of *net* investment (after deduction of depreciation) but as Keynes has shown, from the point of view of the theory of income generation it is *gross* investment which alone matters.

it, if possible), it is a necessary attribute of business profit that a large share of it should be retained in the business, irrespective of the wealth or the psychological proclivities of the owners.

The counterpart of an increase in shareholders' assets attained through retentions is the increase in earnings and dividends per share, and the associated rise in share prices, which may be either greater or less than the (net) profit retentions that gave rise to them, depending on a particular firm's "valuation ratio". The benefits which shareholders receive in the form of capital gains represent an accretion of spending power which is *sui generis*—it gives rise to additional consumption, though not in the same manner as an increase in ordinary income.[1] Consumption out of capital or capital gains is an offset to personal savings, and in the Appendix to this paper on the "Neo-Pasinetti Theorem"[2] I attempted to show how the level of share prices in the capital market will tend to generate a "valuation ratio" for shares at which the net savings of individuals equals the proportion of business investment which enterprises decide to finance through the issue of new securities. This leads to results similar to Dr. Pasinetti's, but by a different route, and one which is proof against the kind of criticism raised by Meade, Samuelson and Modigliani.[3]

This paper marked the last of a series of theoretical papers on growth theory which proceeded by way of deductive reasoning from macro-economic axioms of a rather general character. In my subsequent work I followed a different method: I tried to find what kind of regularities can be detected in empirically observed phenomena and then tried to discover what particular testable hypotheses would be capable of explaining the association. I

---

[1] The typical rentier treats capital gains as an accretion of the value of his assets, so that the consumption generated by it tends to be proportional to the consumption/wealth ratio and not to the consumption/income ratio.

[2] Pp. 94–9 below.

[3] Adrian Wood, *A Theory of Profits* (Cambridge University Press, 1975) obtains the same formulae for the profit ratio by a somewhat different route. He takes the "valuation ratio" as exogenously given (and does not consider consumption out of capital gains or its effects on share prices) but shows that three financial ratios—the retention ratio, the proportion of investment which can be financed externally, and the desired proportion of financial assets to total capital employed—suffice to determine the margin of profit required to finance any particular growth rate; and also shows that, on these assumptions, there will be an optimal profit margin which maximises the (financially attainable) long-run growth rate of the firm.

became aware of this more pragmatic approach during the war when it was used by scientists for the purpose of "operational research". It is an approach which in one sense is more modest in scope (in not searching for explanations that derive from a comprehensive model of the system) and also more ambitious in that it directly aims at discovering solutions (or remedies) for real problems.

In the mid 1960s, when I was working in the Treasury it became obvious to me that the large differences in the economic growth rates of different countries (which had been known for some years) could not be explained by temporary factors, such as the recovery from war-time devastations or dislocations, since the group of fast-growing economies (such as Japan and Germany) continued in their fast growth long after they surpassed, not only their own pre-war productivity levels, but the prevailing productivity levels of the relatively slow-growing countries with whom they were supposed to be catching up. In the search for an explanation of "why growth rates differ" I came across an extraordinarily close correlation between the rate of growth of manufacturing output and the rate of growth of the GDP—relationship of a kind which suggested that the rate of economic growth of a country will depend on how much faster its manufacturing output grows than the rest of the economy. This, combined with the strong correlation between the rate of productivity growth in the economy as a whole and the change in the structure of employment between manufacturing and non-manufacturing (combined with the absence of any correlation between the growth rate and the *overall* growth of employment and of capital) strongly suggested that the key to an explanation of slow and fast growth rates must be sought in demand factors and in particular in the growth of demand for the products of the manufacturing sector, the most important exogenous component of which (in an open economy) is the growth of export demand. The latter hypothesis was confirmed by the strong correlation between the growth of exports and the growth of manufacturing output.[1]

---

[1] Strictly speaking it is the growth of *net* exports of manufactures which correlates with the growth of manufacturing output. But this qualification is only important in

The basic reason for this is that the labour absorbed in manufacturing in the course of industrial growth does not diminish production in the rest of the economy, owing to the existence of surplus labour in agriculture and services—which exists in high-income countries as well as low-income countries. Thus the main message of the neo-classical "paradigm" that the market allocates resources so as to make the marginal product of labour approximately the same in all parts of the economy (i.e. it makes the distribution of "resources" Pareto-optimal) is a false one. In some sectors (such as agriculture and also in some of the service industries) the true marginal product of labour (i.e. the loss of output caused by a small diminution of the labour force) should be zero or even negative. In manufacturing industry on the other hand, owing to increasing returns to scale, the marginal product of labour is likely to be considerably *above* the average product—on the basis of the regression equations used to test the Verdoorn Law it is approximately twice as high.

In my Inaugural Lecture in Cambridge (delivered in November, 1966) where I first expounded these thoughts,[1] my main concern was to give an explanation why Britain's rate of economic growth was so much lower than that of other industrial countries. The hypothesis which suggested itself to me on the basis of these empirical findings was that the U.K. *alone* among the "developed countries" had reached "economic maturity" in the sense that the mechanism which enabled manufacturing industry to expand by drawing labour from the other sectors in response to demand was not functioning in the U.K. because earnings differences between sectors were so largely eliminated. Hence the expansion of manufacturing output was limited by a labour-constraint which did not exist elsewhere.

As an explanation for the peculiarly poor performance of the British economy, this hypothesis, as I afterwards acknowledged,[2]

---

those cases (such as the U.K. or Japan) where the one measure is significantly different from the other, i.e. where the growth rate of exports of manufactures diverges to an important degree from the growth rate of imports of manufacturers.

[1] Reprinted (with Appendices) on pp. 100–38 below.

[2] See "Economic Growth and the Verdoorn Law: A Comment on Mr. Rowthorn's Article", *Economic Journal*, December 1975, pp. 891-896

turned out to be a mistaken one. As later statistical studies have shown,[1] I was wrong in thinking that "low-earnings" sectors have been eliminated in the British economy; the acute labour shortages which limited the expansion of manufacturing output in the growth years were short period phenomena—i.e. the consequence, rather than the cause, of a low trend rate of growth of manufacturing output.[2] And when labour shortages were relieved (in 1966 and after, through S.E.T. as well as general deflationary measures) there was no rebound in exports as would have been expected to occur if my hypothesis had been correct.[3]

But contrary to the view of some critics, this did not reduce the importance of the findings concerning the key rôle of manufacturing industry in determining the growth rate. These empirical findings (which were later confirmed and extended by Cripps and Tarling[4]) were not consistent with the generally accepted notion that an industrially developed economy is "resource-constrained"—in other words that it produces, given the constellation of consumers' wants, as much as it possibly can produce, and no re-organisation of resources can make it produce more; while over time, on the same view, the economy's "productive potential" grows at some pre-ordained rate, determined mainly by some exogenously given rate of productivity improvement caused by technical progress, the growth of the labour force, etc. The regression equations calculated by Cripps and Tarling[5] strongly suggest that the success of an industrial economy, just

---

[1] See Sleeper, R., "Manpower Redeployment and the Selective Employment Tax", *Bulletin of the Oxford Institute of Economics and Statistics*, November 1970.

[2] The critical shortages were in skilled labour (particularly in the engineering industry) which was a reflection of an insufficient growth of demand and the consequent inadequacies in the flow of recruitment; with regard to unskilled labour, there was a considerable transfer of labour from the service sector in boom years, and a reverse flow in recession years.

[3] I should have been forewarned against this hypothesis by the fact that Britain was just as conspicuous for her *relatively* slow rate of growth in the late nineteenth century—indeed, throughout the forty years 1873–1913—when labour shortage could certainly not have played a rôle, considering the large amount of disguised unemployment prevailing in both towns and villages, and the high rate of emigration due to inability to find employment. (For my more recent views of the causes—or at least *some* of the causes—of Britain's low growth rate since the last quarter of the nineteenth century, see the essay "Capitalism and Industrial Development: Some Lessons from Britain's Experience" in volume 6 of this series, *Further Essays in Applied Economics*, pp. 154ff.).

[4] T. F. Cripps and R. J. Tarling, *Growth in Advanced Capitalist Economies*, 1950–70, D.A.E., Occasional Paper No. 40, Cambridge University Press, 1973.

[5] *Ibid.*, p. 30. See also the equations on pp. 134–5 below, and *Economic Journal* December 1975, p. 894.

as the success of an individual business, depends on the demand for its products—or, putting it more finely, on the demand it is able to attract for its products. It is the growth of demand for the products of manufacturing industry, and not the constraints on supply, which determines how fast overall productivity and hence total output will grow in an advanced industrial economy.

The recognition of the key rôle of the growth of manufacturing industry in the general rate of productivity growth of the economy also brought home to me what were the fundamental shortcomings of the post-Keynesian growth and distribution models on which I concentrated my analytical work in the 1950s and the early 1960s (the latest formal presentation of which was that in "New Model of Economic Growth" of 1962). All these models were "single sector models"—not in the precise but trivial sense of assuming that only a single commodity exists (as is the case with some models concerned with capital theory) but in the sense in which the model underlying Keynes's *General Theory* was a single sector model: it considered the working of the economic system as if *all* productive activity exhibited the same characteristics—i.e. those typical of a developed capitalist economy where production is organised in large enterprises, with sufficient command over financial resources to take investment decisions on the basis of sales and profit expectations more or less independently of their current "cash inflow". (This last assumption—which makes incomes the resultant of the expenditure decisions of entrepreneurs, and not the other way round—is the critical feature which distinguishes Keynesian from pre-Keynesian economics.[1]) A logical corollary of these assumptions, in the case of a growth model (as distinct from a stationary equilibrium model), was that the equilibrium growth rate was given exogenously (or quasi-exogenously) by the "natural rate of growth" (i.e., the growth of productivity due to technical progress and the growth of the

---

[1] I would add also the assumption of the prevalence of imperfect markets and oligopolistic competition, where prices are set by the leading firms, based on costs, and the most important determinant of costs is the level of money wages (which is treated as an exogenous variable). Keynes himself had never suggested (to my knowledge) that his *General Theory* was dependent on the assumption of imperfect markets. Yet it is difficult to conceive how production in general can be limited by demand—with unutilised capacity at the disposal of the representative firm as well as unemployed labour—unless conditions of some kind of oligopoly prevail.

labour force), which in turn implied that the model assumed "full employment"—i.e., that in a state of steady growth the level of output at any one time was constrained by the effective supply of labour.

The recognition that the "Keynesian" features of the economy only apply to the secondary or industrial sector of an economy, and that this sector is dependent on a "non-Keynesian" primary sector both for its essential inputs of food and raw materials and for the growth of the "external market" for its products, made me realise that a thorough understanding of the nature of the growth process can only be gained on the basis of a two-sector model of Agriculture and Industry. In such a model the ultimate constraint which governs the growth rate is not population growth or the rate of labour-saving inventions, but the progress of land-saving inventions which determine the growth of the "agricultural surplus" at any given terms of trade between the products of Industry and Agriculture; and in which the equilibrium "terms of trade" between the two sectors are determined by the condition that these relative growth rates must be in a sustainable relationship to each other. In such a model the growth rate of the "Keynesian sector" is determined by the growth of the exogenous components of demand originating outside the sector and this yields a closed model which does *not* require the assumption of full employment.

Though I developed the features of such a "two sector" model progressively in the course of ten years' lectures on the subject in Cambridge, I have never felt that the new theory has reached a sufficiently mature stage to merit publication without further work on it—so its most important basic features are still "on the drawing board", unpublished.

However, thinking around this model and in pursuit of its implications provided the major theme of five subsequent papers written in the years 1970–6, reproduced in this volume.

The paper "The Case for Regional Policies" was the first to set out in some detail the basic differences between the economics appropriate to "land-based activities" (agriculture and mineral exploitation) and the economics of "processing activities" (manufacturing industry). The latter are subject to increasing returns to scale, in a sense in which the former are not,[1] and this difference has far reaching consequences on their laws of development, on the nature of competition and price formation, on the effects of international (or interregional) trade, etc. Industry is subject to the principle of "circular and cumulative causation"—success breeds success, whilst failure begets more failure. Under the benign rule of constant returns to scale, competition and free trade would benefit all participants, leading to a general equalisation of returns even in the absence of free mobility,[2] that is to say, to a convergence of living standards and growth rates. But in reality the existence of increasing returns to scale makes the picture far more complicated. Free trade tends to enlarge differences in comparative costs instead of reducing them, and contrary to Mills' famous principle, trade need not be advantageous to all trading partners —it may be ruinous to some, to the greater benefit of others. Instead of a convergence, it may lead to a divergence—to an increasing gap between prosperous and depressed areas.

Until the second quarter of the nineteenth century the great bulk of international trade was in foodstuffs and raw materials; this explains perhaps why in the theory of international trade and payments Ricardo and the other classical economists reached conclusions that are applicable in the trade between different agricultural areas, or to that between agricultural areas and *one* manufacturing area, but which have no universal application to the trade between *different* manufacturing regions; either in the trade with one another or in competition in third markets.[3]

The paper on "Conflicts in National Economic Objectives", prepared as a Presidential address to the Durham meeting of the British Association, was a critique of British post-war economic

---

[1] Indeed the former, as the classical economists argued, is subject to diminishing returns to scale, which is correct if one regards "land" as a factor specific to agriculture (and mining) and defines (correctly) "returns to scale" as returns in terms of *transferable* factors which have alternative uses. (This is argued in a later paper, on p. 209 below.)

[2] In accordance with the "factor price equalisation theorem" of Stolper and Samuelson.

[3] Whether trade will lead to increasing divergence or not will depend on the "feedback" effects of lower costs on increasing demand being large enough to cause an even greater fall in costs in the next round and so on. (See A. P. Thirlwall and R. Dixon. "A Model of Regional Growth-rate Differences on Kaldorian Lines", *Oxford Economic Papers*, July 1975, pp. 201–14.)

policies written from the perspective of the new theoretical ideas just described and also of the experience gained during my years in the Treasury 1964–8. The main point of the paper—which is not perhaps brought out as succinctly as it should have been—was that in the case of a country in Britain's circumstances the long-term cause of the insufficiency of demand and the consequent unemployment and low growth was not so much an excessive propensity to save in relation to investment opportunities but an excessive propensity to import in relation to our ability to export. In other words the relevant "multiplier" which economic management needs to manipulate is not the Keynesian "savings-investment" multiplier, but Harrod's "foreign trade multiplier".[1] Post-war economic management in Britain, by aiming to secure the "correct pressure of demand" through the instrument of fiscal policy, operated so as to generate additional consumption and thereby reduce "excess savings"; this may be justified as a means of counteracting a slump caused by a "collapse of the marginal efficiency of capital";[2] but it was not appropriate as an instrument for correcting chronic unemployment and an un-satisfactory trend rate of growth in an open economy. For the latter requires an instrument operating on the export/import relationship and not the savings/investment relationship.

This paper introduced the distinction between consumption-led growth and export-led growth which has since become part of "received wisdom" (though not until after the failure of one more grandiose attempt to engineer a boom of the former kind in 1972–3). It also emphasised the internal difficulties of achieving the necessary switch from consumption-led growth to export-led

---

[1] Harrod's foreign trade multiplier made its first appearance in his book *International Economics* published in 1933 (Ch. vi, §§ 2 and 3) which thus preceded Keynes' multiplier theory by three years. Although there were various economists (such as P. Barrett Whale) who recognised its importance in explaining how the foreign trade mechanism worked under the gold standard, it was never put forward as a general theory of *employment*; and interest in the concept rapidly receded after the publication of the *General Theory*. The basic assumption needed to validate the Harrod-multiplier is that the price-elasticities of both exports and imports are small, relatively to the income elasticities—i.e., that changes in the (domestic or foreign) level of incomes are a far more important cause of changes in exports or imports than changes in relative prices. (An analogous assumption underlies the Keynesian multiplier theory as regards the relative price and income elasticities of savings, the price of "savings" being the rate of interest.)

[2] Keynes, *General Theory*, pp. 315 ff.

growth, but on the external side it subscribed to the view that once a "managed floating rate" became an acceptable instrument of policy, it would not prove too difficult to achieve a "target rate of growth of exports" by operating on the exchange rate. In this respect I now feel I was mistaken. Events since 1971 have shown that the exchange rate is neither as easy to manipulate nor as rewarding in its effects on the rate of growth of net exports as I had thought.[1]

The next two papers, "The Irrelevance of Equilibrium Economics" and "What is Wrong with Economic Theory", originally prepared as special lectures at the Universities of York and Harvard, are more particularly addressed to students and teachers of economic theory. Their purpose is to show why the dominant theory of economics taught at most universities, which is some version of the general equilibrium theory based on Walras' model, does not provide an appropriate intellectual framework for understanding how market economies work.

The first paper is really an elaboration of Allyn Young's famous paper on *Increasing Returns and Economic Progress*, written almost fifty years ago, which first pointed out the far-reaching consequences of the "law of increasing returns" on the manner of operation of markets, and on the behaviour of an economic system. He showed that the main function of markets is to transmit impulses to economic change, and thereby *create* more resources through enlarging the scope for specialisation and the division of labour—rather than to secure an optimum allocation of a *given* quantum of resources. And he also showed that with increasing returns continual change is self-generated and "propagates itself in a cumulative way". Hence no analysis which describes the forces operating on the economy as tending towards a state of equilibrium can capture the manner in which the development of markets make for perpetual change.[2]

---

[1] The very fact that the concept of the "foreign trade multiplier" presupposes that the *price* elasticities in foreign trade are small relative to income elasticities should have warned one against being over-sanguine of the possibilities of varying the export/import relationship (or of net exports) through exchange rate manipulations. (This question is further discussed in the Introduction to *Further Essays in Applied Economics*.)

[2] In one of his brilliant flashes of insight which failed to arouse the imagination of the academic community, Young asserted that more "roundabout production" (the

In elaborating this idea, Young relied heavily on the notion of the demand for any one commodity being "elastic" "in the special sense that a small increase in its supply will be attended by an increase in other commodities which can be had in exchange for it". He thought that this condition would ensure that increases in supply of some commodities will evoke an increase in demand for other commodities, which in turn is bound to evoke a further increase in supply.

The main contribution of my paper was in showing that "elastic demand" in the sense in which this term is ordinarily used is neither a necessary nor a sufficient condition for economic progress to be cumulative under conditions of increasing returns. What is necessary is that any initial change, whether it arises on the side of supply or demand, should *induce* additional investment; and that a monetary or banking system should exist capable of financing such induced investment until the savings generated by the process of income expansion provide the finance for it.[1]

The next paper, "What is Wrong with Economic Theory", considers the inappropriateness of the theory of general equilibrium from an aspect which Young did not consider. Suppose that "increasing returns" applies only to *some* activities and not to others, and suppose further that the two kinds of activities—those that are and those that are not subject to increasing returns but are, or may be, subject to diminishing returns—produce goods that are complementary to each other. This is the case if one disaggregates economic activity into two sectors—Agriculture and Industry. In agriculture, which is the land-based activity *par excellence*, the amount of labour that can be efficiently employed at any given time is limited by the scarcity of land. Though this limit is continuously "pushed out" on account of the accrual of land-saving inventions, it is solid enough at any particular point

---

substitution of capital for labour), and the exploitation of the economies of large-scale production, are but two different aspects of a single process. The amount of capital per worker is predominantly a matter of the size of the market, and not of the price of capital relative to labour.

[1] In the paper I show that an increase in *supply* can "induce" investment, and not only an increase in *demand*. In fact, on a more inclusive view, *all* investment can be regarded as the resultant of either a shift in the demand curve or a shift in the supply curve: for the latter, on a broad view, can be taken to embrace all investment induced by technological change.

of time. But this implies also that the demand for industrial goods, and the numbers that can be employed in industry, will also be limited, at a given price ratio (or the terms of trade) between the products of industry and agriculture. However, the fact that, quite irrespective of excess supply, the price of labour in terms of food cannot fall below a certain level, means that there can be only a limited range of feasible price-ratios between products of Agriculture and Industry. Hence no market equilibrium may be possible except in a situation of an excess supply of labour —which does not imply, however, that labour becomes a "free good" since, unlike other "factors", it still has a minimum supply price. This situation of an equilibrium with an excess supply of labour could not happen if agricultural output could be expanded by transferring more labour (and capital) to agriculture under conditions of constant returns, since on that assumption *any* desired "product-mix" could be attained. Hence the general postulate of linearity—of constant returns to scale in all processes or activities—appears to be the condition which is both necessary and sufficient to ensure a Walrasian "resource-constrained" equilibrium under competitive conditions. But once we abandon linearity, as we must if we desire to bring abstract theory into a closer approximation to reality, the result is not just that the theory becomes more complicated—as any theory does in the second approximation—but that the whole structure falls to pieces: the model cannot accommodate diminishing returns to scale, any more than increasing returns.

The last paper included in this volume, "Inflation and Recession in the World Economy", could formally be said to be an essay in applied economics, since its subject matter is to provide an explanation for the different phases of the inflation experienced in the post World War II period. My reason for including it in this volume is that it complements the earlier papers in describing in further detail the properties of the "two-sector" model of Agriculture and Industry. It shows the critical importance of the differences in the nature of markets in the different sectors of the world economy—"demand-pull" inflation operating mainly in the primary commodities and "cost-push" inflation in the secondary and tertiary sectors. (I have little doubt that its analysis and

conclusions will be fiercely contested by adherents of the "monetarist" school, who believe that each nation is responsible for its
own inflation through failure properly to regulate its *own* "money
supply".)

The reader who has managed to peruse this long Introduction
from start to finish may be excused a certain feeling of weariness
or scepticism. It has been a long voyage and in retrospect it can
be seen that there were many false starts. Is there any reason for
thinking that we now stand on more solid ground? Has economics
made any real progress or is it just going round in circles? Will
the recent essays, written in the 1970s, look as dated in, say, ten or
twenty years' time as the single-sector "full-employment"
models of the 1950s do now?

To these major questions I feel quite confidently that one can
give a favourable answer. It was an arduous journey but it *has*
brought solid results—and I am confident that they will be seen
as such by future generations. For the moment the status of
economics appears more chaotic and disjointed than ever—with
theoretical papers becoming ever more abstract and irrelevant,
while politicians and opinion-formers of the mass media revert
to ancient cabals, such as the yearning for more austerity and
more unemployment as remedies for inflation and unemployment.

But all this is likely to pass, just as the influence of the deflation-
ist school of economists, so powerful in the 1920s, had evaporated
by 1935.

In fact, we now have a much better insight into the problem
of managing an economy than we had in the aftermath of the
Keynesian revolution. We are on the verge of evolving an integrated theory of inflation which should be capable of forging the
tools necessary for securing prosperity combined with price
stability, partly through intervention in the commodity markets
and partly through incomes policies in the industrial countries,
the methods and techniques of which are still in their infancy.
There is much better understanding of the processes of "cumulative causation" in the sectors of the economy subject to increasing
returns, and of the importance of maintaining market shares for

safeguarding the balance of payments. Last but not least, there is a far better understanding of the true functions of the market, not just in allocating resources, but in generating and transmitting impulses to technological change and new investment. Once a new consensus emerges (as I am sure it will) we shall be far better equipped in knowing how to run our affairs than we were in the past 25 years, and that in turn was a considerable advance over the age of *laisser faire* prior to World War I, or of the primitive interventionism of the years prior to World War II.

As I explained in the Introduction to an earlier volume,[1] in an academic environment both the evolution of ideas and their formulation emerge as a result of a social process—one derives constant stimulation and criticism from those of one's colleagues who share the same general outlook and the same field of interest. In addition to those whose help I have already acknowledged by specific reference in individual papers or in the Introductions to earlier volumes, I should particularly like to acknowledge the help and stimulus I have received in recent years from Francis Cripps, Wynne Godley and Robert Neild.

King's College
Cambridge
October, 1977

NICHOLAS KALDOR

---

[1] *Essays on Economic Stability and Growth*, p. 14.

1

CAPITAL ACCUMULATION AND
ECONOMIC GROWTH[1,2]

I. INTRODUCTION

A theoretical model consists of certain hypotheses concerning the causal inter-relationship between various magnitudes or forces and the sequence in which they react on each other. We all agree that the basic requirement of any model is that it should be capable of explaining the characteristic features of the economic process as we find them in reality. It is no good starting off a model with the kind of abstraction which initially excludes the influence of forces which are mainly responsible for the behaviour of the economic variables under investigation; and upon finding that the theory leads to results contrary to what we observe in reality, attributing this contrary movement to the compensating (or more than compensating) influence of residual factors that have been assumed away in the model. In dealing with capital accumulation and economic growth, we are only too apt to begin by assuming a "given state of knowledge" (that is to say, absence of technical progress) and the absence of "uncertainty", and content ourselves with saying that these two factors—technical progress and uncertainty—must have been responsible for the difference between theoretical expectation and the recorded facts of experience. The interpretative value of this kind of theory must of necessity be extremely small.

Any theory must necessarily be based on abstractions; but the type of abstraction chosen cannot be decided in a vacuum:

[1] A paper prepared for the Corfu meeting of the International Economic Association in August 1958 and published in *The Theory of Capital* (ed. F. Lutz), London, Macmillan, 1961.
[2] The author is indebted to L. Pasinetti and F. H. Hahn for assistance in setting out the models in algebraic form.

it must be appropriate to the characteristic features of the economic process as recorded by experience. Hence the theorist, in choosing a particular theoretical approach, ought to start off with a summary of the facts which he regards as relevant to his problem. Since facts, as recorded by statisticians, are always subject to numerous snags and qualifications, and for that reason are incapable of being accurately summarised, the theorist, in my view, should be free to start off with a "stylised" view of the facts—i.e. concentrate on broad tendencies, ignoring individual detail, and proceed on the "as if" method, i.e. construct a hypothesis that could account for these "stylised" facts, without necessarily committing himself to the historical accuracy, or sufficiency, of the facts or tendencies thus summarised.

As regards the process of economic change and development in capitalist societies, I suggest the following "stylised facts" as a starting-point for the construction of theoretical models:

(1) The continued growth in the aggregate volume of production and in the productivity of labour at a steady trend rate; no recorded tendency for a *falling* rate of growth of productivity.

(2) A continued increase in the amount of capital per worker, whatever statistical measure of "capital" is chosen in this connection.

(3) A steady rate of profit on capital, at least in the "developed" capitalist societies, this rate of profit being substantially higher than the "pure" long-term rate of interest as shown by the yield of gilt-edged bonds. According to Phelps Brown and Weber[1] the rate of profit in the United Kingdom was remarkably steady around $10\frac{1}{2}$ per cent in the period 1870–1914, the annual variations being within $9\frac{1}{2}$–$11\frac{1}{2}$ per cent. A similar long-period steadiness, according to some authorities, has shown itself in the United States.

(4) Steady capital-output ratios over long periods; at least there are no clear long-term trends, either rising or falling, if differences in the degree of utilisation of capacity are allowed for. This implies, or reflects, the near-identity in the percentage rates of growth of production and of the capital stock—i.e. that for

---

[1] *Economic Journal*, 1953, pp. 263–88.

the economy as a whole, and over longer periods, income and capital tend to grow at the same rate.

(5) A high correlation between the share of profits in income and the share of investment in output; a steady share of profits (and of wages) in societies and/or in periods in which the investment coefficient (the share of investment in output) is constant. For example, Phelps Brown and Weber found long-term steadiness in the investment coefficient, the profit share and the share of wages in the U.K., combined with a high degree of correlation in the (appreciable) short period fluctuations of these magnitudes.[1] The steadiness in the *share* of wages implies, of course, a rate of increase in real wages that is proportionate to the rate of growth of (average) productivity.

(6) Finally, there are appreciable differences in the *rate* of growth of labour productivity and of total output in different societies, the range of variation (in the fast-growing economies) being of the order of 2–5 per cent. These are associated with corresponding variations in the investment coefficient, and in the profit share, but the above propositions concerning the constancy of relative shares and of the capital-output ratio are applicable to countries with differing rates of growth.

None of these "facts" can be plausibly "explained" by the theoretical constructions of neo-classical theory. On the basis of the marginal productivity theory, and the capital theory of Böhm-Bawerk and followers, one would expect a continued *fall* in the rate of profit with capital accumulation, and not a steady rate of profit. (In this respect classical and neo-classical theory, arguing on different grounds, come to the same conclusion— Adam Smith, Ricardo, Marx, alike with Böhm-Bawerk and Wicksell, predicted a steady fall in the rate of profit with economic progress.) Similarly, on the basis of the neo-classical approach, one expects diminishing returns to capital accumulation which implies a steady *rise* in the capital-output ratio *pari passu* with the rise in the capital-labour ratio, and a diminishing rate of growth in the productivity of labour at any given ratio of investment to output (or savings to income). Finally, the fluctuations in the

[1] *Op. cit.* Fig. 7.

B

share of profits that are associated with fluctuations in the rate of investment cannot be accounted for at all on the basis of the marginal productivity theory—if we assume, as I believe we must, that the fluctuations in the level of investment are the causal factor, and the fluctuations in the share of profits consequential, rather than the other way round.

My purpose here is to present a model of income distribution and capital accumulation which is capable of explaining at least some of these "stylised" facts. It differs from the prevailing approach to problems of capital accumulation in that it has more affinities with the classical approach of Ricardo and Marx, and also with the general equilibrium model of von Neumann, than with the neo-classical models of Böhm-Bawerk and Wicksell, or with the theories which start off with the Cobb-Douglas type of production function. It differs from the classical models in that it embodies the basic ideas of the Keynesian theory of income generation, and it takes the well-known "dynamic equation" of Harrod and Domar as its starting-point.

II. THE CHARACTERISTIC FEATURES OF THE
CLASSICAL APPROACH

The peculiarity of classical models as against the neo-classical theories is that they treat capital and labour as if they were complementary factors rather than competitive or substitute factors. Of course Ricardo was well aware that the use of capital is not only complementary to labour but also a substitute for labour— hence the famous "Ricardo effect".[1] This demonstrates that with a rise in wages more machinery will tend to be employed per unit of labour, *because* the price of machinery will fall relatively to labour with any rise in the share of the produce going to labour —but he did not accord this substitution-aspect any major rôle in his distribution or growth theory. As far as his distribution theory is concerned he treated the amount of capital per unit of labour as something given for each industry (and similarly, the distribution of labour between different industries as given by the "structural requirements" of the system). He solved the

[1] *Principles*, ch. i, sec. v.

problem of distribution between wages and profits (after deduction of the share of rent which is determined quite independently of this division) by assuming that the amount going to one of these two factors, labour, is determined by its supply price, whereas the share of the other is residual—the share of profits is simply the difference between output per man (after deduction of rent) and wages per man, the latter being treated as constant, governed by the "natural price" of labour at which alone the working population *can remain* stationary.

Since profits were assumed to be largely saved and invested, whilst wages are consumed, the share of profits in income also determines the share of investment in total production, and the rate of accumulation of capital. The rate of accumulation of capital in turn determines the rate of increase in the employment of labour (since employment was assumed to increase at the same rate as capital, there was no scope for any consequential change in the amount of capital per unit of labour) without enquiring very closely where this additional labour comes from. The model is consistent with the assumption that there is an unlimited labour reserve, say, in the form of surplus population in an under-developed country (the assumption favoured by Marx) or with assuming that the rate of increase in population is itself governed by the rate of growth in the demand for labour (the assumption favoured by Ricardo).

Von Neumann's general equilibrium model,[1] though on a very different level of sophistication, explicitly allowing for a choice of processes in the production of each commodity, and abstracting from diminishing returns due to the scarcity of natural resources to which Ricardo accorded such a major rôle, is really a variant of the classical approach of Ricardo and Marx. Von Neumann similarly assumes that labour can be expanded in unlimited quantities at a real wage determined by the cost of subsistence of the labourers, and that profits are entirely saved and re-invested. These two assumptions enable him to treat the economic problem as a completely circular process, where the outputs of productive processes are simultaneously the inputs of the pro-

[1] *Review of Economic Studies*, 1945-6; originally prepared for a Princeton mathematical seminar in 1932.

ductive processes of the following period; this is achieved by treating not labour, but the commodities consumed by labour, as the inputs of the productive processes, and by treating the surviving durable equipment as part of the outputs, as well as of the inputs, of the processes of unit length. Von Neumann is concerned to show that on these assumptions an equilibrium of balanced growth always exists, characterised by the equi-proportionate expansion in the production of *all* commodities with positive prices: and that this rate of expansion (under perfect competition and constant returns to scale for each process) will be the maximum attainable under the given "technical possibilities" (the real wage forming one of the given "technical possibilities"), and will be equal to the rate of profit (= rate of interest) earned in each of the processes actually used.[1]

The celebrated Harrod-Domar equation can be applied to the Ricardian model and the von Neumann model as well as to other models.[2] Though it can be interpreted in many ways (according to which of the factors one treats as a dependent and which as an independent variable) it is fundamentally a formula for translating the share of savings (and investment) in income (s) into the resulting growth rate of capital (G_K), given the capital-output ratio, $v \left(\equiv \dfrac{K}{Y} \right)$[3]

[1] Von Neumann was only concerned with demonstrating the *existence* of such an equilibrium solution. Later Solow and Samuelson (*Econometrica*, 1953) have shown that on certain further assumptions this solution will be stable both "in the large" and "in the small"—i.e. the balanced-growth equilibrium will be gradually approached from any given set of initial conditions; and it will restore itself if it is disturbed for any reason.

[2] In von Neumann's formulation, where the surviving equipment at the end of each period is treated as a part of the output, v is $1/1 + g$, when Y is defined as the gross output of the period (since then K_t and Y_{t-1} are identical) whilst s is unity if Y is defined as the *net* output (since the wage bill forms part of the commodities consumed in the process of production) so that the net-output/capital ratio is equal to g, the rate of growth of the capital stock. It is possible, however, within the framework of the model, to define Y in the usual way as being the sum of profits and wages—in which case the output-capital ratio (in a state of balanced growth) is identical with the net rate of expansion of the system multiplied by the ratio of Y (thus defined) to net output (i.e. the ratio by which the sum of wages and profits exceeds profits). Given a fixed real wage, and the possibility of expanding the rate of employment at the rate dictated by the requirements of a balanced-growth economy, the ratio of wages to profits is itself determined by the relative input-intensities of labour and non-wage commodities when (at the given wage and with the given range of available processes) the rate of expansion of the system is maximised.

[3] Time subscripts are omitted, except in the formal presentation of the models.

$$G_K = \frac{s}{v}, \tag{1}$$

which can also be written

$$s = \frac{I}{Y} = G_K v. \tag{1a}$$

It further follows that when $s = \frac{P}{Y}$, i.e. all profits are saved and all wages are consumed,

$$\frac{P}{Y} = G_K \frac{K}{Y}.$$

But since

$$\frac{P}{K} \equiv \frac{P}{Y} \cdot \frac{Y}{K}$$

$$\frac{P}{K} = G_K \tag{2}$$

the rate of profit on capital is the same as the rate of growth of capital.

As far as Ricardo and von Neumann are concerned, this is really the end of the story, for they do not introduce any limit to the *speed* with which additional labour can be introduced into the system, so that the rate of growth of employment, and hence of income, is fully determined by the rate of growth of capital. Supposing, however, that even if the supply of labour can be increased to an indefinite extent *ultimately*, there is a maximum to the rate of increase of population and/or of employment per unit of time, determined by biological or institutional factors Writing *L* for the quantity of employment, this gives us another equation

$$G_n = l, \text{ where } l = \frac{1}{L} \cdot \frac{dL}{dt}. \tag{3}$$

The Ricardo-Marx-von Neumann model clearly does not work when $G_K > G_n$ since in that case the rate of growth of production cannot be determined by G_K alone.

In a progressive economy the labour potential increases, however, not only on account of the rise in numbers, but also on account of the rise in the productivity of labour due to technical progress. Hence, allowing for technical progress,

$$G_n = l + t, \text{ where } t = \frac{1}{Y/L} \cdot \frac{d(Y/L)}{dt}, \qquad (3a)$$

which is Harrod's formula for the "natural" rate of growth.

Harrod realised that balanced-growth equilibrium is only conceivable when his "warranted rate of growth" equals the "natural rate",

$$G_K = G_n,$$

in other words $\qquad\qquad \dfrac{s}{v} = l + t.$

Since he assumed, however, that s, v, l and t are all independently given and invariant in relation to each other, such an equality, on his theory, could only be the result of a fortunate accident.

Moreover, he thought that any discrepancy between $\dfrac{s}{v}$ and $(l+t)$ must set up cumulative forces of disequilibrium, so that a moving equilibrium of steady growth, even if momentarily attained, is necessarily unstable.

The problem takes on an entirely different aspect, however, once we recognise (as we must) that these variables are not mutually invariant, but that there are certain inter-relationships between them. Thus, as will be shown, the proportion of income saved s, is by no means independent of $(l+t)$; nor is the rate of increase in productivity, t, independent of the rate of capital accumulation, $\dfrac{s}{v}.$[1]

III. THE NATURE OF GROWTH EQUILIBRIA

In order to exhibit the rôle of these various factors it is best to start from a model based on a number of artificial assumptions which together produce the simplest solution to the problem of growth equilibrium. We shall afterwards remove these assumptions one by one (with the exception of the first assumption

---

[1] In the above equation, in deference to the generally accepted use of symbols, we have denoted the rate of growth of labour by l and the rate of growth of output per man by t. In the rest of this paper, however, we shall denote the *maximum* rate of population growth by λ, and the rate of growth of productivity by G_0; reserving the letter t to denote time

listed below) in the reverse order in which they are presented here. The six critical assumptions of our "basic model" are:

(1) Constant returns to scale in any particular process of production; natural environment does not impose any limitation to expansion (i.e. there are two factors of production, Capital and Labour (K and L), and two kinds of income, Profits and Wages (P and W)).

(2) The absence of technical progress—i.e. the function relating the output of various commodities to the input-coefficients of production remains unchanged over time.

(3) General rule of competition: the prices of commodities in relation to the prime costs of production settle at the point where the market is cleared. Capital earns the same rate of profit, and labour the same rate of wages, in all employments.

(4) All profits are saved and all wages are consumed; the division of output between equipment goods (or "input goods") and wage goods ("consumption goods") is the same as the division of income between Profits and Wages.

(5) There is strict complementarity between Capital and Labour (or commodity-inputs and labour-inputs) in the production of both equipment goods and wage goods; there is therefore a single kind of "equipment good" for the production of each wage good, and the different kinds of wage goods are also complementary in consumption.

(6) There is an unlimited supply of labour at a constant wage in terms of wage goods.[1]

Under these assumptions the rate of growth of the capital stock, G_K, will govern the rate of growth of the economy, G_Y; and G_K in turn depends on the proportion of output saved, s, and the capital-output ratio, v. The proportion of output saved is determined by the condition that the wage rate cannot fall below a certain minimum determined by the cost of subsistence,

$$w = w_{\min} \qquad (4)$$

---

[1] These six assumptions are identical (except (5)) with those underlying von Neumann's model; they are substantially the same as those implicit in Ricardo's theory (except for (1)); and Marx's theory (except of course in its "dynamic" aspect, assumptions (2) and possibly (5)).

so that the excess of output per head over the subsistence wage alone determines the share of profits. Output per head (O), the capital-output ratio (v), and hence capital per head, are given technical constants; and in addition the total amount of capital at some arbitrary point of time, $t = 0$, is taken as given.

These assumptions yield a model which can be formally stated as follows. Using our previously introduced notation[1] and denoting output per worker by O, we obtain a system of six relationships, of which four represent assumptions, one is a definitional identity and one equation the equilibrium condition.

$$O(t) = \overline{O} \quad \text{(i)}$$
$$v(t) = \overline{v} \quad \text{(ii)}$$
$$w(t) = w_{\min} \left.\right\} \text{for all } t \geqslant 0 \quad \text{(iii)}$$
$$s(t) = \frac{P(t)}{\Upsilon(t)} \quad \text{(iv)}$$

$$P(t) \equiv \Upsilon(t) - w(t)L(t) \quad \text{(v)}$$

$$s(t)\Upsilon(t) = \frac{dK(t)}{dt} \text{ for all } t \geqslant 0 \quad \text{(vi)}$$

which are sufficient to determine the six basic variables $O(t)$, $v(t)$, $s(t)$, $P(t)$, $\Upsilon(t)$ and $w(t)$ given the initial values. From (vi) and (ii) we have

$$G_{\Upsilon} = \frac{s(t)}{\overline{v}} \text{ or } \overline{v}G_{\Upsilon} = s(t).$$

From (v) it follows

$$\frac{P(t)}{\Upsilon(t)} = \left[1 - \frac{w_{\min}}{\overline{O}} \right]$$

and hence the share of profit is independent of t. And so, by (iv), $s(t)$ is also independent of t, and hence

$$G_K = \frac{s}{v}$$

---

[1] This notation may be summarised as follows:

$$G_K = \frac{dK}{dt}\frac{1}{K} \qquad G_{\Upsilon} = \frac{d\Upsilon}{dt}\frac{1}{\Upsilon} \qquad v = \frac{K}{\Upsilon} \qquad O = \frac{\Upsilon}{L}$$

and the symbols K, Υ, L, w and s represent the stock of capital, output (or income), labour employed, wage per worker, and the proportion of income saved respectively.

$$G_K = G_Y$$

$$\frac{P}{K} = G_K$$

$$\frac{P}{Y} = G_K \bar{v}. \tag{I}$$

IV. FULL EMPLOYMENT GROWTH

The first modification I shall introduce is the removal of assumption (6), that of an unlimited supply of labour. We may suppose that there is a certain maximum rate of population growth, λ, determined by fertility rates; so that (abstracting from technical progress) this rate determines the long-run "natural rate of growth". Hence

$$G_n = \lambda.$$

If we suppose, further, that initially

$$G_K > G_n,$$

i.e. the rate of capital accumulation, as determined by the conditions of our previous model, exceeds the maximum rate of growth of population, the economy can only grow at the rate G_K as long as there are reserves of unemployed labour to draw upon. But just because the economy grows at a higher rate than λ, sooner or later capital accumulation must overtake the labour supply. According to Marx this is precisely the situation which leads to a crisis. When the labour reserves are exhausted, the demand for labour will exceed (or tend to exceed) the supply of labour, since the amount of capital seeking profitable employment will be greater than the number of labourers available to employ them with. Owing to the competition between capitalists, this will cause wages to rise and profits to be wiped out, until, in consequence, capital accumulation is reduced sufficiently to restore the labour reserve and thus restore profits.

However, there is no inherent reason why this situation should involve a crisis; nor does it follow from the assumptions that the maintenance of accumulation requires the continued existence of a labour reserve. Indeed there is no reason why this situation should not result in a neat balanced-growth equilibrium with a higher rate of wages and a lower share of profits, and with a correspondingly lower rate of capital accumulation that would no longer exceed, but be equal to, the rate of increase in the supply of labour. All that is necessary is to bear in mind that every increase in wages (in terms of commodities) lowers the share of profits in income, and every reduction in the share of profits lowers the rate of accumulation of capital and hence *the rate of increase* in the demand for labour. Hence the situation will lead to a balanced-growth equilibrium in which employment at some arbitrary point of time $t = 0$ is taken as given by the size of the working population at that point of time, and where the rate of growth of population λ is also taken as given.

This gives us an alternative model of seven relationships of which four define the assumptions, one is an identity as before and two are equilibrium conditions. Using, in addition, the notation $L^*(t)$ for the maximum amount of labour available at time t, the relationships are as follows:

$$
\left.
\begin{aligned}
L^*(t) &= L^*_{(0)}e^{\lambda t} \\
v(t) &= \bar{v} \\
O(t) &= \overline{O} \\
s(t) &= \frac{P(t)}{Y(t)}
\end{aligned}
\right\} \text{for all } t \geqslant 0
$$

$$\quad\text{(i)}$$
$$\quad\text{(ii)}$$
$$\quad\text{(iii)}$$
$$\quad\text{(iv)}$$

$$P(t) \equiv Y(t) - w(t)L(t) \qquad\text{(v)}$$

$$
\left.
\begin{aligned}
s(t)\,Y(t) &= \frac{dK}{dt} \\
L(t) &= L^*(t)
\end{aligned}
\right\} \text{for all } t \geqslant 0
$$

$$\quad\text{(vi)}$$
$$\quad\text{(vii)}$$

subject to the inequality

$$w(t) \geqslant w_{\min}$$

which are sufficient to determine the seven basic variables $O(t)$, $v(t)$, $s(t)$, $P(t)$, $Y(t)$, $w(t)$ and $L(t)$, given the initial conditions.

It follows from (i) and (vii) that

$$G_Y = \lambda.$$

From (vi), $s(t) = \lambda v(t)$ and so, by (i) and (ii), $s(t)$ is independent of t. Hence by (iv)

$$G_K = \frac{s}{\bar{v}}$$

$$G_K = G_y$$

$$\frac{P}{\Upsilon} = \lambda \bar{v}$$

$$\frac{P}{K} = \lambda$$

Also, by (v), $\qquad w(t) = (1 - \lambda\bar{v})\overline{O},$

subject to the inequality stated. (II)

The difference between this model and the previous one is that while in both, output per man and capital per man are constant (over time), in this model the rate of profit on capital and the share of profit in income (given v, which is here as a technical constant) are uniquely determined by λ, the population growth rate, which on our present assumptions will alone determine the uniform expansion rate of the economy. There is an equilibrium wage, w, which will exceed the subsistence wage, $w_{\min}$, by the amount necessary to reduce the share of profits to λv. But despite the similarities, this second model is the inverse of the Ricardian (or Marxian) one; for here it is not profits which form a residual after deducting subsistence-wages, but wages form the residual share after deducting profits, the amount of profits being determined independently by the requirements of the (extraneously given) balanced growth rate.[1]

Ricardo did say, in various places scattered around in the

---

[1] This situation is incompatible also with von Neumann's model, which, as mentioned before, implicitly assumes that the effective supply of labour can be increased at the required growth rate, whatever that rate is. But if one introduced labour explicitly as one of the "commodities" into the von Neumann model (instead of the goods consumed by labour) and assumed that the supply of labour was growing at some autonomous rate that was lower than the maximum potential expansion rate of commodities other than labour, the same result would be reached. For then the equilibrium price system which equalised the rate of profit earned in all the "chosen" processes would be the one which made the price of labour in terms of other commodities such as to reduce the rate of profit earned in the production of commodities (other than labour) to the expansion rate of labour.

Principles, that as capital accumulation runs ahead of population, or the reverse, wages will rise above the "natural price of labour" or may fall below it. But he never drew the immanent conclusion (though in several places he seemed almost on the point of saying it) that the rise or fall in wages resulting from excessive or insufficient rates of accumulation *will itself change the rate of accumulation of capital through changing the profit share,* and thereby provides a mechanism for keeping the rate of accumulation of capital in step with the rate of increase in the labour supply—i.e. that there is an "equilibrium" level of wages which maintains the increase in the demand for labour in step with the increase in supply. (Had he said so, with some emphasis, one cannot help feeling that the subsequent development of economics, both Marxist and orthodox, might have taken a rather different turn.)

Marx's view that where excessive accumulation leads to a crisis due to the scarcity of labour there is nothing to stop wages from rising until profits are wiped out altogether, clearly assumes a *constant* supply of labour over time. If population is rising, profits cannot fall below the level which provides for a rate of accumulation that corresponds to the rate of growth in the supply of labour; and once "full employment" has been reached (i.e. the "reserve army" is exhausted) there is no reason why wages should not settle down to a new equilibrium level, divorced from the cost of subsistence of labour.

There is one other important assumption implicit in this, and in the other growth models, which may be conveniently introduced at this stage. In a capitalist economy continued investment and accumulation presupposes that the rate of profit is high enough (in the words of Ricardo) to afford more than the minimum necessary compensation to the capitalists "for their trouble, for the risk which they must necessarily encounter in employing their capital productively".[1] Hence growth-equilibrium is subject to a further condition which can be written in the form

$$\frac{P}{K} \geqslant r + \rho, \tag{5}$$

i.e. the rate of profit as determined by the model (under our

[1] *Principles*, Sraffa edition, p. 122.

present assumption by λ alone) cannot be less than the sum of the "pure" rate of interest on financial assets of prime security, and the additional premium required for the risks involved in productive employments of wealth.

We know, since Keynes, that there is a minimum below which the pure long-term rate of interest cannot fall, and that this is determined by the minimum necessary compensation for the illiquidity risk entailed in holding long-term bonds as against cash (or other short-term financial assets which are close sub-stitutes for cash). We also know (though this has received far less emphasis in the literature) that the risks (whether illiquidity risks or other risks) associated with the direct investment of capital in business ventures are quantitatively far more important than the risks entailed in holding long-term financial assets of prime security. (The rate of profit on business investments in fixed capital (in plant and equipment) in the U.S., for example, is generally taken to be 20 per cent gross, or say 10 per cent net, of taxation, when the "pure" long-term rate of interest is around 4 per cent.)

The (expected) marginal return on investments in circulating capital (which, by universal convention, are treated as part of the "liquid assets" of a business) is much more in line with the money rates of interest, though here also, the expected return is likely to be appreciably higher than the (pure) short-term rate of interest. It is indeed highly unlikely that in an economy *without* technical progress, and where *all* profits are saved and re-invested, the rate of profit (as determined by population growth) could be anywhere near high enough to satisfy the above condition. If it is not, there cannot be a moving equilibrium of growth, though this does not mean that the economy will lapse into perpetual stagnation. Accumulation could still take place in periodic spurts, giving rise to a higher-than-trend rate of growth for a limited period.

We must now proceed with the relaxation of the various simplifying assumptions made. As we shall see, until we come to technical progress, none of these introduces a vital difference to our results.

V. NEO-CLASSICAL GROWTH

We can allow for variable proportions, instead of strict complementarity, between capital and labour, by postulating that there is a choice of processes of production involving differing quantities of capital per man (i.e. a differing ratio between "commodities" and "labour" as inputs). Thus output per man, O ($O \equiv Y/L$), will be a function of K/L, capital per man, the increase in the former being less than proportionate to the latter, if the production function for labour and capital together is homogeneous and linear. Hence

$$O \equiv Y/L = f_1(K/L), \text{ where } f_1' > 0, f_1'' < 0. \qquad (6)$$

Assuming that each entrepreneur at any one time has a limited amount of capital at his disposal, the amount of capital per man employed will be such as to maximise the rate of profit; and this optimum amount of capital per man will be all the greater the higher are wages in terms of commodities, hence

$$K/L = f_2(w), \text{ where } f_2' > 0, f_2'' < 0. \qquad (7)$$

(6) in combination with (7) also implies that the capital-output ratio in the "chosen" process will be all the greater, the higher the rate of wages, hence

$$v \equiv \frac{K}{Y} = f_3(w), \text{ where } f_3' > 0, f_3'' < 0. \qquad (8)$$

Further, it also follows that output per man will be the greater the higher the capital-output ratio

$$O = f_4(v), \text{ where } f_4' > 0, f_4'' < 0. \qquad (9)$$

Hence as wages rise (with the approach to full employment and the slowing down of the rate of accumulation) v will rise as well; this in turn will increase the share of investment in output $\left(\dfrac{I}{Y}\right)$ at

any *given* rate of growth of output, and hence the share of profits. It *may* also slow down the rise in wages in terms of commodities, but since the rise in v will increase output per man, as well as the share of profits, this does not necessarily follow. However, on the assumption of diminishing returns (which, as we shall argue later, comes to much the same as the assumption that there is no technical progress) $f_1'' < 0$, the rise in the investment ratio and in the share of profits will not be sufficient to prevent a continued fall in the rate of growth of capital with the continued increase in v. Hence this process of adopting more labour saving techniques by increasing capital per head will come to an end when the rate of growth of capital declines sufficiently to approach the rate of increase in the supply of labour, λ. From then onwards the system will regain a balanced-growth equilibrium with unchanging techniques and capital per head and proceeding at the uniform expansion rate λ.

Thus the introduction of a choice of processes permitting the substitution of capital for labour will mean that there will be an intermediate stage between the equilibrium of Model I (where G_Y was determined by G_K) and of Model II (where G_Y was determined by G_n, and G_K by G_Y), characterised by the condition

$$G_K > G_Y > G_n,$$

i.e. where the actual rate of growth is greater than the natural rate, as determined by population growth, and lower than the rate of capital accumulation. In other words, the rate of growth of capital will be higher than that of output, and the latter will be declining. The difference thus introduced is best shown in a diagram (Fig. 1) where output (Y_t) is shown vertically (on a

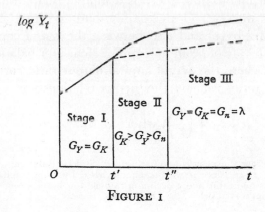

FIGURE I

logarithmic scale) and time horizontally. Assuming that from $t = 0$ onwards the economy is in a growth equilibrium with unlimited supplies of labour with $G_Y = G_K$, G_K being determined by the ratio of savings to income when wages are at the minimum subsistence level; and assuming further that the labour reserves are exhausted at the point of time t', then, in the absence of a choice of "techniques" of a more or less labour-saving character, wages will immediately rise to the point where the share of profits is cut down to the level where the rate of accumulation is brought down to $G_n = \lambda$ and the system attains a new balanced-growth equilibrium at this lower rate. If we assume, however, that there are technical possibilities for increasing output per head by using more capital per unit of labour, the transition will be gradual. Wages will rise more gradually, and accumulation will be maintained (temporarily) at a higher rate, serving both the requirements of the growing working population and the increasing amount of capital per unit of labour. But since during this stage the rate of growth of production will be declining, and will be constantly smaller than the rate of capital accumulation, balanced-growth equilibrium will be regained at a certain point (shown by t'' in the diagram). This will occur when wages have risen to the point at which accumulation is brought down to the rate corresponding to the rate of growth of population, and from then onwards the economy will attain the same constant growth rate, determined by λ.[1]

Given the range of alternative processes represented by our f functions, it follows that there is a unique relationship between output per worker and the capital-output ratio (as stated in equation (9) above) and also between the *desired* capital-output ratio and the rate of profit on capital. Hence for balanced-growth equilibria (where the actual capital-output ratio corresponds to the desired ratio) we have the further relationship

$$v = \phi\left(\frac{P}{K}\right), \text{ where } \phi' < 0, \ \phi'' > 0. \tag{8a}$$

---

[1] The first of our three stages may be termed the "classical" stage, the second the "neo-classical" stage (since it will be characterised by rising capital per man, a rising capital-output ratio, and a declining rate of growth and profit) and the third stage, for reasons set out below, the "Keynesian" stage.

Writing these relationships in this form, this model will be characterised by seven relationships, of which three are equilibrium conditions.

$$L^*(t) = L^*(0)e^{\lambda t} \tag{i}$$
$$O(t) = f(v(t)), f' > 0, f'' < 0 \quad \text{for all } t \geqslant 0 \tag{ii}$$
$$s(t) = \frac{P(t)}{Y(t)} \tag{iii}$$

$$P(t) \equiv Y(t) - w(t)L(t) \tag{iv}$$

$$s(t)Y(t) = \frac{dK(t)}{dt} \tag{v}$$
$$L(t) = L^*(t) \quad \text{for all } t \geqslant 0 \tag{vi}$$
$$v(t) = \phi\left(\frac{P(t)}{K(t)}\right) \tag{vii}$$

where
$$\phi' < 0, \quad \phi'' > 0$$
subject to the inequalities
$$w(t) \geqslant w_{min}$$
$$\frac{P(t)}{K(t)} \geqslant r + \rho.$$

By the same argument as employed in Model II above it follows that
$$G_Y = \lambda.$$

Hence by (v), $\frac{s(t)}{v(t)}$ is independent of t. By (iii) we have $\frac{P(t)}{Y(t)} = \lambda v(t)$ and so
$$\frac{P}{K} = \lambda$$

and using (vii) we obtain $\frac{P}{Y} = \lambda\phi(\lambda).$ \tag{III}

As a comparison with the corresponding equations for Model II shows, the introduction of a "production function" which makes the capital-output ratio dependent on the rate of profit will not affect the equilibrium growth-rate, or the rate of profit on capital.

But it will have an influence on the share of profits, and hence on the savings coefficient, s, for any given rate of growth, since λ and $\phi(\lambda)$ are inversely related to one another: the higher the value of λ, the lower the equilibrium value $\phi(\lambda)$. In the special case where the function $\phi(\lambda)$ is one of constant unit elasticity (i.e. when doubling the rate of growth and the rate of profit involves halving the capital-output ratio, etc.) the investment coefficient, $\lambda\phi(\lambda)$, will be invariant with respect to any change in the rate of growth and the rate of profit on capital, and, in that sense, the share of profits and wages can be said to be uniquely determined by the coefficients of the production function. But the assumption of constant unit elasticity for the ϕ function is by no means implicit in the assumption of homogeneous and linear production functions, and indeed it cannot hold in all cases where there are limits to the extent to which any one factor can be dispensed with. If, in the relevant range, the elasticity of this function is appreciably smaller than one, the share of profit will predominantly depend on the rate of economic growth (and on the propensities to save out of profits and wages discussed below) and only to a minor extent on the technical factors, the marginal rates of substitution between capital and labour (which determine the elasticity of the ϕ function).[1]

VI. THE PROPENSITIES TO SAVE

We can now relax our fourth assumption, the one implicit in all "classical" models, that there is no consumption out of profits and no saving out of wages. We can allow both for the fact that profits are a source of consumption expenditure and that wages may be a source of savings—provided that we assume that the proportion of profits saved is considerably greater than the proportion of wages (and other contractual incomes) saved.[2]

[1] Empirical evidence, such as it is, lends little support to the supposition that the capital-output ratio is smaller in fast-growing economies than in slow-growing economies, or in economies where the amount of capital per head is relatively small as against those where it is large. But the reason for this, as we shall argue later, is not the lack of substitutability between capital and labour, but the unreality of the postulate of a ϕ function which abstracts from all technical progress.

[2] I am assuming here, purely for simplicity, that the savings functions for both profits and wages are linear (with a zero constant) so that the average and marginal propensities are identical. If this were not so, it would be the difference in marginal propensities which was critical to the theory.

This assumption can be well justified both by empirical evidence and by theoretical considerations. Thus, on U.S. data, gross savings out of gross (company) profits can be put at 70 per cent, whereas savings out of personal incomes (excluding unincorporated businesses) are only around 5 per cent. Statistical evidence from other countries yields very similar results. On theoretical grounds one can expect the propensity to save out of business profits to be greater than that of wage and salary incomes (i) because residual incomes are much more uncertain, and subject to considerable fluctuations, year by year; (ii) because the accumulation of capital by the owners of the individual firms is closely linked to the *growth* of the firms: since a firm's borrowing power is limited to some proportion of its equity capital, the growth of the latter is a necessary pre-condition of the growth in its scale of operations. Apart from this, it could be argued on Keynesian considerations that it is precisely this difference in savings-ratios which lends stability to a capitalist system, under full employment or near-full employment conditions. For if these differences did *not* exist, any chance increase in demand which raised prices would bring about a cumulative tendency: a rise in prices is only capable of eliminating the disequilibrium in so far as the transfer of purchasing power from "contractual" to "residual" incomes which it represents reduces effective demand in real terms.

If we denote by α the proportion of profits saved and β the proportion of wages saved,

$$I = \alpha P + \beta W, \text{ where } 1 > \alpha > \beta > 0 \tag{10}$$

$$s \equiv \frac{I}{Y} = (\alpha - \beta)\frac{P}{Y} + \beta \tag{10a}$$

and

$$\frac{P}{Y} = \frac{1}{\alpha - \beta}\frac{I}{Y} - \frac{\beta}{\alpha - \beta}. \tag{10b}$$

If, in the first approximation, we assumed that βW is zero the equilibrium relationships will remain the same as in Model III, with the exception of (ii) which becomes

$$s(t) = \alpha\frac{P(t)}{Y(t)}.$$

This modification implies that in equilibrium

$$\frac{P}{K} = \frac{\lambda}{a}$$

$$\frac{P}{Y} = \frac{\lambda}{a} \cdot \phi\left(\frac{\lambda}{a}\right). \tag{IV}$$

In other words, the rate of profit on capital will now exceed the rate of growth by the reciprocal of the proportion of profits saved. Similarly, the share of profit in income will also be raised, except in so far as the rise in $\frac{P}{K}$ will reduce v, and hence the investment-output ratio at any given rate of growth.

VII. COMPETITION AND FULL EMPLOYMENT

Before examining the implications of assumption (3), the general rule of competition, I should like to translate our results into terms that are in accord with the Keynesian techniques of analysis. So far we have assumed that the level of production at any one time is limited not by effective demand but by the scarcity of resources available; which meant in the case of Model I that it was limited by the amount of capital (i.e. physical capacity) and in the case of Model II by the available supply of labour. In the "Keynesian" sense, therefore, the equilibrium in both cases is one of "full employment". This is ensured, in the case of Model I, through the assumption, implicit in the model, that it is the "surplus" remaining after the payment of subsistence wages which determines the rate of accumulation. In the case of Model II, where investment demand per unit of time is independently determined by the accrual of new investment opportunities resulting from the given rate of increase in the labour supply, it is ensured through the fact that the level of wages in real terms, and thus the share of profits, is assumed to settle at the point where savings out of profits are just equal to the required rate of investment. This latter presumes in effect a "Keynesian" model where investment is the independent variable, and savings are the dependent variable: but the process of adjustment is assumed to take place not in a Keynesian but in a classical manner through forces operating in the labour market. An excess of savings over investment manifests itself in an excess of the demand for labour over the supply of labour; this leads to a rise in wages which reduces profits, and thus savings, and hence diminishes the rate of increase in the demand for labour. There is therefore some particular real wage at which the rate of increase in the demand for labour, resulting from capital accumulation, keeps in step with the rate of increase in the supply of labour, and which therefore is alone capable of maintaining the labour market in equilibrium.

But we are not *obliged* to look upon the equilibrating mechanism in this way; we could equally describe the equilibrating process in the "Keynesian" manner, through the forces of adjustment operating not in the labour market, but in the commodity markets. In the Keynesian system an excess in the demand for labour in the labour market can only cause a rise in *money* wages, not of *real* wages, since a rise in *money* wages, *ceteris paribus*, will raise monetary demand, and thus prices, in the same proportion. To explain movements in *real* wages (output per man being assumed as given) we need to turn to the commodity markets and examine the conditions of equilibrium for the demand and supply of commodities. It is the most significant feature of Keynes' theory to have shown that equilibrium between savings (*ex ante*) and investment (*ex ante*) is secured through forces operating in the commodity markets. When investment exceeds savings, the demand for commodities will exceed the supply. This will lead *either* to an expansion of supply (assuming the prevalence of "Keynesian" unemployment and hence a state of affairs where production is less than the short-period maximum) *or* to a rise in prices relatively to costs (assuming "full employment" in the Keynesian sense, i.e. that supply is limited by physical bottlenecks). In both cases an increase in the demand for commodities will lead to an increase in savings; in the first case, because savings are an increasing function of real income, at any *given* relationship of prices to costs (or of profits to wages); in the second case, because the rise in prices relative to costs implies a rise in profits and a fall in wages (in *real* terms) which increases savings.

Keynes, in the *General Theory*, writing in the middle of the big slump of the 1930s, concentrated on the under-employment case, and conceived of the mechanism which equates savings with investment as one which operates through variations in the general level of employment. But in his previous book, *A Treatise on Money* (written in the late 1920s), he described essentially the same mechanism as determining the relationship of prices to costs, with output and employment as given.[1]

To illustrate the nature of this process and to analyse the conditions under which the forces equalising savings and investment determine the price-cost relationship at full employment, rather than the level of employment at some *given* relationship of prices to costs, I should like to make use of the time-honoured device of the "representative firm" which is assumed to behave like a small-scale replica of the economy as a whole. I shall assume, in other words, that variations in the output of the "representative firm" reflect equivalent variations in total production, and that the firm employs a constant fraction of the total employed labour force.

I shall ignore falling average prime costs in the short period and shall assume that average and marginal prime costs are constant up to the point where the optimum utilisation of capacity is reached and begin to rise afterwards, as shown by the curves APC and MC in Fig. 2. I shall assume that our representative firm is fully integrated vertically, so that its average and marginal prime costs consist only of labour cost. (The rate of money-wages is assumed to be given.) And I shall further assume, as is appropriate for a "developed" economy under conditions of imperfect competition, that the effective bottleneck setting an upper limit to production is labour rather than physical capacity: there is more than enough capacity to employ the available labour force. Hence, since our firm accounts for a constant fraction of total employment, it cannot produce at a rate higher than that indicated by the full-employment position (as shown by the dashed line in Fig. 2.)[2]

---

[1] *A Treatise on Money* (London, 1930), vol. I, p. 139.
[2] The assumption that physical capacity is more than sufficient for the employment of the available labour force in "developed" capitalist economies is empirically supported by the fact that even in times of very low unemployment, double or treble

Finally, I shall assume that whatever the state of demand, our firm will not be forced to reduce prices to the bare level of prime costs; there is a certain *minimum margin of profit* which competition cannot succeed in eliminating. We can call this minimum profit margin the "degree of monopoly", or the "degree of market imperfection", remembering, however, that it does not necessarily *set* the price (in relation to costs), it merely sets a rock-bottom to prices. (In Fig. 2 the dot-and-dash line indicates the minimum price at the given level of prime cost per unit of output.) The greater the intensity of competition the lower will be this minimum margin of profit.

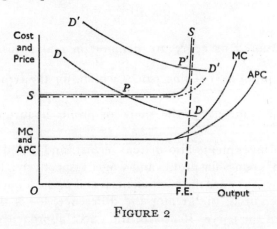

FIGURE 2

The assumption that prices cannot fall below some minimum determined by the degree of market imperfection, and that production cannot exceed a certain maximum determined by full employment, yields a short-period supply curve (the curve S–S in Fig. 2) which exhibits the familiar reverse L-shaped feature: the curve is horizontal up to a certain point (when the supply price is set by the minimum profit margin) and well-nigh vertical afterwards (when production is limited by full employment).

We can now introduce the Keynesian demand function which shows the demand price for each level of output—i.e. it shows for

---

shift utilisation of capacity is fairly rare. And it is the existence of considerable spare capacity under conditions of imperfect competition which alone explains the absence of diminishing productivity to labour with increasing employment in the short period, despite the co-existence of physical equipment of varying degrees of efficiency.

any particular output (and employment) that excess of price over prime cost which makes the effective demand in real terms equal to that output. (The excess of price over prime cost is of course the same thing, on our assumptions, as the share of profits in output.) Assuming that investment, I, is an independent variable invariant with respect to changes in output, this demand curve will be falling from left to right, much like the Marshallian demand curve, and its equation, according to the well-known multiplier formula, will be

$$D = \frac{1}{(a - \beta)\dfrac{p - c}{p} + \beta}I, \tag{11}$$

where D represents aggregate demand in real terms, $\dfrac{p - c}{p}$ the margin of profit over selling price (which, for the representative firm, is the same as $\dfrac{P}{Y}$, the share of profits in income), I the

amount of investment (also in real terms), and a and β the co-efficients of savings for profits and wages respectively. The higher is I, and the lower are the coefficients a and β, the higher the position of the curve; the greater the difference, $a - \beta$, the greater elasticity of the curve. If $\beta = 0$, the curve approaches the APC curve asymptotically; if $a = \beta$ the curve becomes a vertical straight line.

Depending on the relative position of the two curves, this intersection can yield either an under-employment equilibrium (when the demand curve cuts the supply curve in the horizontal segment of the latter, as shown by $D - D$, with the point of intersection P) or a full-employment equilibrium (as shown by $D' - D'$, with the point of intersection P'). In the former case the price-cost relationship (the distribution of income) will be independently given by the degree of market imperfection (marginal productivity plays no rôle in this case since the average productivity of labour is assumed to be constant) whilst the level of output is determined by the parameters of the demand function (the savings-investment relationship). In the latter case, output is independently given, and it is the price-cost relationship which will be determined by the demand function, i.e. by the savings-investment relationship.[1]

However, our demand curve has so far been based on the postulate that the rate of investment is invariant with respect to changes in output. In fact, it is the rate of growth of output which governs investment demand; and, in addition to the growth of output due to the natural rate of growth of the economy, investment in the short period will also vary with the change in output reflecting a change in the level of unemployment. Such "induced" investment will only come into operation, however, when the degree of utilisation of capacity permits a normal rate of profit to be earned; in other words when receipts cover, or more than cover, *total* costs, including "normal" profits on the capital invested.

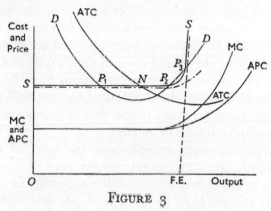

FIGURE 3

In Fig. 3 the curve *ATC* indicates average total costs (including "normal" profits) and the point N (where the curve *ATC* intersects the *S–S* curve) the level of production which yields a "normal" profit on the existing capital equipment. Beyond N, any further increase in production will "induce" investment in the shape of additions to productive capacity, and it is reasonable to suppose that the increase in investment associated with an

[1] It follows also that in so far as β (savings out of wages) is zero or negligible, under-employment equilibrium necessarily presupposes some degree of market imperfection; for if competition were perfect and the minimum profit margin were zero, the inter-section of the demand curve with the supply curve would necessarily fall on the vertical section of the latter.

increase in output will exceed the increase in savings for any *given* distribution of income. Hence the savings-investment relationship will yield a U-shaped demand curve; the curve will be falling up to N (when induced investment is zero)[1] and will slope upwards to the right of N (when induced investment is positive). As shown in Fig. 3 this will yield multiple positions of equilibrium, P_1, P_2 and P_3, of which only P_1 and P_3 are stable positions whereas P_2 is unstable (since at P_2, where the demand curve cuts the supply curve from below, a small displacement in either direction will set up cumulative forces away from P_2 until either P_1 or P_3 is reached).

It follows that an under-employment equilibrium is only *stable* under slump conditions when induced investment is zero.

It also follows that it is impossible to conceive of a *moving* equilibrium of growth being an under-employment equilibrium. Such an equilibrium is necessarily one where productive capacity is growing, and where therefore induced investment is positive, and hence the $D - D$ curve slopes upwards and not downwards. It therefore postulates the equilibrium of the P_3 type and not of the P_1 type. In that situation the profit margin must be above the minimum level, and the distribution of income will tend to be such as to generate the same proportion of income saved as the proportion of investment in output.

In a balanced-growth equilibrium, the level of investment must of course also correspond to the rate of accumulation appropriate to the rate of growth of the economy, in other words (in terms of Model II) to $(\lambda v) Y$. This is not necessarily the rate of investment reflected by our (short-period) demand curve at the point P_3; if it is not, the adjustment takes the form of a change in capacity in relation to output (a shift in point N in the diagram) and a consequent change in the investment "induced" by the excess of actual output over N sufficient to make the volume of induced investment equal to $(\lambda v) Y$.

It further follows that a moving equilibrium of growth is only possible when, given the savings propensities, the profit margin

[1] Up to point N, the position of the demand curve may be regarded as being determined by the existence of some "autonomous" investment which is independent of the current level of activity, or else by a negative constant in the savings functions, which makes savings zero at some positive level of income and employment.

resulting from the equilibrium rate of investment is higher than the minimum profit margin indicated by the height of the horizontal section of the S–S line; and there must be sufficient competition to ensure this. If this were not so, the point P_3 would lie below the S–S line, and the only equilibrium conceivable in that case would be that of the P_1 type at which, as we have seen, induced investment is zero, and the level of output remains stationary over time, irrespective of the growth in population. *It is only under conditions of "Keynesian" full employment that the growth-potential of an economy (indicated by its "natural" rate of growth) is exploited in terms of actual growth.*

We must therefore add a further restriction to our models which can be written (putting m for the minimum profit margin, reflecting the degree of market imperfection):

$$\frac{P}{Y} \geqslant m \qquad (12)$$

which, under the assumption of Model II where $\frac{P}{Y} = \lambda v$, can be written in the form

$$m \leqslant \lambda v. \qquad (12a)$$

If this condition is not satisfied, the economy will lapse into stagnation.

So far we have not mentioned marginal productivity. Clearly, the equilibrium real wage cannot *exceed* the short-period marginal product of labour: for if it did, the position of full employment could not be reached. Under our present assumptions, where the full-employment position falls within the range of the horizontal section of the average prime cost curve (or very near it), this does not impose any further restriction. For when productivity is constant, the marginal product of labour is the same as the average product, and the condition therefore is necessarily satisfied, so long as the equilibrium wage is lower than output per head (i.e. so long as the equilibrium share of profits is positive). In order to generalise our results, however, to cover the case of diminishing (short-period) returns (i.e. when the full-employment line in Figs. 2 and 3 cuts the average prime cost curve in the *rising* section of the latter and marginal costs exceed average prime costs), we need to introduce a further restriction to the effect that the share of wages cannot exceed the marginal product of labour. Writing for a *given* value of K,

$$\Upsilon = \Psi(L), \text{ where } \Psi' > 0,\ \Psi'' \leqslant 0$$

for the *short-period* relationship between output and employment (L denoting the amount of employment) the condition is

$$\frac{W}{\Upsilon} \leqslant \frac{L\Psi'(L)}{\Psi(L)}. \qquad (13)$$

Under conditions of our Model II, where $\dfrac{P}{\Upsilon} = \lambda v$, this could also be written in the form

$$\frac{\Psi(L) - L\Psi'(L)}{\Psi(L)} \leqslant \lambda v, \qquad (13a)$$

i.e. the equilibrium share of profits, as determined by the "dynamic" conditions, cannot be less than the excess of the average product of labour over the marginal product. We can assume, however that the system will tend to generate sufficient excess capacity (in relation to the labour supply) for this condition to be satisfied.

These two restrictions, (12) and (13), together with that given in (5), are not additive but alternative, and only the higher of them will apply. For our minimum margin of profit in (12) is not the same thing as the "optimum" monopoly profit of the text-books, which is the outcome of short-period profit-maximisation with reference to some given marginal-revenue schedule to the individual firm. It is more akin to Marshall's notion of a minimum margin of profit on turnover below which producers refuse to go "for fear of spoiling the market",[1] but which tends to be the lower, the more intense the competition among producers. As such it is related to the average cost of production and not to marginal cost; and as an obstacle to a fall in the profit-share, it overlaps with the technical barrier set by the excess of short-period marginal cost over average prime cost.

---

[1] *Principles* (8th ed.), Book V, ch. 5, section 5, pp. 374–6.

VIII. TECHNICAL PROGRESS

We must now proceed to remove the most important of our "simplifying" assumptions, the absence of technical progress. A moving equilibrium of growth involves continued increase in the productivity of labour and not only in the working population, *pari passu* with a continued increase in the amount of capital per worker; though in the absence of any reliable measure of the quantity of capital (in a world where the technical specification of capital goods is constantly changing, new kinds of goods constantly appear and others disappear) the very notion of the "amount of capital" loses precision. The terms "income" or "capital" no longer have any precise meaning; they are essentially accounting magnitudes, which merely serve as the basis of calculations in business planning; the assumption that money has a stable value in terms of some price index enables us to think of "income" and "capital" as *real* magnitudes only in a limited, and not precisely definable, sense.[1]

Orthodox theory attempts to deal with these problems in terms of the traditional tools—the assumption of a linear and homogeneous production function, coupled with the assumption that with the changing state of knowledge this function is continually shifting upwards and outwards. As depicted in Fig. 4

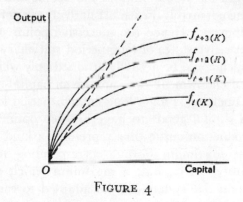

FIGURE 4

[1] These problems do not appear in a von Neumann type of model of balanced-growth equilibrium with constant technical functions, precisely because the technical specification of goods, their relative composition and their relative values remain unchanged through time; everything remains the same, except for the actual quantities of goods, and there is no problem involved in aggregation.

at any one *point* of time, *t*, there is assumed to be a unique relationship between capital and output, which conforms to the general hypothesis of diminishing productivity, but this relationship is constantly shifting with the passage of time. The assumption of "neutral" technical progress means that the production curve shifts in such a manner that the slope of the tangents of the functions f_t, f_{t+1}, f_{t+2}, etc., remain unchanged along any radius from the origin. This hypothesis is necessary in order to make it possible for a constant rate of profit over time to be consistent with a constant rate of growth and a constant relationship between capital and output (since the rate of profit on capital is uniquely related to the slope of the production function).

There are, however, several basic faults in this procedure—quite apart from the inherent improbability that technical progress should obey any such rigid rules.

(1) In the first place the production function assumes that the capital stock in existence at any one time is perfectly adapted to any given capital-labour ratio—that there is a particular assortment of equipment goods corresponding to each successive point of the production curve which is different from the assortment associated with any neighbouring point. (This will be true even in the absence of "technical progress" so long as the substitution of capital for labour implies the use of different *kinds* of equipment, and not merely the use of relatively greater quantities of the *same* equipment.) Hence the successive points on this curve represent alternative states of long-period stationary equilibrium any one of which could be actually attained only when any given state of capital endowment (i.e., any given capital-output ratio) has obtained unchanged for a long enough period for the actual assortment of capital goods to have become optimally adapted to it. The production curve thus represents a kind of boundary indicating the maximum output corresponding to each particular "quantity" of capital, a maximum which assumes that the whole productive system is fully adapted to each particular state of accumulation. In an economy where capital accumulation is a continuous process this boundary is never attained—since the actual assortment of capital goods at any one time (even with a *constant* state of knowledge, whatever that assumption may be

taken to mean) will consist of items appropriate to differing states of accumulation, and the output corresponding to any particular "quantity" of capital will be less than the equilibrium (or maximum) output associated with that quantity. This is only another way of saying that in a society which is *not* in continuous long-run stationary equilibrium, output cannot be regarded as a unique function of capital and labour; and the slope of the production curve cannot be relevant to the pricing process, since the system does not move *along* the curve, but *inside* it.

(2) In the second place (and quite independently of the first point) the assumption that there is a curve which continually shifts upwards means that technical progress is treated as a variable of the function in a manner perfectly analogous to a second factor of production, like labour (or land). This is evident from the consideration that if, instead of postulating rising technical knowledge and a constant labour force, we postulated a constant state of technical knowledge and a rising labour force, the nature of the shift of the curve (under the hypothesis of a homogeneous and linear function) would be exactly the same. A given rate of shift of the curve, along any radius from the origin, could equally well result from a given percentage increase in the labour supply as from the same percentage increase in the state of "knowledge". But unlike labour, the state of knowledge is not a quantifiable factor. A *given* or a *constant* state of knowledge is only capable of being defined implicitly: there is no possible way in which, comparing two different positions, at two different points of time, the change due to the movement along the curve could be isolated from the change due to the shift of the curve. The whole procedure by which this separation is attempted is purely circular: since the *slope* of the curve (under the additional hypothesis that the function is not only homogeneous and linear but a constant-elasticity function *à la* Cobb-Douglas!) is supposed to determine the share of profits in income, the share of profits is taken to be an indication of its slope, and the residual is then attributed to the shift of the curve! There could be no better example of *post hoc ergo propter hoc*.

(3) The hypothesis that the *slope* of the curve determines the share of profits, in accordance with the marginal productivity

principle, despite the continued shift in the curve, presumes of
course that the factor responsible for the shift is itself rewarded
on the same principle, since it is the marginal product of *all*
factors taken *together* which exhausts the total product. This
condition can be satisfied when the shift of the curve is due to,
say, a certain rate of increase in the quantity of labour, since that
part of the increase in the product which is due to the shift is
definitely imputed to labour in the form of wages. But knowledge,
just because it is not a quantifiable factor which can be measured,
or brought under exclusive ownership, or bought and sold, cannot
receive its *own* marginal product. It is like other scarce but un-
appropriated agents of production (like the sea in the case of the
fishing industry) whose existence causes divergences between the
private and the social product of the *other* factors. This is only
another way of saying that we are not free to elevate to the
rôle of a "factor of production" anything we like; the variables of
the production function must be true inputs, and not vague
"background elements", like the sun or the sea or the state of
knowledge, any of which may be thought to cause the results
to diverge from the hypothesis of the homogeneous-and-linear
production function. In terms of the *true* variables, Capital and
Labour, the production function will not be linear-homogeneous
but will be a function of a higher order, when technical knowledge
is increasing over time.[1] It is therefore illegitimate to assume
that factor rewards are allocated in accordance with their marginal productivities, since the sum of the marginal products
of the factors will exceed the total product. When, the quantity
of labour being given, an increase in capital by a given proportion yields an increase in output in the same proportion,
the "true" marginal product of capital will *alone* exhaust the
total product.[2] For this reason any postulate derived from the

---

[1] It is a well-known dodge that any function whatsoever in n variables can be
converted into a homogeneous-and-linear function of $n+1$ variables by adding a
further variable which is *implicitly* defined. But as Samuelson has pointed out (*Foundations of Economic Analysis*, p. 84), any such procedure is illegitimate, since factor
rewards will not conform to the partial differentials of this wider function.

[2] Supporters of the neo-classical approach would argue that the increase in product
in this case is not *due* to the change in the quantity of capital alone—it is the joint
result of the change in the quantity of the "factor" capital, and the shift in the "state
of knowledge" which is presumed to have occurred in the interval of time during
which the increase in capital occurred. But this is precisely the point: since the accumu-

hypothesis of diminishing productivity (such as our $v = \phi\left(\dfrac{P}{K}\right)$ function, given in equation (8a) above) is illegitimate when productivity, for whatever reason, is *not* diminishing. Given the fact of constant or increasing productivity to capital accumulation, the share of profit must necessarily be *less* than the marginal product of capital, and there is no reason why a given capital-output ratio should be associated with a particular rate of profit, or indeed, why the two should be functionally related to each other on account of any technical factor.

(4) Added to this is the further complication that the rate of shift of the production function due to the changing state of "knowledge" cannot be treated as an independent function of (chronological) time, but depends on the rate of accumulation of capital itself. Since improved knowledge is, largely if not entirely, infused into the economy through the introduction of new equipment, the rate of shift of the curve will itself depend on the *speed of movement* along the curve, which makes any attempt to isolate the one from the other the more nonsensical.[1]

The most that one can say is that whereas the rate of technical improvement will depend on the rate of capital accumulation, any society has only a limited capacity to *absorb* technical change in a

---

lation of capital is necessarily a process in time, and cannot be conceived of in a time-less fashion, a movement *along* the curve cannot be isolated from the shift of the curve; indeed it is illegitimate to assume the existence of a "curve" independently of its shift, since there is no conceivable operation by which the slope of this "curve" could be identified.

[1] None of the above strictures against the postulate of a "production function" which continually shifts with technical progress invalidates the assumption of a *short-period* relationship between employment and output, which takes the character and composition of fixed equipment of all kinds as given. This short-period production function (as employed in equations (13) and (13a) above) implies that for any given volume of employment a definite "marginal product" can be imputed to labour, which, as we have seen, sets an *upper limit* to the share of wages in output (the "rents" to be imputed to capital being the residual, i.e. the difference between the average and the marginal product of labour). This limit, however, only becomes significant when diminishing returns prevail, so that an increase in production is associated with a more-than proportionate increase in employment—with constant or increasing returns, the marginal product of labour will be equal to, or exceed, the average product, and the former *cannot* therefore be the governing factor determining distributive shares. Whether diminishing returns prevail or not will predominantly depend on the output capacity represented by the existing capital stock and its degree of utilisation when labour is fully employed. Under conditions of imperfect competition it is perfectly compatible with "profit-maximising behaviour" to suppose that the representative firm will maintain a considerable amount of spare capacity even in relation to the output attainable under full-employment conditions.

C

given period. Hence, whether the increase in output will be more or less than proportionate to the increase in capital will depend, not on the state of knowledge or the rate of progress in knowledge, but on the *speed* with which capital is accumulated, relatively to the capacity to innovate and to infuse innovations into the economic system. The more "dynamic" are the people in control of production, the keener they are in search of improvements, and the readier they are to adopt new ideas and to introduce new ways of doing things, the faster production (per man) will rise, and the higher is the rate of accumulation of capital that can be profitably maintained.

These hypotheses can, in my view, be projected in terms of a "technical progress function" which postulates a relationship between the rate of increase of capital and the rate of increase in output and which embodies the effect of constantly improving knowledge and know-how, as well as the effect of increasing capital per man, without any attempt to isolate the one from the other.

It is the shape and position of this "technical progress function" which will exhibit features of diminishing returns. If we plot percentage growth rate of output per head, $\overset{\circ}{Y}/Y$, along the abscissa and percentage growth rate of capital per head, $\overset{\circ}{K}/K$, along the ordinate (Fig. 5), the curve will cut the y-axis positively (since a certain rate of improvement would take place even if capital per head remained unchanged) but it will be convex upwards, and reach a maximum at a certain point—there is always a maximum beyond which a further increase in the rate of accumulation

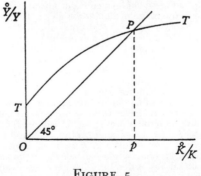

FIGURE 5

will not enhance further the *rate* of growth of output (Fig. 5). This means that the increase in capital (per head) will yield increasing or diminishing returns in terms of output according as the rate of accumulation is relatively small or large. If the rate of accumulation is less than Op, output will increase faster than capital, and vice versa.

The *height* of the curve expresses society's "dynamism", meaning by this both inventiveness and readiness to change or to experiment. But the convexity of the curve expresses the fact that it is possible to utilise as yet unexploited ideas (whether old ideas or new ideas) more or less fully; and it is always the most profitable ideas (i.e. those that raise output most in relation to the investment which they require) which are exploited first. Some are old ideas; some are new ideas; most of the technical improvement that takes place embodies both. We cannot isolate the element of pure novelty in a world where knowledge is constantly improving, and where the techniques actually used constantly lag behind the very latest techniques that would be selected if everything were started afresh. When capital is accumulated at a faster rate (and technical improvement goes on at a faster rate), productivity will also increase at a faster rate, but the growth in the latter will lag behind the growth in the former, and beyond a certain point a further increase in the rate of accumulation ceases to be "productive"—it is incapable of stepping up the rate of growth of productivity any further.

There is therefore no *unique* rate of technical progress—no *unique* rate at which alone a constant rate of growth can be maintained. There is a whole series of such rates, depending on the rate of accumulation of capital being relatively small or large.

On this analysis, it is the "technical dynamism" of the economy, as shown by the height or position of our technical progress curve, which is responsible, in a capitalist economy, both for making the rate of accumulation of capital and the rate of growth of production relatively small or relatively large. It explains why there is no long-run tendency to a *falling* rate of profit, or for a continued increase in capital in relation to output, either in slow-growing or in fast-growing economies. In economies whose technical dynamism is low, both the rate of accumulation and the growth of production will be relatively low, but in either case, growth can go on at a steady rate, without any necessary tendency to diminishing returns and thus to a gradual approach to a stationary state.

On the assumption that this function cuts the y-axis positively (i.e. that there would be some positive rate of growth in output per man, even if capital per man remained unchanged—an assumption which is justified by the fact that even a zero rate of net investment implies a certain rate of infusion of new techniques or new designs, through the replacement of worn-out capital; and that there are always *some* improvements which may require no investment at all) and that the curve is convex upwards, there is necessarily a certain point on the curve at which it is intersected by a radius of 45 degrees from the origin—i.e. where the rate of growth of output is equal to the rate of growth of capital (P in Fig. 5). At that point *all* the conditions of "neutral" technical progress are satisfied: the capital-output ratio will remain constant at a constant rate of growth, constant distributive shares, and a constant rate of profit on capital.

In order to "close" our model—that is, to produce a model that would account for the empirical features of the growth process as summarised by our "stylised facts" at the beginning—it is necessary to show, not merely that such a point exists, but that in a capitalist system there is a tendency to move towards this point, which thus represents a long-run equilibrium rate of growth, and which is also stable in the sense that displacements due to shifts in the curve, etc., set up forces to re-establish it.

The hypothesis that *given* the technical progress function, the system tends towards that particular rate of accumulation where the conditions of "neutral progress" are satisfied, cannot of course be justified on *a priori* grounds; it must be based on empirical evidence—at least in the sense that it can be shown to be consistent with facts which are more difficult to explain on any alternative hypothesis. Supposing that the statisticians were to agree that the capital-output ratio tends to be constant in periods in which the rate of growth of production is constant (in which therefore the rate of technical progress is neither increasing nor decreasing) whilst the capital-output ratio tends to decrease in periods of accelerating growth and vice versa. This would support the hypothesis that the system *tends* towards P: and variations in the rate of growth, and in the movements in the capital-output ratio, are then to be explained in terms of the unequal incidence of technical progress—i.e. in terms of shifts of our technical progress function. If, on the other hand, the statisticians were to agree that there is no correlation between these magnitudes, that periods of steady growth are just as likely to be associated with a steadily decreasing or a steadily increasing ratio of capital to output, this would support the hypothesis that the system tends towards some point on the curve—to some equilibrium rate of growth of output and of capital—which is not necessarily the one at which the two growth rates are *equal*.

IX. ASSUMPTIONS ABOUT INVESTMENT BEHAVIOUR

In either event, to obtain an equilibrium solution—to assert, in other words, that there is some particular equilibrium rate of growth of output and of capital towards which the system is tending—we need to introduce an "investment function" based on entrepreneurial behaviour. Since we *cannot* say that the rate of capital accumulation depends on the community's propensity to save (since the latter is a dependent variable, depending on the share of profits, and thus on the share of investment) nor on the requirements of the "natural rate of growth" (because one of the two constituents at least of the natural rate of growth, the rate of growth of productivity, is a dependent variable, depending on the rate of accumulation of capital and thus on the share of investment), we need to introduce, in order to close our model, an independent function describing the investment decisions of entrepreneurs. There are various alternative assumptions that can be made about investment behaviour which lead to divergent results; and at the present stage we cannot say that our knowledge of entrepreneurial behaviour is sufficient to rule out any particular assumption in preference to some other. Hence our final choice of assumption must be based on the admittedly weaker procedure of its yielding results that are more in conformity with the facts of experience than its alternatives.

(1) One hypothesis, originally advanced by Kalecki,[1] is that the subjective risks assumed by entrepreneurs are an increasing function of the rate of capital accumulation (or, as Kalecki put it, the rate of investment decisions is an increasing function of the gap between the prospective rate of profit and the rate of interest). This assumption, at any rate for a given market rate of interest, makes the rate of capital accumulation a single-valued function of the rate of profit on capital, and since the latter, in a state of balanced-growth equilibrium, is a single-valued function

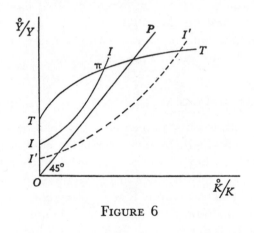

FIGURE 6

of the rate of growth, it makes the desired rate of accumulation a single-valued function of the rate of economic growth. Such an "inducement to invest" function is shown by the curve *I–I* in Fig. 6. The height of this curve (i.e. the point at which it cuts the *y*-axis) reflects the market rate of interest, while the slope of the curve reflects increasing marginal risk. This postulate yields an equilibrium position at point *π* where the rate of economic growth resulting from the given rate of capital accumulation coincides with the rate of economic growth that is required in order to induce entrepreneurs to accumulate capital at that particular rate. On this hypothesis the equilibrium rate of growth can be anywhere on the *T–T* curve, depending only on the position of the risk preference function (governing the inducement to invest) relatively to the technical progress function (governing

[1] "The Principle of Increasing Risk", *Economica*, 1937, p. 440.

the rate of growth resulting from varying rates of accumulation). Thus if π is to the left of P, the equilibrium rate of growth will involve a constantly falling capital-output ratio, and if it is to the right of P (as with the dotted line $I'-I'$ in Fig. 6) it involves a constantly rising capital-output ratio. In both cases the rate of growth will be constant over time, but in the first case the equilibrium will involve a steadily falling share of profit in income and in the second case a steadily rising share of profit. On this hypothesis therefore the "neutral" position at P will only be reached as a result of a coincidence—of the $I-I$ curve cutting the $T-T$ curve at that point.

(2) An alternative hypothesis, which is a variant of the one put forward in my paper "A Model of Economic Growth",[1] makes the principle of increasing risk applicable, not to the volume of investment decisions as such, but only to that part of investment which is in excess of that required to maintain a constant relationship between output capacity and prospective output. Whenever sales are rising, entrepreneurs will in any case increase the capital invested in the business by the amount necessary to enable them to increase their productive capacity in line with the growth of their sales—there are no greater risks involved in a larger business than a smaller one; and no greater risks are entailed in a higher rate of growth of employed capital, if this proceeds *pari passu* with a higher rate of growth of turnover. Hence if their actual sales are rising at the rate of g (where g may be any particular point on the $T-T$ curve in Fig. 6) we may suppose, in accordance with the "acceleration principle", that the growth in output in itself will "induce" sufficient investment to enable that rate of growth of production to be maintained, without requiring a higher prospective rate of profit. As far as this "induced investment" is concerned, any particular point on the curve could be an equilibrium point. But if a particular rate of growth of output and capital involves the expectation of a *rising* rate of profit in the minds of investors, it will induce an acceleration in the rate of accumulation and hence will cause the system

---

[1] *Economic Journal*, 1957, p. 604. The form of the "investment function" given in that paper was justly criticised; the present version, I hope, meets the objections raised against the earlier version by Professor Meade, Mr. Hudson and others.

to move to the right (on the curve); if it involves the expectation of a falling rate of profit, it will cause it to move to the left.

The *prospective* rate of profit in the minds of entrepreneurs is based on two things: on the amount of capital required per unit of output, and on the expected profit margin per unit of output. If we assume that all savings come out of profits (i.e. $\beta = 0$) then, given constant rates of accumulation and growth, the realised rate of profit on capital will also be constant over time, irrespective of whether capital per unit of output is constant, rising or falling (since any reduction in the capital-output ratio will be matched by a corresponding reduction in the share of profits in output, and vice versa). But we cannot assume that the *prospective* rate of profit on current investment will be the same as the *realised* rate of profit on existing capital—the prospective rate of profit will be higher, precisely because the capital required for producing a unit-stream of future output is less than the amount of capital that was (historically) invested in producing a unit-stream of current output. Nor can it be assumed that the prospective rate of profit on new investment will be the same as the actually realised rate of profit in future periods, since the latter magnitude will itself depend on the investment decisions currently made by entrepreneurs. Thus if at some particular rate of accumulation the trend of progress causes a continued fall in the amount of capital required per unit of output,

$$\frac{P}{K} \equiv \frac{P}{Y} \cdot \frac{Y}{K}$$

will remain constant if the rise in Y/K is offset by a corresponding fall in P/Y. This would occur if the fall in K/Y involved a corresponding reduction in I/Y; if, in other words, it left the rate of expansion of capacity unchanged. But if this consequential fall in profit margins is *not* foreseen, or not sufficiently foreseen, the rise in Y/K will involve the expectation of a higher prospective rate of profit, which by increasing the rate of investment may prevent the fall in P/Y from occurring at all. This is a case, therefore, where the movement of the economy, and the nature of the final equilibrium, cannot be predicted independently of the nature of the expectations of entrepreneurs. The assumption of "static fore-sight" (i.e. the projection of existing prices, costs and output levels to the future) leads to a different result from the assumption of "perfect foresight"; the latter assumption moreover leaves the situation indeterminate since the expectations that are capable of being actually realised are by no means unique. It is only in the "neutral" equilibrium case (at point P) that the two kinds of assumptions (static foresight and perfect foresight) lead to consistent results.

Expectations are invariably based on past experience, and in that sense, are of the "static" rather than of the "perfect" kind. In addition, they can be defined as being more or less "elastic" according as the projections into the future are based on the events of the very recent past, or on the average experience of a longer interval of elapsed time. Expectations are likely to be the more elastic the less past experience justifies the assumption of some norm around which short-term movements fluctuate; the more, in other words, past movements have been subject to a trend. For that reason, business expectations are far more likely to be elastic with respect to volume of sales than with respect to the margin of profit on turnover; the future expectation concerning the margin of profit per unit of sales, which is taken as the basis of business calculations, is far more likely to reflect some standard, or norm, than the experience of the most recent period alone. This provides a further reason for supposing that in situations in which production rises faster than the stock of capital, the prospective rate of profit will be rising relatively to the realised rate of profit; and if, in response to this, the rate of accumulation is accelerated, the rate of growth of production, and the realised rate of profit, will rise as well.

Hence the tendency of the system to move towards a position where output and capital both grow at the same rate, and where therefore the rate of profit on capital will remain constant at a constant margin of profit on turnover, can be justified by the suppositions (i) that the prospective rate of profit on investments will be higher than the currently realised rate of profit on existing capital whenever production is rising faster than the capital stock; (ii) that a rise in the prospective rate of profit causes an increase in the rate of investment, relative to the requirements of a state of steady growth, and vice versa.[1]

X. THE FINAL MODEL

The equilibrium relationships of this final model can thus be set out as follows. It is based on three functions: first, on a savings function on the lines of equation (10) above, which can be written in the form

$$\frac{S}{Y} = (a - \beta)\frac{P}{Y} + \beta, \tag{10a}$$

where $1 > a > \beta \geqslant 0.$

Second, on a technical progress function showing the relationship between the rate of growth of output per worker (G_0) and the rate of growth of capital per head $(G_K - \lambda)$, and which (using a linear equation for the sake of convenience)[2] can be written in the form

$$G_0 = a' + \beta'(G_K - \lambda), \text{ where } a' > 0, \ 1 > \beta' > 0. \tag{14}$$

[1] In the first version of the present growth model (published in the *Economic Journal*, December 1957 and reprinted in *Essays on Economic Stability and Growth*, pp. 259–300) I postulated an investment function which made current investment depend (*inter alia*) on the change in the *realised* rate of profit as compared with the previous period. This was unsatisfactory in that it failed to take into account the fact that the inducement to invest depends on the prospective rate of profit, and not on the actual profit earned on existing capital; and that quite apart from the question of expectations, the prospective rate of profit will differ from the currently realised rate whenever (owing to technical progress, etc.) the "productivity" of capital on new investment (i.e. the amount of investment required per unit of future output capacity) differs from the existing capital-output ratio.

[2] It has been pointed out to me by Professor Meade, Mr. Hahn and others that whilst, in general, the technical progress function cannot be integrated in terms of a production function with a particular rate of time shift, a *linear* technical progress function as given in (14) can be integrated to obtain

$$Y_t = Be^{a't}K_t{}^\beta \tag{14a}$$

which appears to be the same as the Cobb-Douglas function (remembering that Y_t and K_t refer to the output and the capital *per unit* of labour). However, as was pointed out to me by H. Uzawa of Stanford University, in integrating the technical progress function, the constant of the integral $B = B(Y_0, K_0)$ is a function dependent on the initial amount of capital K_0 and of output Y_0, whereas a production function of the type

$$Y_t = f(K_t, t) \tag{14b}$$

requires that the function should be independent of the initial conditions.

Apart from this, the aggregative production function of the type (14b), a special case of which is the Cobb-Douglas function, implies the assumption that at any given time t, the output Y_t is uniquely determined by the aggregates, K_t and L_t, irrespective of the age-and-industry composition of the capital stock. However,

Third, on an investment function based on the assumptions already described, and which makes investment a combination of two terms. The first term of the equation relates to the amount of investment *induced* by the change in output the previous period, and assumes that this investment will be such as to make the growth in *output capacity* in period $(t + \theta)$ equal to the growth in output in period t. Since in view of (14), the rate of capital accumulation per worker $(G_K - \lambda)$, which is required to increase output capacity by G_0 will not (necessarily) be equal to G_0 but to

$$\frac{G_0 - a'}{\beta'}$$

and since $\qquad\qquad G_K \equiv \frac{I}{K},$

the rate of *induced* investment in period $(t + \theta)$ and which is the first term of our investment equation, will be equal to

$$(G_0(t) - a')\frac{K(t)}{\beta'} + \lambda K'(t).$$

The second term of our investment equation depends on the change in the prospective rate of profit which, on our assumptions concerning the expected margin of profit turnover (i.e., that the *expected* value of Γ/Υ is based on an average past values), will be a rising function of the *change* in Υ/K over time. Assuming this latter relationship to be linear for the sake of convenience the whole function can be expressed in the following form:

---

when the technical progress of an economy depends on its rate of capital accumulation (when, in other words, the improvements in techniques require to be embodied in new equipment before they can be taken advantage of), no such functional relationship exists. To describe the relationship between capital, labour and output we require a function in the form

$$\Upsilon_t = \phi(A_t) \qquad\qquad (14c)$$

where A_t specifies the distribution of capital according to age as well as (in a multi-commodity world) the distribution of both capital and labour between industries and firms. In that case the postulate of a linear technical progress function is perfectly consistent with the ϕ function being neither homogeneous in the first degree nor of constant elasticity. In the short run the age-and-industry distribution is of course given as a matter of past history. But even in a long-run growth equilibrium with technical progress, A_t could not be treated as a unique function of K_t and L_t, since it will also depend on λ and (in view of the varying incidence of obsolescence at differing rates of progress) on γ', the equilibrium value of G_0.

$$I(t+\theta) = (G_0(t) - a')\frac{K(t+\theta)}{\beta'} + \lambda K(t+\theta) + \mu\frac{d}{dt}\left(\frac{Y(t)}{K(t)}\right), \quad (15)$$

where $\mu > 0$.

The first term of this equation gives rise to an amount of investment at any given rate of growth of output that is sufficient to maintain that rate of growth of output—i.e. sufficient to keep the system on any particular point on the $T-T$ curve. It can also be seen immediately that when

$$G_Y > G_K,$$

the second term of the expression is positive, hence G_K will be rising over time. A rise in G_K, in accordance with (14), will raise G_Y but less than proportionately, and hence lead to a further rise in investment in accordance with the first term at the same time as it diminishes the second term. Hence, whatever initial position we start from (defined by given values of K, L, and O at some initial point $t = 0$), this process will gradually lead to a situation in which the second term of equation (15) dependent on $\frac{d}{dt}\left(\frac{Y(t)}{K(t)}\right)$ vanishes to zero and where therefore

$$\frac{dv(t)}{dt} = 0. \quad (16)$$

This implies that
$$G_0 = \frac{a'}{1 - \beta'} = \gamma', \quad (17)$$

and
$$G_Y = G_K = \lambda + \gamma'. \quad (18)$$

Hence this model, like the earlier ones, also yields a state of moving equilibrium, where the rate of growth, the capital-output ratio and the distributive shares are constant over time—the main difference being that the output per worker, capital per worker and wages per worker are now no longer constant but rising at the equilibrium rate of growth productivity, γ'. However, these assumptions are not yet sufficient to set out a full equilibrium model. The reason is that since we no longer have a technical equation for v on the lines of equation (8a) which was incorporated in Models III and IV, the actual value of v is here left undetermined. From this model it only follows that at the position of equilibrium v will be constant (since this is implicit in equation (15), as shown by (16)); but this is consistent with any particular value for v—or rather v could only be determined in this model historically, if we assumed that it had a certain initial value at some particular point of time, and followed its resulting movement through the successive steps to final equilibrium.

Hence, in order to close the model, we shall introduce two more variables and three additional relationships. These are strictly "Keynesian"—since they are, on the one hand, necessary to ensure that the reaction-mechanism of the model follows the Keynesian system in which the inducement to invest is independent of the propensities to save; and on the other hand because they incorporate Keynesian notions of the rate of interest and the supply price for risk capital based on liquidity preference and the aversion to risk taking.

We have already argued in connection with (5) above[1] that the inequality

$$\frac{P}{K} \geqslant r + \rho$$

is a necessary boundary condition of the model in the sense that the continued accumulation of capital cannot go on unless the ruling rate of profit is *at least* as high as the necessary compensation for risk and illiquidity involved in the productive employment of wealth.[2] Further consideration shows that in order that the investment equation in (15) should hold, it is not enough to make equation (5) into a boundary condition; for so long as P/K is higher than the supply price of risk capital, there is no reason to suppose that investment outlay will be confined to that necessary for the increase in output capacity (i.e. to that given by "the acceleration principle") or to that resulting from a given increase in the prospective rate of profit in a particular period.

[1] P. 15 above.
[2] A more precise statement of this condition would break down $r + \rho$ further into its component elements, distinguishing between the expected average of short rates of interest and the premium of the long rate over the expected average short rate on the one hand, and the additional lenders', borrowers' and speculative risks, etc., involved in direct investment, on the other hand, but this is not necessary for our present purposes.

Indeed, unless the rate of profit actually corresponds to the supply price of risk capital, one cannot assume that the investment of each period will be confined to the *new* investment opportunities accruing in that period—an assumption necessary for an equilibrium of steady growth. Hence equation (5) should be converted into an equilibrium condition

$$\frac{P}{K} = r + \rho. \tag{19}$$

The second relationship concerns the behaviour of the rate of interest, r, and here we shall follow orthodox Keynesian lines in assuming that the rate of interest is determined by the liquidity preference function and/or monetary policy (summarised in the function $\pi\left(\dfrac{M}{Y}\right)$, where $\pi' \leqslant 0$ and M is the real quantity of money), subject to the condition that there is a minimum $(\bar{r})$ determined by the risk premium associated with the holding of long-term financial assets, below which the rate of interest cannot fall. This relationship can therefore be expressed in two alternative forms

$$r \geqslant \bar{r}$$

when $r > \bar{r}$, $$r = \pi\left(\frac{M}{Y}\right). \tag{20}$$

The third relationship concerns the behaviour of ρ, and though this equation can be fully supported on *a priori* grounds, it is put forward here more tentatively, as at present there is insufficient empirical evidence available to support it. It is based on the following considerations.

(1) First, as explained earlier in this paper,[1] it may be assumed that at any given rate of interest the minimum rate of profit necessary to provide inducement for any particular kind of investment will be higher the riskier (or the more "illiquid") that investment is considered to be;

(2) Second, as was also argued,[2] investment in "fixed assets" (plant and equipment, etc.) is considered to be far more risky or

---

[1] P. 40–2 above.
[2] *Ibid.*

illiquid than either investment in financial assets or in working capital;

(3) Third, it may be assumed that the turnover-period of circulating capital is invariant (or practically invariant) with respect to changes in the techniques of production, so that circulating capital stands always in a linear relationship to output; hence any increase in the ratio of fixed to circulating capital involves an increase in the capital-output ratio.

It follows as a joint result of (2) and (3) that a higher capital-output ratio (including both fixed and circulating capital in the capital employed) requires for any given rate of interest a *higher* minimum rate of profit. Hence when the stage of accumulation is reached in which the actual rate of profit becomes *equal* to this minimum, the capital-output ratio will be uniquely related to the rate of profit; and, as we have seen, it is only under these conditions that the actual investment in each period is limited by the "new" investment opportunities becoming available in that period (through λ and γ').

Writing F for fixed capital and C for circulating capital, k for the turnover-period of circulating capital, ρ_F and ρ_C for the marginal risk premium on the two types of investments respectively, and ρ for the marginal risk premium on investment in general, we thus have the following additional assumptions and relationships:

$$K \equiv F + C$$

$$C = kY$$

$$v \equiv \frac{K}{Y} \equiv \frac{F + kY}{Y}$$

$$\rho_F > \rho_C$$

$$\therefore \rho \equiv \frac{\rho_F F + \rho_C kY}{F + kY} = \xi_1\left(\frac{F}{Y}\right)$$

$$\rho = \xi_2(v), \text{ where } \xi_2' > 0. \tag{21}$$

It will be noted that the relationship expressed in (21) operates in a reverse manner to equation (8a) which determines v in the "neo-classical" model; since in the case of (8a), ϕ' is negative, not positive.

We have argued at some length that equation (8a) can no longer be assumed to hold when technical progress is a continuing process and there is *no* unique function relating output to the capital stock, in which case, depending on the factors determining the rate of growth, varying shares of profit in income and varying rates of profit on capital can be associated with any *given* capital-output ratio. It is now seen that when equation (21) holds, equation (8a) *cannot* hold—at least not within the framework of a model which assumes that the money rate of interest is determined by "monetary" factors and that there is a minimum below which the rate of interest cannot fall.[1]

We can now set out our final Model V in a formal manner. It contains ten equations and ten variables—$Y(t)$, $O(t)$, $L(t)$, $P(t)$, $v(t)$, $s(t)$, $w(t)$, $G_0(t)$, $\rho(t)$ and $r(t)$. We shall continue to assume for simplicity that β is zero (there are no savings out of wages) and we shall take the simpler form of (20), treating the money rate of interest as a constant. We shall also bring together the various boundary conditions that emerged in the course of the analysis (cf. equations (4), (12) and (13) above, including a further one that is implicit in the relationship expressed in (21)).

Assumptions

$$L^*(t) = L^*(\text{o})e^{\lambda t} \tag{i}$$

$$G_0(t) = \alpha' + \beta'(G_K(t) - \lambda) \tag{ii}$$

$$s(t) = \alpha\frac{P(t)}{Y(t)} \tag{iii}$$

$$\frac{dv(t)}{dt} = \text{o} \tag{iv}$$

for all $t \geqslant \text{o}$

$$r(t) = \bar{r} \tag{v}$$

$$\rho(t) = \xi(v(t)) \tag{vi}$$
$$\xi' > \text{o}$$

[1] It might be argued that the two equations could be made compatible with one another by an appropriate movement of the money price level which brought the "real" rate of interest (*à la* Fisher) into an appropriate relationship with the other factors. But the movement of the price level depends on the behaviour of money wages (relatively to the change in productivity, γ') and this factor cannot, in turn, be treated as a function of the other variables.

Identity

$$P(t) \equiv \Upsilon(t) - w(t)L(t) \qquad \text{(vii)}$$

Equilibrium Conditions

$$s(t)\Upsilon(t) = \frac{dK(t)}{dt} \qquad \text{(viii)}$$

$$L(t) = L^*(t) \qquad \text{for all } t \geq 0 \qquad \text{(ix)}$$

$$\frac{P(t)}{K(t)} = r(t) + \rho(t) \qquad \text{(x)}$$

subject to the inequalities

(a) $\qquad\qquad w(t) \geq w_{min}$

(b) $\qquad\qquad \dfrac{P(t)}{\Upsilon(t)} \geq m$

(c) $\qquad\qquad \dfrac{W(t)}{\Upsilon(t)} \leq \dfrac{\dfrac{d\Upsilon(t)}{dL(t)}(Lt)}{\Upsilon(t)}$

(d) $\qquad\qquad \rho_F + \bar{r} > \dfrac{\lambda + \gamma'}{a} > \rho_C + \bar{r}. \qquad$ **(V)**

It is readily seen that the above yields a determinate system provided that the solutions fall within the limits indicated by the boundary conditions (a)–(d). By (ii) and (iv) we have

$$G_n = \frac{a'}{1 - \beta'} \equiv \gamma' \text{ (say)}.$$

Hence by (i) and (ix) $\quad G_Y = \lambda + \gamma'.$

But by (vii) $\qquad G_Y(t) = \dfrac{s(t)}{v(t)} = \lambda + \gamma' \equiv N \text{ (say)}.$

By (iii), (v), (vi) and (x)

$$\frac{P(t)}{K(t)} = \frac{s(t)}{av(t)} = \frac{N}{a} = \bar{r} + \xi(v(t)).$$

Hence by solving the last equality for $v(o)$, we can obtain all the remaining unknowns of the system.

If inequality (a) does not hold, $\dfrac{P}{Y}$ will be compressed below its equilibrium level, and hence the rate of accumulation and the rate of growth will be less than that indicated. As long, however, as we abstract from diminishing returns due to limited natural resources, and assume continuous technical progress, so that $G_0(t)$ rises over time, sooner or later the point must be reached where this inequality becomes satisfied.[1]

If, on the other hand, any one of the inequalities (b), (c) or (d) is not satisfied, $\dfrac{P}{Y}$ will be larger than its equilibrium value, and full-employment growth equilibrium becomes impossible. As regards (c) we may assume that there is always some degree of excess capacity (i.e., some relationship between output capacity and the full-employment labour supply) which satisfies this condition, and the system will tend to generate the required amount of excess capacity, if it did not obtain initially.[2] It is possible however, that the conditions (b) or (d) represent genuine obstacles to the attainment of balanced-growth equilibrium.[3] In that case the system cannot grow at a steady rate. This does not mean, however, that the economy will lapse into permanent stagnation. As investment opportunities accumulate during periods of stagnation (owing to continued technical progress and population growth), it becomes possible for the system to grow, for a limited period, at a rate appropriately higher than $(\lambda + \gamma')$, thus generating the required value of $\dfrac{P(t)}{K(t)}$.

Finally, if condition (d) is not satisfied, a steady rate of growth is incompatible with the assumed rate of interest $\bar{r}$. Two

---

[1] Allowing for diminishing returns, however, it is possible that (depending on the relative values of λ, α' and β') balanced-growth equilibrium will necessarily settle at the point where the fall in $G_0(t)$ due to λ is precisely offset by the rise in $G_0(t)$ due to γ'; where, in other words, constancy of $G_0(t)$, and $w(t)$ over time, becomes a necessary condition of equilibrium. (This case seems to have application for many of the underdeveloped countries.)

[2] Page 28 above. One may assume that the reaction mechanism here operates via the in- and out-flow of new firms as well as the investment behaviour of the representative firm.

[3] It is evident that these two restrictions are alternatives, of which only the higher one will apply.

cases are possible. If $\dfrac{\lambda+\gamma'}{a} > \rho_F + \bar{r}$, equilibrium requires a higher money rate of interest. If $\dfrac{\lambda+\gamma'}{a} < \rho_C + \bar{r}$, and the money rate of interest is already at its minimum level, it requires a rate of increase in money wages that would permit a rate of increase in the price level which reduced the real rate of interest to the appropriate figure.

Of all the relationships assumed in this model, that represented by (vi) and the inequality (d) are perhaps most open to doubt. Yet it can be shown that the assumption that ρ is a variable of v is the only one which makes the condition expressed in (x)—that the rate of profit is *equal* to the supply price of risk capital—consistent with the rate of profit being also determined by the growth factors, λ and γ' and by a. Equation (x) taken alone is incompatible with the rest of the model if the money rate of interest is assumed to be determined independently. But as indicated earlier, until there is more empirical evidence available to show that ρ_F is *appreciably* higher than ρ_C (or alternatively, that ρ_F itself is a rising function of the fixed-capital-output ratio, $\dfrac{F}{Y}$) and in consequence, the rate of profit is higher in industries and/or economies where the capital-output ratio is higher, I hesitate to put forward the relationship expressed in (vi) as more than a tentative suggestion, which I would be prepared to discard in favour of a better alternative, if such could be found.[1]

---

[1] For the reasons given I regard Kalecki's assumption

$$\rho = \theta(G_K), \text{ with } \theta' > 0$$

as a worse alternative, apart from the fact that in the context of the present model it serves as a substitute for equation (15), not for equation (21), and hence is not sufficient for closing the model.

2

A NEW MODEL OF ECONOMIC GROWTH[1]

1. The purpose of this paper is to present a "Keynesian" model of economic growth which is an amended version of previous attempts put forward by one of the authors in three former publications.[2] This new theory differs from earlier theories mainly in the following respects:

(1) it gives more explicit recognition to the fact that technical progress is infused into the economic system through the creation of new equipment, which depends on current (gross) investment expenditure. Hence the "technical progress function" has been re-defined so as to exhibit a relationship between the rate of change of gross (fixed) investment per operative and the rate of increase in labour productivity on *newly installed* equipment;

(2) it takes explicit account of obsolescence, caused by the fact that the profitability of plant and equipment of any particular "vintage" must continually diminish in time owing to the competition of equipment of superior efficiency installed at subsequent dates; and it assumes that this *continuing obsolescence is broadly foreseen by entrepreneurs* who take it into account in framing their investment decision. The model also assumes that, irrespective of whether plant and equipment has a finite physical lifetime or not, its *operative* life-time is determined by a complex

[1] Written in collaboration with J. A. Mirrlees and originally published in the *Review of Economic Studies*, vol. XXIX (1962) no. 3.
[2] Cf. N. Kaldor, "Alternative Theories of Distribution", *Review of Economic Studies*, 1955–6, (reprinted in *Essays on Value and Distribution*, pp. 228–36). A Model of Economic Growth," *Economic Journal*, December 1957 (reprinted in *Essays in Economic Stability and Growth*, pp. 256–300) and "Capital Accumulation and Economic Growth" (presented in Corfu, September 1958 and published in *The Theory of Capital*, London, Macmillan, 1961, pp. 177–220; reprinted in this volume.) N. Kaldor's ideas in connection with the present model were worked out during his tenure as Ford Research Professor in Economics in Berkeley, California.

of economic factors which govern the rate of obsolescence, and not by physical wear and tear;

(3) in accordance with this, the behavioural assumptions concerning the investors' attitudes to uncertainty in connection with investment decisions, which are set out below, differ in important respects from those made in the earlier models;

(4) account is also taken, in the present model, of the fact that some proportion of the existing stock of equipment disappears each year through physical causes—accidents, fire, explosions, etc.—and this gives rise to some "radioactive" physical depreciation in addition to obsolescence;

(5) since, under continuous technical progress and obsolescence, there is no way of measuring the "stock of capital" (measurement in terms of the historical cost of the surviving capital equipment is irrelevant; in terms of historical cost *less* accrued "obsolescence" is question-begging, since the allowance for obsolescence, unlike the charge for physical wear and tear etc., depends on the share of profits, the rate of growth, etc., and cannot therefore be determined independently of all other relations), the model avoids the notion of a quantity of capital, and its corollary, the rate of capital accumulation, as variables of the system; it operates solely with the value of current gross investment (gross (fixed) capital expenditure per unit of time) and its rate of change in time. The macro-economic notions of income, income per head, etc., on the other hand are retained.

2. The present model is analogous to the earlier models in the following main features:

(1) like all "Keynesian" economic models, it assumes that "savings" are passive—the level of investment is based on the volume of investment decisions made by entrepreneurs, and is independent of the propensities to save; it postulates an economy in which the mechanism of profit and income generation will create sufficient savings (at any rate within certain limits or "boundaries") to balance the investment which entrepreneurs decide to undertake;

(2) the model relates to an isolated economy with continuous

technical progress, and with a steady rate of increase in the working population, determined by exogenous factors;

(3) the model assumes that investment is primarily *induced* by the growth in production itself, and that the underlying conditions are such that growth-equilibrium necessarily carries with it a state of continuous full employment. This will be the case when the purely "endogenous" growth rate (as determined by the combined operation of the accelerator and the multiplier) which is operative under conditions of an unlimited supply of labour, is appreciably higher than the "natural rate of growth", which is the growth of the "labour potential" (i.e., the *sum* of the rate of growth of the labour force and of (average) labour productivity). In that case, starting from any given state of surplus labour and under-employment, continued growth, as determined by these endogenous factors, will necessarily lead to full employment sooner or later; and once full employment rules, continued growth involves that the "accelerator-multiplier" mechanism becomes "tethered" (through variations in the share of profits and through the imposition of a quasi-exogenous growth rate in demand) to the natural rate of growth.

3. In a situation of continuing full employment the volume of investment decisions for the economy as a whole will be governed by the number of workers who become available, per unit period, to "man" new equipment, and by the amount of investment per operative. It may be assumed that each entrepreneur, operating in imperfectly competitive markets, aims at the maximum attainable growth of his own business (subject, as we shall explain below, to the maintenance of a satisfactory rate of return on the capital employed) and for that reason prefers to maintain an appreciable amount of excess capacity so as to be able to exploit any chance increase in his selling power either by increasing his share of the market or by invading other markets. However, when gross investment per period is in excess of the number of workers becoming available to "man" new equipment, the degree of excess capacity must steadily rise; hence whatever the desired relationship between capacity and output, sooner or later a point will be reached when the number

of workers available for operating new equipment exerts a dominating influence (via the mechanism of the accelerator) on the
volume of investment decisions in the economy.[1]

We shall assume that the equipment of any given vintage is in
"limitational" relationship to labour—i.e. that it is not possible
to increase the productivity of labour by reducing the number of
workers employed in connection with already existing equipment
(though it is possible that productivity would, on the contrary,
be *reduced* by such a reduction, on account of its being associated
with a higher ratio of overhead to prime labour). This does not
mean that the equipment of any vintage requires a fixed amount
of labour to keep it in operation. The latter would assume the
case not only of "fixed coefficients" but of complete indivisibility
of the plant and equipment as well.

Writing n_t for the number of workers available to operate
new equipment per unit period and i_t for the amount of investment per operative on machines of vintage t, and I_t for gross
investment in fixed capital

$$i_t = \frac{I_t}{n_t}.\qquad(\text{I})$$

We shall use the symbols Y_t for the gross national product at
t, N_t for the working population, and y_t for output per head, so
that

$$y_t = \frac{Y_t}{N_t}.$$

4. We shall assume that "machines" of each vintage are of
constant physical efficiency during their lifetime, so that the
growth of productivity in the economy is entirely due to the
infusion of new "machines" into the system through (gross)
investment.[2] Hence our basic assumption is a technical progress

---

[1] We may assume that for the average, or representative, firm, sales grow at the
same rate as production in the economy as a whole. But there will always be of course
the exceptional firms who grow at a higher rate, and sub-average firms who grow
at a lower rate. Investment in all cases serves the purpose of keeping productive
capacity in some desired relationship with expected sales.

[2] It is probable that in addition to "embodied" technical progress there is some
"disembodied" technical progress as well, resulting from increasing know-how in the
use of existing machinery. On the other hand it is also probable that the physical
efficiency of machinery declines with age (on account of higher repair and main-

function which makes the annual rate of growth of productivity per worker *operating on new equipment* a function of the rate of growth of investment per worker, i.e., that

$$\dot{p}_t/p_t = f(\dot{i}_t/i_t) \text{ with } f(0) > 0, f' > 0, f'' < 0 \qquad (2)$$

This function is illustrated in Fig. 1. It is assumed that a constant rate of investment per worker over time will itself increase productivity per worker, but that the rate of growth of productivity will also be an increasing function of the rate of growth of investment per worker, though at a diminishing rate.[1]

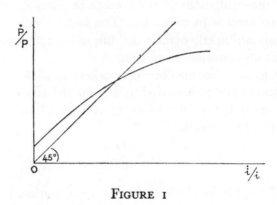

FIGURE I

Both output per operative and investment per operative are measured in terms of money values deflated by an index of the prices of "wage goods" (i.e., consumption goods which enter into the wage-earners' budget). This means that changes in the prices of equipment goods in terms of wage-goods (and also of such consumption goods which only enter into consumption out

tenance expenditures, etc.); our assumption of constant physical efficiency thus implies that these two factors just balance each other.

[1] It should be noted that the "technical progress function" in this model relates to the rate of growth of output per man-hour of the workers operating newly installed equipment (the equipment resulting from the investment of period t), *not* to the rate of growth of productivity in the economy in general (though in full steady-growth equilibrium, as we shall see, the two will correspond to each other); and to the rate of growth of gross investment per worker from year to year, not the rate of accumulation of capital (which may not be a meaningful or measurable quantity). It is plausible that, with technical progress, the same investment per operative should yield a higher output per operative in successive years, and that this rate of growth will be enhanced, within limits, when the value of investment per operative is increasing over time.

of profits) will in general cause shifts in the f-function. Provided, however, that there is a reasonably stable trend in the prices of these latter goods in terms of wage goods, we can still conceive of the function as stable in time for any particular value of I_t/Y_t in money terms, and the system may still possess a steady growth equilibrium with a constant (equilibrium) value of I_t/Y_t. A full demonstration of this would require, however, a fully fledged 2-sector model in which the technical progress functions of the consumption goods sector and the capital goods sector, the distribution of employment and of savings between the two sectors, etc., are all treated separately. Since this would go far beyond the scope of this paper, it is better to assume, for present purposes, that the rate of technical progress, as measured by productivity growth, is the same in all sectors, and hence that relative prices remain constant, bearing in mind, however, that the model could probably be extended to cover a wider range of possibilities.

5. With regard to the manner in which entrepreneurs meet risk and uncertainty, we shall make two important assumptions. In the first place we shall assume that entrepreneurs will only invest in their own business in so far as this is consistent with maintaining the earning power of their fixed assets above a certain minimum, a minimum which, in their view, represents the earning power of fixed assets in the economy in general. This is because, if the earnings of a particular firm are low in relation to the capital employed, or if they increase at a lower rate than the book value of the fixed assets, fixed assets will take up an increasing proportion of the total resources of the firm (including its potential borrowing power) at any given rate of growth, with the result that the financial position of the firm will become steadily weaker, with enhanced risks of bankruptcy or take-over bids. Hence we may assume that the sum of the expected profits anticipated from operating the equipment during its anticipated period of operation (or lifetime), T, will earn after full amortisation, a rate of profit that is at least equal to the assumed rate of profit on new investment in the economy generally. Hence for any particular investor

$$i_t \leqslant \int_t^{t+T} e^{-(\rho+\delta)(\tau-t)} \left(p_t - w_\tau^*\right) d\tau \qquad (3)$$

where ρ stands for what the entrepreneur assumes the general rate of profit to be, w_τ^* for the expected rate of wages which is a rising function of future time[1] and δ is the rate of "radioactive" decay of machines (we take it that the investor assumes his machine is an average machine).[2]

In the second place, under conditions of continuing technical progress, the expectations concerning the more distant future (whether in regard to money wages or in regard to the prices—or demands—of the particular products produced by a firm, both of which are projected in w_τ^*) are regarded as far more hazardous or uncertain than the expectations for the near future, where the incidence of unforeseeable major new inventions or discoveries is less significant. Hence investment projects which qualify for adoption must pass a further test—apart from the test of earning a satisfactory rate of profit—and that is that the cost of the fixed assets must be "recovered" within a certain period—i.e., that the gross profit earned in the first h years of its operation must be sufficient to repay the cost of investment. Hence

$$i_t \leqslant \int_t^{t+h} \left(p_t - w_\tau^*\right) d\tau. \qquad (4)$$

We shall assume, for the purposes of this model, that (3) is satisfied whenever (4) is satisfied—hence in (4) the = sign will

[1] In a golden age equilibrium, the inequality (3) should be replaced by an equality, and since all the variables will be determined independently by the other equations, (3) can then be taken as determining the rate of profit on investment. Cf. pp. 70–1 below.

[2] Our equation (3) thus postulates conditions under which the amount of "finance" available to the firm is considerably greater than its fixed capital expenditure, so that the firm is free to vary its total investment expenditure per unit of time; and that it will adopt projects which pass the tests of adequacy as indicated by (3) even though it could earn a higher *rate* of profit on projects involving a smaller volume of investment and yielding a smaller *total* profit. (In other words we assume that the firm is guided by the motive of maximising the rate of profit on the shareholders' equity, which involves different decisions from the assumption of maximising the rate of profit on its fixed investment.)

apply, i.e., the undiscounted sum of profits over h periods must be equal to i_t. There is plenty of empirical evidence that the assumption underlying (4) is a generally recognised method of meeting the uncertainty due to obsolescence in modern business, though the value of h may vary with the rate of technical progress, and also as between different sectors. (In the U.S. manufacturing industry h is normally taken as 3 years; in other sectors—e.g., public utilities—it is much higher.)[1]

6. It is assumed, as in the earlier Keynesian growth models, that the savings which finance business investment come out of profits, and that a constant proportion, s, of *gross* profits are saved.[2] Hence (dividing income into two categories, profits and wages, which latter comprise all forms of non-business income) the share of (gross) profits, π_t, in the gross national product will be given by the equation

$$\pi_t = \frac{1}{s}\frac{I_t}{Y_t} \tag{5}$$

which, by virtue of equation (1), reduces to

$$\pi_t = \frac{r}{s}\frac{i_t}{y_t} \tag{5a}$$

where r is defined by

$$r_t = n_t/N_t,$$

[1] The assumptions represented by these two equations should be contrasted with the assumptions made in "Capital Accumulation and Economic Growth," according to which

$$\frac{P}{K} = r + \rho$$

$$\rho = \xi(v) \quad (\xi' > 0)$$

where P/K the rate of profit, r the money rate of interest, ρ the risk premium, v the capital/output ratio. ρ was assumed to be a rising function of v, because v reflects the ratio of fixed to circulating capital, and investment in the former is considered far more risky or "illiquid" than investment in the latter. The present assumptions are not inconsistent with the former hypothesis concerning the higher returns demanded on fixed investments; but they also take into account that the "riskiness" of the investment in fixed capital will be all the greater the longer the period over which the cost of the investment is "recovered" out of the profits—a matter which depends not only on the capital/output ratio (or rather, the investment/output ratio) but also on the share of gross profits in output. "Gross profits" should for this purpose be calculated net of other charges, including a notional interest charge on the "liquid" business assets (i.e., the investment in circulating capital associated with the investment in fixed capital).

[2] Savings out of wages are ignored—i.e., they are assumed to be balanced by non-business (personal) investment (i.e., residential construction). The assumption that business savings are a constant proportion of *gross* profits (after tax) is well supported by data relating to gross corporate savings.

where N_t is the total labour force at time t and n_t, as earlier defined, is the number of workers available to operate new equipment per unit period.

We shall assume that once equipment is installed the number of workers operating it will only fall in time by the physical wastage of equipment, caused by accidents, fires, etc.—until the whole of the residual equipment is scrapped on account of obsolescence. Writing δ for the rate of (radioactive) depreciation per unit period, and $T(t)$ for the age of the equipment which is retired at t (i.e., the lifetime of equipment as governed by obsolescence), we have the following relationship for the distribution of the labour force:

$$N_t = \int_{t-T}^{t} n_\tau e^{-\delta(t-\tau)}\, d\tau \qquad (6)$$

and for total output

$$Y_t = \int_{t-T}^{t} p_\tau n_\tau e^{-\delta(t-\tau)}\, d\tau. \qquad (7)$$

Since output Y_t is divided into two categories of income only, wages and profits, the residue left after profits is equal to the total wages bill. Writing w_t for the rate of wages at t, we further have

$$Y_t(1 - \pi_t) = N_t w_t. \qquad (8)$$

Finally, since equipment will only be employed so long as its operation more than covers prime costs, the profits on the oldest yet surviving machinery must be zero. Hence

$$p_{t-T} = w_t. \qquad (9)$$

We shall assume that population grows at the constant rate λ, hence

$$\dot{N}_t = \lambda N_t. \qquad (10)$$

We shall also assume that businessmen anticipate that wages in terms of output units will rise in the foreseeable future at the same rate as they have been rising during the past l periods.

Hence the expected wage rate at a future time T will be

$$w_T^* = w_t \left(\frac{w_t}{w_{t-l}}\right)^{\frac{T-t}{l}}. \tag{11}$$

Finally, the model is subject to two constraints (or "boundary conditions") which are known from earlier models:

$$w_t \geqslant w_{\min}$$
$$\pi \geqslant m.$$

In other words, the wage rate resulting from the model must be above a certain minimum (determined by conventional subsistence needs) and at the same time the share of profits resulting from the model must be higher than a certain minimum (the so-called "degree of monopoly" or "degree of imperfect competition").

7. The above system gives 10 independent equations (regarding (3) only as a boundary condition) which are sufficient to determine the 10 unknowns: I_t, i_t, n_t, p_t, w_t, w^*_t, π_t, T, y_t, N_t, given the parameters, s, h, δ and λ, and the function f.

We shall investigate whether this system yields a solution in terms of a steady growth (or golden age) equilibrium where the rate of growth of output per head is equal to the rate of growth of productivity on new equipment and both are equal to the rate of growth of (fixed) investment per worker, and to the rate of growth of wages; i.e., where

$$\dot{p}/p = \dot{y}/y = \dot{i}/i = \dot{w}/w;$$

and where the share of investment in output I/Y, the share of profits in income π, and the period of obsolescence of equipment, T, remain constant. Finally we shall show that there is a unique rate of profit on investment in a steady growth equilibrium.

The assumptions about the technical progress function imply that there is *some* value $\dot{p}/p$ (let us call it γ) at which

$$\dot{p}/p = \dot{i}/i = \gamma.$$

Equilibrium is only possible when this holds.

If we integrate equation (4) using (11), we see that

$$i_t = hp_t - w_t \frac{e^{vh} - \mathrm{I}}{v}, \qquad (12)$$

where v is the expected rate of growth of w. Hence p could only grow faster than i in the long run if w was growing faster than p: that would imply a continuous reduction in T, which would lead to unemployment and stagnation before T fell to h (at which point the rate of profit would be negative). On the other hand, p cannot grow more slowly than i in the long run, since w cannot fall below w_{min} (and there would in fact be an inflation crisis before that point was reached).

It is clear too that, so long as $\dot{w}/w$ does not diverge too far from $\dot{p}/p$, $\dot{i}/i$ would increase if it were less than $\dot{p}/p$, and decrease if it were greater than $\dot{p}/p$. For if $\dot{p}/p$ were less than γ, it would breed, by equation (4), a rate of growth of investment, $\dot{i}/i$ that would require higher $\dot{p}/p$, and so on, until the equilibrium position is reached. A similar mechanism would be at work if $\dot{p}/p$ were greater than γ. Thus the equilibrium would in general be stable; but instability cannot be excluded, and a movement away from equilibrium would be possible in either of the two ways described above. For example a downward drift of the technical progress function might allow the rate of growth of p to fall off, and remain below the rate of growth of w (which reflects the rate of growth of y over the recent past) sufficiently long until with falling investment, unemployment and stagnation set in.[1] Conversely an upward shift in the technical progress function might lead to an inflationary situation in which investment, by one means or another, would be compressed below that indicated by (4) and (13).

Hence, excluding the case where $\dot{p}/p$ is significantly different from $\dot{w}/w$, when

$$\frac{\dot{p}}{p} > \dot{i}$$
$$\frac{\dot{p}}{p} < \dot{i}$$

there will be a convergent movement until (12) is obtained.

8. It will be convenient to deduce two further relations from

---

[1] For example, a slowing down of technical progress in the late 1920s may have been responsible for that "sudden collapse of the marginal efficiency of capital" which ed to the crisis and stagnation of the 1930s.

the above equations. The first one relates to n_t, the amount of labour available for new equipment: it is obtained by differentiating (6) with respect to t.

$$n_t = \dot{N}_t + \delta N_t + n_{t-T}\left(1 - \frac{dT}{dt}\right)e^{-\delta T}. \qquad (13)$$

This equation says that n_t will be composed of three elements: (i) the growth in working population, $\dot{N}_t$; (ii) the labour released by physical wastage of equipment of all vintages, which is δN_t; (iii) and finally the labour released by the retirement of obsolete equipment.

Differentiating equation (7) in the same way we obtain

$$\dot{Y}_t = p_t\, n_t - p_{t-T}\, n_{t-T}\left(1 - \frac{dT}{dt}\right)e^{-\delta T} - \delta Y_t.$$

Substituting w_t for p_{t-T} in accordance with (9) and using (13) this becomes

$$\dot{Y}_t = p_t\, n_t - w_t(n_t - \dot{N}_t - \delta N_t) - \delta Y_t.$$

Dividing both sides by $Y_t = N_t y_t$ we obtain

$$\frac{\dot{Y}_t}{Y_t} = r\frac{p_t}{y_t} - \frac{w_t}{y_t}(r - \lambda - \delta) - \delta.$$

Using

$$\frac{\dot{Y}_t}{Y_t} = \frac{\dot{y}_t}{y_t} + \lambda$$

and re-arranging we finally obtain

$$\frac{\dot{y}_t}{y_t} + \lambda + \delta = r\frac{p_t}{y_t} - (r - \lambda - \delta)\frac{w_t}{y_t}. \qquad (14)$$

9. In order that entrepreneurial expectations should be fulfilled, it is necessary that wages should grow at constant rate in time, β.

$$\frac{\dot{w}_t}{w_t} = \beta \text{ (constant)} \qquad (15)$$

We shall now proceed to demonstrate that when β is constant, T will also be constant, provided that $\gamma < \frac{s}{h} - \lambda - \delta$.

If follows from (9) that

$$\frac{\dot{w}_t}{w_t} = \frac{\dot{p}_{t-T}}{p_{t-T}}\left(1 - \frac{dT}{dt}\right).$$

Hence

$$1 - \frac{dT}{dt} = \frac{\beta}{\gamma}, \text{ a constant.}$$

Integrating with respect to t we obtain

$$T = T_0 + \left(1 - \frac{\beta}{\gamma}\right)t \tag{16}$$

where T_0 is the lifetime of equipment at some initial date, $t = 0$.

Substituting (16) into (13) and remembering that $r_t = n_t/N_t$, we obtain

$$r_t = \lambda + \delta + r_{t-T}e^{-(\lambda+\delta)T}\frac{\beta}{\gamma}. \tag{17}$$

In order to show that, in a state of steady-growth equilibrium $T = T_0$ and $\beta = \gamma$, we shall first consider the cases where $\beta \neq \gamma$.

(i) When $\gamma < \beta$, clearly steady growth cannot continue since entrepreneurs' profits would become negative sooner or later.

(ii) when $\gamma > \beta$, it follows from equation (16) that T becomes indefinitely large with time (and perhaps this is enough to dispose of this case, since for most goods there may be a maximum physical lifetime, quite apart from obsolescence). In any case this implies, in accordance with (17), that r ultimately tends to $\lambda + \delta$; and since w/y must tend to zero, so that the share of profits, π, tends towards unity,

$$i/y \text{ tends to } \frac{s}{\lambda+\delta}. \tag{18}$$

Also from (4):

$$i/p \text{ tends to } h.$$

Hence from (14):

$$\dot{y}/y \text{ tends to } \frac{s}{h} - \lambda - \delta.$$

(18) shows that y ultimately grows at the same rate as i, which grows at the rate γ.

Therefore

$$\gamma = \frac{s}{h} - \lambda - \delta \tag{19}$$

which implies, in Harrod's terms, that the "natural rate" (here, $\gamma + \lambda + \delta$) is equal to what the "warranted rate" would be if $\gamma + \lambda + \delta$ were zero and profits absorbed the whole output (since then s would equal the proportion of Y saved, and $h = i/p$).

10. It is easy to see that in fact the rate of growth of output per head cannot in the long run be greater than this quantity $\frac{s}{h} - \lambda - \delta$. By (5), i/y can rise no higher, ultimately, than s/r; hence by (4), even if (as might happen ultimately) the wage rate were negligible in relation to output per head, p/y could not be greater than $s/(rh)$. Turning to equation (14), we see that it implies the inequality

$$\dot{y}t/yt + \lambda + \delta \leqq r. \frac{s}{rh} = \frac{s}{h}.$$

Hence there can be no steady-growth equilibrium unless

$$\gamma \leqq \frac{s}{h} - \lambda - \delta.$$

Normally we would not expect to have to worry about this constraint, for the quantity s/h will be large—especially when we remember that h will be small when there is a high rate of growth. If it is asked what would happen if the equilibrium growth rate given by the technical progress function really did fail to satisfy this inequality, the answer must be that the wage rate would be driven down to its minimum level and entrepreneurs would then find themselves unable to invest as much as the prospects would warrant: the equality (4) would become an inequality again. The rest of the discussion will be carried on under the assumption that the equilibrium rate of growth γ does satisfy this inequality.

We can see that, quite apart from the unrealistic value of γ implied by equation (19), equilibrium with $\gamma > \beta$ is a freak

D

case; the slightest shift in γ would either render equilibrium impossible, or make it possible only with $\beta = \gamma$.

11. (iii) It is clear from the above that steady-growth equilibrium will involve

$$\beta = \gamma$$

in which case it also involves a constant T.
(17) has now become

$$r_t = \lambda + \delta + r_{t-T}\, e^{-(\lambda+\delta)T},$$

where T is constant, so that r_t will tend to the equilibrium value

$$r = \frac{\lambda + \delta}{1 - e^{-(\lambda+\delta)T}}. \tag{20}$$

From equation (5)

$$y_t = w_t + \frac{r}{s}\, i_t,$$

so that, since r is constant in equilibrium, y_t also grows at the equilibrium growth rate γ. It is convenient to write this last equation as

$$\frac{r}{s}\frac{i}{y} + \frac{w}{y} = 1. \tag{21}$$

In equilibrium, expectations are fulfilled, so that $w_t{}^* = w_t$. Since $w_t = w_0\, e^{\beta t} = w_0\, e^{\gamma t}$ (where w_0 is the wage rate at some initial time), the integral in equation (4) can be evaluated, so that

$$i_t = hp_t - \frac{e^{\gamma h} - 1}{\gamma} w_t,$$

which we can write

$$\frac{1}{h}\frac{i}{y} + \frac{e^{\gamma h} - 1}{\gamma h}\frac{w}{y} - \frac{p}{y} = 0. \tag{22}$$

(14) can now be rewritten

$$(r - \lambda - \delta)\frac{w}{y} - r\frac{p}{y} = -(\gamma + \lambda + \delta). \tag{23}$$

Equations (21), (22), (23) can be treated as three simultaneous equations for $\frac{i}{y}$, $\frac{w}{y}$, and $\frac{p}{y}$ (which are all constant in a state of steady growth).

Now equation (9) provides an equation for T:

$$e^{\gamma T} = \frac{p}{w} = \frac{p/y}{w/y}. \tag{24}$$

Using the values of r, $\frac{p}{y}$, $\frac{w}{y}$ found by solving (21), (22) and (23), we obtain:

$$e^{\gamma T} = \frac{1 - \dfrac{h(\gamma + \lambda + \delta)}{s} \dfrac{e^{\gamma h} - 1}{\gamma h} + \dfrac{\gamma}{r}}{1 - \dfrac{h(\gamma + \lambda + \delta)}{s}}. \tag{25}$$

And from (20), since $e^{\gamma T} = [e^{-(\lambda+\delta)T}]^{-\gamma/(\lambda+\delta)}$

$$e^{\gamma T} = \left[1 - \frac{\lambda+\delta}{r}\right]^{-\frac{\gamma}{\lambda+\delta}}. \tag{26}$$

(25) and (26) determine T and r simultaneously in terms of the parameters λ, δ, h, s, and the steady-growth rate γ (which was determined by the technical progress function). Equation (20) is not valid when $\lambda + \delta = 0$. In that case we go back to equation (6); integration gives

$$rT = 1, \tag{27}$$

which replaces (26) in this particular case.

12. Although (25) and (26) are rather cumbersome equations, numerical solution for particular values of the parameters presents no particular difficulty. Once T and r are calculated, simultaneous solution of (23) and (24) yields the values of $\frac{p}{y}$ and $\frac{w}{y}$ (the share of wages). Then $\frac{i}{y}$ is found from (22). A demonstration of the existence of a unique meaningful solution to the equations is given in the Appendix.

If capital stock were valued at historic cost, without any allowance for reduction in value through obsolescence, we should have

$$K = \int_{t-T}^{t} i_\tau \, n_\tau \, e^{-\delta(t-\tau)} \, d\tau,$$

and

$$Y = \int_{t-T}^{t} p_\tau \, n_\tau \, e^{-\delta(t-\tau)} \, d\tau, \tag{28}$$

so that the aggregate capital-output ratio,

$$\frac{K}{Y} = \frac{i}{p},$$

since this latter is constant.

However, when obsolescence is *foreseen* the knowledge of the share of profits, π, and of the historical cost of invested capital as shown by (28), does not enable us to calculate either net profits or the rate of profit on capital. The value of capital at any one time will be lower than K_t by the accrued provision made for obsolescence, and the appropriate obsolescence provision—which must take into account the annual reduction in the profits earned on equipment of a given vintage, as well as the retirement of equipment when it becomes T years old—cannot be calculated without knowing the capital on which the profit is earned, which in turn cannot be known without knowing the rate of profit.

13. In a state of fully-fledged golden age equilibrium, where (1) expectations are (in general) fulfilled and the expected profit on new investments is therefore the same as the realised profit, and (2) the rate of profit earned on all investment will be the same, the inequality (3) above can be replaced by an equality and regarded as an additional equation determining ρ (since i_t, p_t, w_t and T are all determined by the other equations of the system).

$$i_t = \int_0^T e^{-(\rho+\delta)\tau} (p_t - W_{t+\tau}) \cdot d\tau; \tag{3a}$$

ρ is constant, so the familiar relation

$$\gamma + \lambda = \rho\sigma, \tag{29}$$

where σ is the proportion of *net* profits saved, holds; for it is easy to check that the value of capital—in terms of output to come—grows at the equilibrium growth rate $\gamma + \lambda$, and that ρ defined by (3a) is equal to the ratio of net profit to the stock of capital. In general, of course, σ depends on ρ, and is best calculated from the relation (29). But when $s = 1$, i.e., when all (gross) profits are invested, σ must also be equal to unity, so that the rate of profit is equal to the rate of growth of output: $\rho = \gamma + \lambda$. On the face of it, it is not clear that this value of ρ satisfies (13a): yet it must do. To show that it does, we use the fact that total output,

$$Y_t = \int_0^T p_{t-\tau}\, n_{t-\tau}\, e^{-\delta\tau}\, d\tau,$$

$$= p_t n_t \int_0^T e^{-(\gamma+\lambda+\delta)\tau}\, d\tau.$$

Thus, when we put $\rho = \gamma + \lambda$ in the right hand side of (3a), we get:

$$\frac{y_t}{r_t} - w_t \int_0^T e^{-(\lambda+\delta)\tau}\, d\tau.$$

This last integral $= \dfrac{1 - e^{-(\lambda+\delta)T}}{\lambda + \delta} = \dfrac{1}{r}$, by equation (20). Hence the right hand side of equation (3a) is equal to $(y_t - w_t)/r$, which is equal to i_t when $s = 1$ (by equation (21)).

If $s \neq 1$, we must find ρ from equation (3a). If we perform the integration (which we can do, since p and w are growing exponentially), we get the following relation, which can be solved numerically for $\rho + \delta$:

$$\frac{i}{y} = \frac{1 - e^{-(\rho + \delta)T}}{\rho + \delta} \frac{p}{y} - \frac{1 - e^{-(\rho + \delta - \gamma)T}}{\rho + \delta - \gamma} \frac{w}{y}. \tag{30}$$

Outside a golden age equilibrium a rate of profit on investment does not exist except in the sense of an *assumed* rate of profit, based on a mixture of convention and belief, which enables entrepreneurs to decide whether any particular project passes the test of adequate profitability.

14. *Some Numerical Results*

The following are the solution of the equations for various arbitrarily selected values of the parameters.[1]

For $s = 0.66$:

h years	$\lambda + \delta\%$	$\gamma\%$	T years	r	$\pi\%$	$I/Y\%$	i/p	$\rho + \delta\%$
3	2	2	8·03	0·135	8·0	5·3	0·367	21·7
		2·5	8·15	0·133	10·1	6·7	0·459	22·1
		3	8·27	0·131	12·2	8·1	0·551	22·4
	4	2	8·68	0·136	8·9	5·9	0·401	23·0
		2·5	8·82	0·135	11·2	7·5	0·501	23·4
		3	8·97	0·133	13·5	9·0	0·601	23·7
4	2	2	11·20	0·100	11·2	7·5	0·672	17·0
		2·5	11·44	0·098	14·1	9·6	0·839	17·3
		3	11·68	0·096	17·1	11·4	1·006	17·6
	4	2	12·54	0·101	12·9	8·6	0·759	18·2
		2·5	12·84	0·100	16·3	10·9	0·948	18·6
		3	13·15	0·098	19·8	13·2	1·136	18·9
5	2	2	14·69	0·078	14·6	9·7	1·080	14·1
		2·5	15·10	0·077	18·5	12·3	1·348	14·4
		3	15·53	0·075	22·4	14·9	1·615	14·7
	4	2	17·13	0·081	17·8	11·9	1·267	15·4
		2·5	17·71	0·079	22·5	15·0	1·579	15·7
		3	18·34	0·077	27·4	16·4	1·888	16·0

[1] We are indebted to D. G. Champernowne for programming these calculations, and to the Director of the Mathematical Laboratory of Cambridge University for making the computer available.

Some representative values for different s:

s	h	$\lambda+\delta\%$	$\gamma\%$	T	r	$\pi\%$	$I/\Upsilon\%$	i/p	$\rho+\delta\%$
0·33	3	2	2	20·66	0·059	20·4	6·8	0·955	30·6
			2·5	21·26	0·058	25·6	8·5	1·169	30·8
0·50	4	4	2	19·98	0·073	20·7	10·3	1·207	21·7
			2·5	20·66	0·071	26·2	13·1	1·490	22·0
			3	21·42	0·070	31·8	15·9	1·765	22·3
	5	2	2	22·61	0·055	22·2	11·1	1·655	17·0
			2·5	23·47	0·053	28·1	14·0	2·038	17·3
			3	24·41	0·052	34·1	17·0	2·407	17·6
1·00	4	4	2·5	6·08	0·185	7·7	7·7	0·387	6·5
			3	6·22	0·182	9·4	9·4	0·474	7·0
	5	2	2·5	7·20	0·140	9·0	9·0	0·561	4·5
			3	7·49	0·144	11·1	11·1	0·691	5·0
		4	2·5	8·20	0·143	10·4	10·4	0·662	6·5
			3	8·44	0·140	12·7	12·7	0·812	7·0

For the U.S. in the 1950s, reasonable values of the parameters are γ = 2 to $2\frac{1}{2}\%$, $\lambda+\delta$ = 2 to 4%, s = 0·66, h = 4 to 5 years. The average lifetime of equipment in manufacturing industry has been estimated at 17 years. π as indicated by the ratio of gross corporate profit after tax to the gross income originating in corporations after corporation tax has been 21%, and the ratio of business fixed capital to business gross product around 1·5. These, as the table shows, are close to the results of the model when s = 0·66, h = 5, $\lambda+\delta$ = 4%, and when γ is 2 to 2·5%.[1]

The rate of profit on investment, on the other hand, appears rather high. However, it must be remembered that our equation (3) derives the rate of (net) profit from the stream of gross profit *after* tax, and not (as is usually done) from the gross profit before tax. This involves a smaller provision for obsolescence, and consequently a higher net profit, than in the usual method of calculation. It also implies that in "grossing up" for tax, the relevant rate is the effective tax charge on profits before depreciation, and

---

[1] It should be borne in mind, of course, that no allowance was made in the model for net investment in working capital (inventory accumulation) which would affect the values of T, π, I/Υ and i/p, but the effect of which can be subsumed in h. Equally, the model assumes that government savings and investment are equal—i.e., that there is no financial surplus or deficit arising out of government operations, and that personal savings and personal investments (mainly in housing) are equal.

not the rate of tax on profits net of depreciation. Hence, if the tax on corporation profits is one third of gross profits before tax, a rate of net profit (net of tax) of 12·5% (assuming $\lambda = 1\%$, $\delta = 3\%$) corresponds to a rate of net profit *before* tax of 18·5%.[1]

It can be seen from the figures, too, that π and i/p are quite sensitive to changes in the technical progress function (i.e. in γ), and highly sensitive to changes in s and h, but stable for changes in λ and δ. T is only sensitive to changes in s and h, but *not* to γ. These results may sound surprising at first. One would expect T to be inversely related to γ, and one would also expect r ($= n_t/N_t$) to be positively correlated with $(\lambda + \delta)$. However, a rise in γ leads to a rise in i/p, and hence of π, which more than compensates for the rise in γ in determining the associated change in T; a rise in $(\lambda + \delta)$ reduces (as between one steady-growth equilibrium and another) the amount of labour released through obsolescence in relation to the current labour force (since the labour force T years ago was that much smaller, when λ is larger; and of the equipment built T years ago so much less survives to be scrapped when δ is larger) so that it compensates for the increase in $(\lambda + \delta)$, leaving the value of r pretty much the same.

15. *General Conclusions*

The model shows technical progress—in the specific form of the rate of improvement of the design, etc., of newly produced capital equipment—as the main engine of economic growth, determining not only the rate of growth of productivity but—together with other parameters—also the rate of obsolescence, the average lifetime of equipment, the share of investment in income, the share of profits, and the relationship between investment and potential output (i.e., the "capital/output ratio" on new capital).

The model is Keynesian in its mode of operation (entrepreneurial expenditure decisions are primary; incomes, etc., are secondary) and severely *non*-neo-classical in that technological factors (marginal productivities or marginal substitution ratios)

---

[1] U.S. estimates put the average rate of profit on (business) investment at 16% before tax and 8% after tax.

play no role in the determination of wages and profits. A "production function" in the sense of a single-valued relationship between *some* measure of capital, K_t, the labour force N_t and of output Y_t (all at time t) clearly does not exist. Everything depends on past history, on how the collection of equipment goods which comprises K_t has been built up. Thus Y_t will be greater for a given K_t (as measured by historical cost) if a greater part of the existing capital stock is of more recent creation; this would be the case, for example, if the rate of growth of population has been accelerating.

Whilst "machines" earn quasi-rents which are all the smaller the older they are (so that, for the oldest surviving machine, the quasi-rents are zero) it would be wrong to say that the position of the marginal "machine" determines the share of quasi-rents (or gross profits) in total income. For the total profit is determined quite independently of the structure of these "quasi-rents" by equation (5), i.e., by the factors determining the share of investment in output and the proportion of profits saved and therefore the position of the "marginal" machine is itself fully determined by the other equations of the system. It is the macro-economic condition specified in (5), and not the age-and-productivity structure of machinery, which will determine what the (aggregate) share of quasi-rents will be.

The technical progress function is quite consistent with a technological "investment function", i.e., a functional relationship (shifting in time) between investment per worker and output per worker.[1] However, owing to anticipated obsolescence and to uncertainty, it would not be correct to say that the "marginal product" of investment, dp_t/di_t, plays a role in determining the amount per man. Since the profitability of operating the equipment is expected to diminish in time, the marginal addition to

---

[1] On the relationship of a technical progress function and a production function cf. John Black, "The Technical Progress Function and The Production Function", *Economica*, May 1962. Whilst it is possible to make assumptions under which a technical progress function is merely one way of representing an (ex-ante) production function of constant elasticity which shifts at some pre-determined rate in time, the postulate of a technical progress function is also consistent with situations in which the rate of technical progress does not proceed at some pre-determined rate (where the shift of the "curve" is bound up with the movement *along* the "curve") and where therefore one cannot associate a unique production function with a given "state" of knowledge.

the stream of profits (which we may call the "marginal value productivity") will be something quite different from the marginal product in the technological sense, and unlike the latter, it will not be a derivative of a technological function alone but will depend on the whole system of relationships. Further, owing to the prevailing attitude to uncertainty, it would not even be correct to say that "profit-maximising" will involve adding to investment per man until the marginal increment in anticipated profits, discounted at the ruling rate of interest or at some "assumed" rate of profit, becomes equal to the marginal addition to investment. Whenever the desire to recover the cost of investment within a certain number of years—owing to the greater uncertainty of the more distant future—becomes the operative restriction (as is assumed in equation (4)), investment per man will be cut short before this marginal condition is satisfied.

The inequality (3) together with equation (4) enables us to specify an investment function in terms of the parameters of the system which determine both n_t and i_t without regard to the relationship between the expected rate of profit on investment and the rate of interest. In previous "Keynesian" models the existence of an independent investment function was closely tied to the postulate of some relationship between the "marginal efficiency" of investment and—an independently determined—rate of interest. This was a source of difficulty, since it either caused such models to be "over-determined"[1] or else it required the postulate that the capital/output ratio (or the amount of investment per worker) itself varied with the excess of the rate of profit over the money rate of interest.[2] The weakness of this latter approach has been that it assigned too much importance to the rate of interest. So long as one could assume that the rate of interest was a constant, determined by some psychological minimum (the "pure" liquidity preference of Keynesian theory), this did not matter very much. But it was unsatisfactory to rely on the *excess* of the rate of profit over the rate of interest as an important element—determining the chosen capital/output ratio

---

[1] Cf. R. C. O. Matthews, "The Rate of Interest in Growth Models", *Oxford Economic Papers,* October 1960, pp. 249–68.
[2] Cf. "Capital Accumulation and Economic Growth", above, p. 53.

and through that, the other variables—considering that this excess is under the control of the monetary authorities; if the authorities were to follow a policy of keeping the money rate of interest in some constant relationship to the rate of profit— which they may be easily tempted to do—this would have endowed them with an importance in the general scheme of things which is quite contrary to common experience.

The present model, by contrast, allows the money rate of interest to move up and down, without the slightest effect on investment decisions, provided such movements do not violate certain constraints.[1] This is in much better accord with the oft-repeated assertions of business men (both in the U.K. and the U.S.) that the rate of interest has *no* influence on their investment decisions, at least as far as investment in fixed capital is concerned.

Finally there is the question how far the postulate of a "technical progress function" as specified in (2) implies some restraint on the *nature* of technological change. Every change in the rate of investment per worker implies a change in the extent to which new ideas ("innovations") are actually exploited. Since the "capital saving" innovations—which increase the output/capital ratio as well as the output/labour ratio—are much more profitable to the entrepreneur than the "labour-saving" ones that yield the same rate of increase in labour productivity, clearly the former are exploited first and the balance of technological change will appear more "capital-using" (or the less "capital-saving") the greater the rate of increase in investment per man. There is therefore always *some* rate of increase in investment per worker which allows output per man to grow at the same rate as investment per man and in that sense takes on the appearance of "neutral" technical progress; to assume that this rate of increase in investment per man remains unchanged over time implies also assuming that the relative importance of "capital saving" and "capital using" innovations in the total flow of innovations remains unchanged. To assume this is really

---

[1] For it must still remain true, of course, that the expected rate of profit on (fixed) investment must exceed the rate of interest by more than some minimum compensation for the "illiquidity" or other risks.

implied in the assumption that the rate of technical progress is *constant*; since a growing incidence of "capital saving" innovations is the same thing as an upward drift in the technical progress function, and *vice versa*. Therefore the only sense in which the technical progress function postulates some "neutral" technical progress is the sense in which "unneutral" technical progress necessarily involves either a continuous acceleration or deceleration in the rate of increase in productivity for any given value of i/i.

The main "practical" conclusion for economic policy that emerges from this model is that any scheme leading to the accelerated retirement of old equipment (such as a tax on the use of obsolete plant and equipment) is bound to accelerate for a temporary period the rate of increase in output per head $\dot{y}/y$, since it will increase n_t (the number of workers "available" for new machines) and hence I_t; and will thus involve a reduction in p_t/y_t. A more permanent cure, however, requires stimulating the technical dynamism of the economy (*raising* the technical progress function) which is not only (or perhaps mainly) a matter of more scientific education and more expenditure on research, but of higher quality business management which is more alert in searching for technical improvements and less resistant to their introduction.

APPENDIX

We must enquire whether the solution of the equations for a state of steady growth is unique. Equation (25) is a linear equation for $e^{\gamma T}$ in terms of $\dfrac{1}{r}$; it can be represented on a diagram, with

$\dfrac{1}{r}$ measured along one axis and $e^{\gamma T}$ along the other, by a straight line.

Equation (26), on the other hand, represents a curve of increasing slope (as shown in the diagram). The curve representing equation (26), BB', passes through the point $e^{\gamma T} = 1$, $\dfrac{1}{r} = 0$;

AA', which represents equation (25), has $e^{\gamma T} < 1$ when $\dfrac{1}{r} = 0$.

We shall prove that (1) AA', in fact cuts BB', and cuts it in two points, to which correspond the values r_1 and r_2 of r, and T_1 and T_2 of T; (2) $T_1 < h$, so that this case is in fact impossible (for entrepreneurs will make losses). It follows that there is a single possible steady growth state.

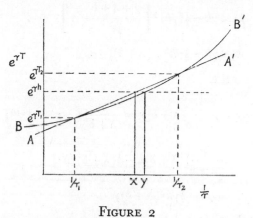

FIGURE 2

(1) To prove that AA' does not fail to cut BB', we show that there are points of BB' lying *below* AA'. Let x be the value of $\dfrac{1}{r}$ corresponding to $T = h$ on the curve AA' (i.e., found by solving equation (25)); and let y be the value of $\dfrac{1}{r}$ corresponding to $T = h$ on the curve BB' (i.e., found by solving equation (26)).

Then

$$\gamma x = e^{\gamma h}\left[1 - \frac{h(\gamma + \lambda + \delta)}{s}\right] + \frac{h(\gamma + \lambda + \delta)}{s}\,\frac{e^{\gamma h} - 1}{\gamma h} - 1$$

$$= e^{\gamma h} - 1 - \frac{(\gamma + \lambda + \delta)}{\gamma s}\left[\gamma h \cdot e^{\gamma h} - e^{\gamma h} + 1\right]$$

$$= \gamma h + \tfrac{1}{2}(\gamma h)^2 + \tfrac{1}{6}(\gamma h)^3 + \ldots$$

$$- \frac{\gamma + \lambda + \delta}{\gamma s}\left[\tfrac{1}{2}(\gamma h)^2 + \tfrac{1}{3}(\gamma h)^3 + \tfrac{1}{8}(\gamma h)^4 + \ldots\right]$$

$$= \gamma h + \tfrac{1}{2}(\gamma h)^2\left[1 - \frac{\gamma + \lambda + \delta}{\gamma s}\right] + \tfrac{1}{6}(\gamma h)^3\left[1 - 2\frac{\gamma + \lambda + \delta}{\gamma s}\right]$$

$$+ \tfrac{1}{24}(\gamma h)^4\left[1 - 3\frac{\gamma + \lambda + \delta}{\gamma s}\right] + \ldots$$

Clearly $\gamma + \lambda + \delta > \gamma s$, so that all the terms in square brackets are negative. Hence:

$$\gamma x < \gamma h - \tfrac{1}{2}(\gamma h)^2\left[\frac{\gamma + \lambda + \delta}{\gamma s} - 1\right],$$

so that $\gamma x < \gamma h - \tfrac{1}{2}\gamma h^2 . (\lambda + \delta),$ (28)

since $s \leqq 1.$

Also, $$\gamma y = \frac{\gamma}{\lambda + \delta}(\lambda + \delta)y = \frac{\gamma}{\lambda + \delta}[1 - e^{-(\lambda + \delta)h}]$$

$$> \frac{\gamma}{\lambda + \delta}[(\lambda + \delta)h - \tfrac{1}{2}(\lambda + \delta)^2 h^2]$$

$$= \gamma h - \tfrac{1}{2}\gamma h^2(\lambda + \delta),$$

which, as we have just shown, $> \gamma x.$

Hence $y > x$;

which is to say, that when $T = h$, the curve BB' lies to the right of AA'. Hence AA' meets BB'; for AA' cuts the $e^{\gamma T}$-axis below BB', and BB' eventually rises above AA'.

(2) It also follows from the fact that BB' lies to the right of AA' when $T = h$ that one of the points at which AA' and BB' cut has $t < h$; i.e., $T_1 < h.$ Thus only T_2 (which is $> h$) is a possible value for T.

What we have shown is that there exists a single possible solution to our equations for the state of steady growth at rate γ. [The case $\lambda + \delta = 0$ follows in the same way; from (28), $\gamma x < \gamma h$; and $h = y$ in this case.]

3

MARGINAL PRODUCTIVITY AND THE MACRO-ECONOMIC THEORIES OF DISTRIBUTION[1]

COMMENT ON SAMUELSON AND MODIGLIANI[2]

Professors Samuelson and Modigliani have written a long critical essay on macro-economic theories of distribution which demonstrates not only the splendid analytical powers of the two authors, but also the intellectual sterility engendered by the methods of Neo-classical Economics. The assumption of Profit Maximisation under conditions of Universal Perfect Competition involves, as a logical step (given the postulate of substitute relationships between factors), the assumption of production functions which are linear-homogeneous and "well-behaved" (with isoquants asymptotic to the axes). In addition, it has also been found necessary to assume either that capital is completely "malleable", or else that capital-labour intensities are identical in all industries in all circumstances—so that *real* capital can be uniquely measured in value (money) terms —and that there is no technical progress, except of the "Harrod neutral" type which falls like manna from Heaven. Given sufficient refinement of analysis no doubt many other such "assumptions" may have to be added. (One obvious candidate which has not been incorporated yet in neo-classical models is the absence of "Sraffa effects"—though it may be difficult to formulate the necessary conditions explicitly.) There is no room here for increasing returns, learning by doing, oligopolistic competition, uncertainty, obsolescence and other such troublesome things which mar the world as we know it. Markets operate in such a way that "competition will *enforce* [their italics] *at all times* [my italics] equality

---

[1] Originally published in the *Review of Economic Studies*, vol. XXXIII (1966) no. 4.
[2] Their paper was published in the same issue of *Review of Economic Studies*.

of factor prices to factor marginal productivities" (p. 271) and even if marginal productivities did not exist (in the "fixed co-efficient case" on pp. 287–89) "markets" would still operate in such a way as to punish immediately a factor in excess supply, be it Capital or Labour, with a zero price.

I would not wish to deny that these "abstractions" are necessary to make the system logically consistent, given the basic assumptions concerning how markets behave and how entre-preneurs behave (profit maximisation *combined with* universal perfect competition). But one must not fall into the error of supposing that assertions about reality can be derived from *a priori* assumptions. Whether well-behaved homogeneous-and-linear production functions exist or not is a question of fact. They cannot be presumed to exist as a consequence of some basic postulate, such as "profit maximisation under competitive con-ditions". If adequate empirical observation *established* the existence of production functions of constant returns to scale; if entrepreneurs can be *shown* to be confronted by infinitely elastic demand and supply curves; if the progress in technical knowledge could be *shown* to be of the kind which affected the productivity of all resources equally, and which proceeded at some autonomous rate in time, independently of entrepreneurial decisions concerning production and investment, the situation would be different. But all that we can tell from empirical observation is that output per unit of labour increases with the passage of time— to an extent that varies significantly between different industries and different countries—whilst output per unit of capital shows no systematic trend, upwards or downwards. We know that in a majority of cases, if not all, there is a positive association between the rate of increase of output-per-man and the rate of increase of output. But it is not possible to isolate the element of "autonomous" technological change from elements which are induced by, or associated with, changes in output or in investment.

However, for Professors Samuelson and Modigliani, assump-tions like homogeneous-linear and "well-behaved" production functions, or autonomous "Harrod-neutral" technical change, are not meant, I suppose, to be descriptions of reality (though in many places they argue as if they were)—they are "abstractions" which are intended merely as intermediate stages in the process of analysis. It is the hallmark of the neo-classical econo- mist to believe that, however severe the abstractions from which he is forced to start, he will "win through" by the end of the day— bit by bit, if he only carries the analysis far enough, the scaffolding can be removed, leaving the basic structure intact. In fact, these props are *never* removed; the removal of any one of a number of them—as, for example, allowing for increasing returns or learning-by-doing—is sufficient to cause the whole structure to collapse like a pack of cards.[1] It is high time that the brilliant minds of M.I.T. were set to evolve a system of non-Euclidean economics which starts from a non-perfect, non-profit-maxi- mising economy where such abstractions are initially unnecessary. (Of course the neo-classical purist would argue, again on *a priori* grounds, that in the long run the non-profit-maximisers will fall by the wayside—profit-maximisation will emerge by a Darwinian process of selection. This *may* be true in a static world with perfect foresight, in which profits can be made *only* through the relentless pursuit of the principle of substitution. But in a world of imperfect foresight and changing technology, the Darwinian process may favour the successful innovator who operates on hunches rather than the *homo oeconomicus* of the more pedestrian type, the careful equator of marginal substitution ratios.)

These general observations will, I think, be helpful in appreci- ating the particular comments that follow.

(1) *Capitalists and Workers*

Samuelson and Modigliani assume that any macro-economic theory which makes use of the notion of differences in savings propensities between profits and wages requires an identifiable class of hereditary barons—a class of capitalists "with permanent membership"—distinguished by a high savings propensity and of

[1] This is occasionally admitted—cf. e.g. footnote 7 which says that "the assumption of constant returns to scale is essential both to Pasinetti's and our own analysis, for otherwise the concept of a golden age steady state becomes self-contradictory". If the specification of a "golden age steady state" includes perfect competition, profit maximisation, *et al.*, this is obviously true. But if by a "golden-age steady state" no more is meant than a steady rate of growth with a constant rate of profit, the pro- position is not true.

a "permanent" class of workers distinguished by a low savings propensity. I cannot of course speak for Dr. Pasinetti, but as far as my own ideas are concerned, I have always regarded the high savings propensity out of profits as something which attaches to the nature of business income, and not to the wealth (or other peculiarities) of the individuals who own property. It is the enterprise, not the particular body of individuals owning it at any one time, which finds it necessary, in a dynamic world of increasing returns, to plough back a proportion of the profits earned as a kind of "prior charge" on earnings in order to ensure the survival of the enterprise in the long run. This is because: (i) continued expansion cannot be ensured in an uncertain world, and in the long run, unless *some proportion* of the finance required for expansion comes from internal sources; (ii) the competitive strength of any one enterprise, in a world of increasing returns, varies with the enterprise's share of the market—it declines with any decrease in that share, and improves with an increasing share; hence (iii) in a world of expanding markets, continued expansion (by the individual firm) is necessary merely to maintain the competitive strength of the enterprise. Hence the high savings propensity attaches to profits as such, not to capitalists as such.

In the early days of industrial capitalism when the ownership and management of businesses were united in the same person (as in the case of the early ironmasters of England, or, in more recent times, of Henry Ford) a high propensity to plough back business profits inevitably entailed a high propensity to save out of individual income. The capitalists of the nineteenth century, as Keynes once said, "were allowed to call the best part of the cake theirs, and were theoretically free to consume it, on the tacit underlying condition that they consumed very little of it in practice".[1] But nowadays businesses are to a large extent owned by rentier-capitalists (shareholders) whose personal savings-propensity need bear no relation to the savings propensity of the enterprises which they own. They are free to consume, in addition to their dividend income, as much of their capital (or their capital gains) as they like; in so far as they do so, this goes to offset the net acquisition of business assets by the "workers":

[1] *The Economic Consequences of the Peace*, p. 17.

it does *not* reduce, but on the contrary, enhances, the difference in savings propensities between business income and personal income. (For reasons explained in the Appendix, the shareholders' consumption out of capital gains cannot be treated as a reduction of s_c; it has exactly the same effect as a reduction of s_w, since it causes a reduction of the net savings of persons that is available to finance business investment.)

(2) The "Anti-Pasinetti Theorem"

The foregoing remarks are sufficient, I think, to refute the authors' contention that provided the savings propensity of workers is high enough, the "capitalists" (distinguished by their high savings propensity) will be gradually eliminated so that, in a Golden Age equilibrium, only one "savings propensity" is left. For this purpose they consider a situation in which the basic "Pasinetti inequality" (i.e. that the share of investment in total income is higher than the share of savings in wages, or in total personal income) does not hold as regards the "equilibrium" level of investment. They then proceed to demonstrate that the "capitalists" will be gradually "squeezed out". However, the end of it all is not a violent revolution, à la Marx, but the cosy world of Harrod, Domar and Solow, where there is only a single savings propensity applicable to the economy—where in other words,

$$sY = s_w Y.$$

The simple answer to all this is that, if the basic Kaldor-Pasinetti inequality is not satisfied, no Keynesian macro-economic distribution theory could survive for an instant, let alone in Golden Age equilibrium. If the "equilibrium" level of investment was less than the workers' savings, it is impossible to contemplate that investment should play the active role, and savings the passive role; for if we postulated that investment decisions were autonomous, either the full employment assumption would break down, or profits would have to be negative; and in either case it is clearly inconceivable that profits should be determined by the need to generate sufficient savings to finance investment. Moreover if we assume that profits are determined quite independently of this relation—either by marginal productivities in the Wonderland of Perfect Competition, etc., or by, say, Kalecki's "degree of monopoly"—we need further to assume a purely non-Keynesian system where there is necessarily just enough investment to finance full employment savings—where, in other words, savings *govern* investment, not the other way round.[1] It is easy to refute Pasinetti by postulating conditions in which the Pasinetti model could not possibly work, and where therefore something else must take its place—whatever that something else may be. Professors Samuelson and Modigliani assume, as a matter of course, that it must be Walras. In disproving Pasinetti they conjure up a Walrasian world in all its purity—a world in which all savings get invested somehow, without disturbing full employment: because any excess of savings over its equilibrium level induces a corresponding excess of investment over its equilibrium level. It is a world in which excess savings in search of investment necessarily depress the rate of interest (r) to whatever level is required to induce the necessary addition to investment, which means that, given a sufficient fall in r, a value of k/y can always be found (this is where "well-behaved" production functions come in) to make $nk/y = s_w$.

The validity of the Pasinetti inequality, $s_w < I/T$—or, in the Samuelson-Modigliani way of looking at it, $s_w < a(k)s_c$—is a matter of fact, just as perfect competition, constant returns to scale, *et al.* are matters of fact. Empirical investigation can disprove the former, just as it can disprove the latter. The question is, does it, and if so, which?

(3) *A Side Glance to Reality*

There is just one occasion where the two authors find it neces-

[1] On the subject of "full employment" the two halves of the Samuelson-Modigliani paper take up wholly contradictory positions. In the first half it is automatically (and continually) ensured by the marginal productivity equations. But in the second half, dealing with macro-economic theories, they become highly sceptical of its ever occurring, and pour scorn on people like Marshall, Pigou or myself for suggesting that unemployment has been small or trendless. (Compare, for example, the statement on p. 277 that "as long as the production function is well behaved, failure of (8) or even (7) to hold *cannot interfere* with full employment" (my italics) with footnote 3, p. 294, which says that if you believe in a mechanism making for full employment, "You can—as the Duke of Wellington once said—believe in anything".) Is there nothing, literally nothing, in a capitalist system which makes for full employment equilibrium—outside the cosy world of neo-classical theory?

sary to discuss the realistic values of the variables in order to justify their concern with the "anti-Pasinetti" case where "capitalists" are saved out of existence by the "workers". It occurs in footnote 1, p. 274, which is adduced in support of the statement that values of $\frac{P}{Y} = a(k^*) = \frac{1}{4}$, $s_c = \frac{1}{3}$ and $s_w = 0.05$, which (in their view) rule out the Pasinetti theorem, "are econometrically reasonable for a mixed economy like the U.S., U.K. or Western Europe".[1] In this demonstration, however, they make no less than four slips:

(i) The "corporate savings propensity of $\frac{1}{3}$" relates to savings out of net profits, after capital consumption allowances. The share of corporate profits of $\frac{1}{4}$ relates to the share of *gross* profits in the GNP. The empirical "savings propensity" out of gross profits after tax is not $\frac{1}{3}$, but 0.7 for the United States and the United Kingdom, and somewhere around 0.8 for Germany and Japan. (From the point of view of the mechanics of a Keynesian model, it is *gross* savings out of *gross* profits, and *gross* investment, that are relevant, not *net* savings and *net* investment; indeed in a more realistic "vintage" model it is not even possible to say *ab initio* what the latter are.)

(ii) The value $s_w = \frac{1}{12}$ is probably a realistic one for the net savings of wage and salary earners (i.e. net of dis-savings of retired workers); it is not, however, an indication of the savings available for the acquisition of business capital or for lending to the business sector, since a large part of it goes to finance personal investment in consumer durables. The only consumer durable which is statistically relevant in this connection is residential housing (since furniture, cars, etc. are statistically reckoned in consumption, not in investment, in official national income

---

[1] Incidentally, the very demonstration that these figures are inconsistent with the Pasinetti theorem is based on a piece of circular reasoning—it assumes what it intends to prove. For it supposes that the share of profits is determined by the technical coefficients of the production function, irrespective of anything else, in particular the investment coefficient, I/Y, which is here supposed to be governed by the savings generated by a predetermined profits share, dictated by the production function— whereas the whole dispute between Keynesian and non-Keynesian theories is whether investment determines savings, or *vice versa*. (I admit that they do not quite go the whole hog and postulate a world under a full Cobb-Douglas dictatorship where the share of profit is a technologically given constant, irrespective of anything else.)

accounts) and the latter must be deducted before the value of "s_w" relevant to the model can be estimated.

The net acquisition of financial assets by the personal sector—which is the measure of the personal saving available for lending to other sectors—appears to be very much smaller, as the following estimates show:[1]

Percentage of personal
disposable income
(average 1960 to 1965)

	United Kingdom	United States
Personal saving	6·9	10·3
less investment in dwellings	−2·8	−4·7
less investment in fixed assets and stock by unincorporated businesses	−1·8	−4·5
equals net acquisition of financial assets by the personal sector	2·3	1·1
of which increase in life assurance and pension funds	4·7	2·6
increase in other financial assets (net)	−2·4	−1·5

In the United Kingdom personal savings as a percentage of personal disposal income appears to be lower than in the United States. But because investment in dwellings by the personal

---

[1] The figures are derived from the official national income accounts for the United States and the United Kingdom and are, as far as possible, on a comparable basis. The source of the figures for the United States is the *Survey of Current Business*, May 1966; for the United Kingdom, *Financial Statistics*, June 1966 and *Economic Trends*, April 1966.

Personal disposable income, as defined here, is reckoned before deducting capital consumption. Gross personal saving includes any capital transfers received *less* any capital transfers paid. For both countries independent estimates of identified acquisitions of financial assets *less* liabilities exceed the residual figures obtained from the official national income accounts; it is impossible to say how far the discrepancy is due to an underestimate of personal savings in the national accounts (and an over-estimate of corporate etc. savings) and how far to under-recording of financial transactions between the personal sector and the others. For the U.S. estimates based on identified financial transactions may be deduced from the May 1966 issue of the *Federal Reserve* Bulletin:

sector and investment by unincorporated businesses is relatively less important in the United Kingdom, net acquisition of financial assets appears to be somewhat higher.

Hence, whether we take the U.S. or the U.K. figures, the value of s_w—in the only sense in which this is relevant to the Pasinetti theorem or the anti-Pasinetti theorem—is more like $\frac{1}{50}$ or $\frac{1}{100}$ than $\frac{1}{12}$.

(iii) In the above figures the "increase in life assurance and pension funds" is probably a good indication of the net savings of wage and salary earners (after deduction of the savings that go to repay mortgages on houses), since these are so largely contractual in character. On the other hand, the net diminution in "other financial assets" is probably a good measure of the net consumption of property-owners out of capital or capital gains. Since net spending in excess of dividend-income involves a net sale of securities, which goes to offset at least a part of the net demand for securities originating from wage and salary earners' savings, it should be evident that spending out of capital gains is indistinguishable in its effects from a reduction in workers' savings. The fact that some of the capital gains are spent is thus in no sense a criticism of the "realism of the strict Pasinetti assumptions". There is nothing in the model which requires s_w to be positive—the model works just as well when it is negative, with the business sector being a net lender, not a net borrower, to the personal sector.[1] Despite the laborious attempt to "generalise" the model to all kinds of cases—Pasinetti and Paanti-sinetti—

	Percentages of personal disposable income Average 1961–1965
Increase in life assurance and pension funds	3·4
Increase in other financial assets	−0·5
Net acquisition of financial assets by personal sector	2·9

For both countries the figures of personal saving and of net acquisitions relate to the personal sector as a whole, including unincorporated enterprises. Since the income of these enterprises is small in relation to total of personal income (14 to 15 per cent in the United States and 9 to 10 per cent in the United Kingdom) no great error can result from assuming that the saving (covering both capital consumption and other additions to reserves) of unincorporated enterprises is roughly balanced by their investment. (I am indebted to Mr. L. S. Berman of the Central Statistical Office for these estimates.)

[1] Cf. *Appendix* below, on "A Neo-Pasinetti Theorem".

Samuelson and Modigliani ignore the "super-Pasinetti" case of $s_w < 0$ or the special "arch-Pasinetti" case of $s_w = 0$.

(iv) With a "realistic" value of s_w of, say, $0 \cdot 01 - 0 \cdot 03$, and a "realistic" value of $s_c = 0 \cdot 7$, one would have thought that the Kaldor-Pasinetti type of model is safe enough on empirical grounds—even allowing for "Kuh-Meyer" effects, the validity of which is in any case highly questionable.[1] However, if one goes in for "realism", surely one cannot ignore the existence of a third class, which is more likely to overspend its income than either "workers" or "capitalists", namely the Government. The "net acquisition of financial assets by the personal sector" need not in fact finance business investment: it often goes to finance (probable only a part of) the net borrowing of the public sector. To find out whether "the realistic value of the variables" threatens the Pasinetti model in an anti-Pasinetti direction, one should pose another question: how much of business investment is in fact financed out of personal savings? This information is found by looking at the net acquisition of financial assets of the (private) corporate sector; in the U.S. this item has been positive for three out of the last six years, and in the U.K. it has been positive for five out of the six years (even after adjustment for net long-term investment abroad). In such years the corporate sector is a net lender to the rest of the economy, and not a net borrower. This comes to the same, from the point of view of the mechanics of the Keynesian-type distribution theory, as assuming a negative value of s_w; in its effects on profits it makes no difference whether the net dis-saving is due to the activities of the personal sector or of the Government.

(4) The "Generalised" Neo-Classical Theory

In section X of their paper the two authors discover that their

---

[1] The correlation found by Kuh and Meyer between corporate savings and corporate investment does not in any way prove that corporate investment is confined by, or governed by, corporate savings: they may both reflect a common factor, the rate of return on capital employed. A company's retention ratio is clearly influenced by its long-run capital requirements: the raison d'être of the plough back is to preserve a company's liquidity and thus to prevent its long-run expansion from being hampered by financial embarrassments. But there is always a "liquidity cushion" (in Anglo-Saxon countries, often a pretty large cushion) between the current cash inflow of savings and the current cash outflow on capital expenditure; the purpose of retention is to protect the cushion, rather than to finance expenditure on a day-to-day basis.

results do not, after all, depend on "marginal productivity notions of the Clark-Wicksteed-Solow-Meade type". *All* that they require is the postulate that the rate of profit, or interest, should be a single-valued function, ϕ, of the capital/labour ratio (K/L), with $\phi' < 0$. No reason whatever is adduced to show why this assumption is any less restrictive than the whole bag of tricks specified in equations (1) and (2). The assumption of a functional relation between the rate of profit and the capital/labour ratio is *implied* in the assumption underlying equations (1) and (2); but without them it is purely arbitrary. Nor is any attempt made to support the validity (or plausibility) of such an assumption empirically. The K/L ratio, unlike the K/Y ratio, shows the widest of variations between the different countries—it is perhaps twenty times as high in the U.S. as in India—whilst the rate of profit is often found to be higher in countries with a relatively high K/L ratio than with a low K/L ratio. (Of course they might have argued, in the manner of the Stanford inquiry, that in terms of "corrected" labour units—corrected for Harrod-neutral differences in "efficiency"—capital/labour ratios are everywhere the same!)

(5) *Fixed Coefficients*

Finally, they assert that macro-economic distribution theories "fare best" under the assumption of fixed coefficients "for under variable coefficients one would have *no need* [my italics] for a genuinely alternative theory of distribution"—why search for something new when you have such a satisfying explanation already?

It is at this point that they should have taken another side-glance into reality and adduced some empirical evidence to show that the most important "predictions" of the marginal productivity theory—diminishing productivity to labour in the short period, constant returns to scale to both labour and capital in the long period—are valid, as a matter of fact. However they could not have done this, because:

(i) all empirical studies concerning the short-period relationship between output and employment (at least in manufacturing activities) show the elasticity of the former with regard to changes in the latter to be greater, not less, than unity ("Okun's Law" makes it 3) which implies of course that the short-period marginal product of labour exceeds the average product. Since profits are non-negative, the proposition that the price of each factor is "at all times" equal to its marginal product cannot possibly hold. Another way of putting the same point is that in order to get diminishing short-period marginal productivity for labour (or increasing marginal labour cost) firms must operate plant near full (or maximum) capacity. Experience shows that even in times when production is limited by labour shortages, plant is not (normally) fully utilised.

(ii) All empirical studies concerning the relationship of productivity and production (again, for manufacturing activities) reveal the existence of (long-run) increasing returns, both on account of the economies of large-scale production, and of the subdivision of processes (and of industries) with an increase in the scale of activities. Again the proposition that factor prices are equal to their marginal products cannot hold, because the marginal products do not "add up" to the total product.

However, the authors believe they have demonstrated (by *a priori* reasoning) that there is no room for anything other than marginal productivity if there are possibilities of factor substitution. Hence "recognising the empirical oddity of the postulate" they proceed to explore the case of fixed coefficients, and find that here at last the Kaldor-Pasinetti proposition has some "definite meaning" as an explanation of relative shares. However, they hasten to add that "whatever value the above model has as an exercise, its economic relevance is in our view very dubious" because an economic system of this kind would be subject to the wildest instability: if the capital/labour ratio wasn't exactly right, either profits would be zero, or wages would be zero (according to whether capital were just a little too much or a little too little); and there is no guarantee that a system fluctuating between the extremes of zero profits and zero wages would tend to generate just the right amount of capital to be consistent with positive values for both.

But what kind of an "economic system" are they "observing"?

Is it Ruritania, Solovia, Cloud-Cuckooland, or the U.S.A. and other members of the Group of Ten? If "excess" labour caused wages to fall to zero, how could there ever be unemployment— of the Keynesian or any other kind? And if "excess" capital caused profits to fall to zero, how could there ever be profits, considering that the employment-capacity of the prevailing capital equipment, in any advanced community, is always larger and often very considerably larger, than what is needed to secure full employment for the existing labour force? Indeed how could capacity ever be under-utilised and still earn a profit?

The whole antithesis that *either* marginal productivity "must explain" pricing and distribution *or else* there must be fixed coefficients, is neo-classical circular reasoning carried *in extremis*. The proposition is true but only in the abstract Wonderland of perfect competition, profit maximisation plus the etceteras specified at the beginning. Their appeal, however, to the need to reconcile "the relatively smooth functioning of behaviour and of share imputation in *observed* economic systems" is an appeal, not to the Wonderland, but to the Real World. Can't they see that it is *possible* for a market economy to be "competitive" without satisfying the neo-classical equations? Can't they imagine a world in which marginal productivities are *not* equal to factor prices, and are not in any definite relationship to factor prices—a world, for example, in which, with the approach of labour scarcity, the share of wages is falling, not rising, despite the fact that the marginal productivity of labour is constant or rising and Capital (in the relevant sense) is redundant in relation to Labour? Unless they make a more imaginative effort to reconcile their theoretical framework with the known facts of experience, their economic theory is bound to remain a barren exercise. One is reminded of what Clapham wrote 44 years ago: "I have a fear lest a theory of value which should prove permanently unable to state of what particular and individual values some of its more important conclusions were true might in the long run be neg- lected by mankind."[1]

[1] *Economic Journal*, December 1922, p. 561.

Dr. Pasinetti has shown that on certain conditions the rate of profit, in a true long-run Golden Age equilibrium, will be independent of the rate of savings of "workers", because the additional consumption generated out of the worker's property income will offset their savings out of wage-income. The difficulty with this proposition (apart from the fact that it is "very long run") is that it assumes that workers spend the same fraction of their income, irrespective of whether it accrues to them as property income or wages. In a world where enterprises are organised as corporations, and property-income takes the form of dividends, this would imply (as Professors Samuelson and Modigliani point out) overspending their dividend income by the exact fraction required to make their consumption equal to $(1 - s_w)P_w$, irrespective of the division of profits between corporate retentions and dividends.

Moreover once we allow spending in excess of dividend income, there is no reason to confine such spending to workers. "Capitalists" also spend some part of their capital gains (or even their capital, in the absence of such gains), and as Professor Modigliani has reminded us, the limited length of human life must add to such temptations.

Hence at any time there must be capitalists (or shareholders) who overspend their current (dividend) income (and the same must be true, of course, of retired workers who consume over the years of retirement their accumulated savings) just as there are active workers who save a certain fraction of their income for retirement. Just as net saving out of income sets up a demand for securities, net dis-saving out of income (= net consumption out of capital or capital gains) sets up a supply of securities. There is also a net supply of new securities issued by the corporate sector. Since, in the securities' market, prices will tend to a level at which the total (non-speculative) supply and demand for securities are equal (at least over longer periods), there must be some

[1] I should like to acknowledge benefits from discussions with F. H. Hahn, L. Pasinetti and J. A. Mirrlees.

mechanism to ensure that the spending out of capital (or capital gains) just balances the savings out of income *less* any new securities issued by corporations.

Let us divide the community into wage and salary earners (W) who save (through the intermediaries of pension funds and insurance companies) some fraction of their income during their working life and consume it in retirement; so long as the population is rising and income per head is rising, the savings of the working population must exceed the dis savings of the retired population by an amount which can be expressed as some fraction (s_w) of current wage-and-salary income. (I am assuming also that s_w is net of personal investment in consumer durables, i.e. in housing.)

Let us further suppose that the shareholders' net consumption out of capital (i.e. their consumption in excess of their dividend income) is some fraction (c) of their capital gains G.

And finally, let us suppose that corporations (having decided on retaining a fraction, s_c, of their profits) decide in addition to issue new securities equal to some fraction, i, $(|i| < 1)$, of their current investment expenditure, gK (where K = capital, g = the growth rate).

Equilibrium in the securities market then requires that

$$s_w W = cG + igK.$$

For such an equilibrium to exist, at least one of these items must be responsive to changes in the market prices of securities. Such an item is cG, since G is nothing else than the change in the market value of securities. This varies not only with the rise in dividends and earnings per share, but also with the "valuation ratio" (v)—i.e. the relation of the market value of shares to the capital employed by the corporations (or the "book value" of assets). In other words, if the market value of securities is pN (where N = number of shares, p = price per share) and given a constant valuation ratio

$$G = N \Delta p = v \Delta K - p \Delta N \tag{1}$$

(i.e. the increase in the corporations' assets *multiplied* by the valuation ratio *less* the value of new securities issued). Since

$$\Delta K = gK$$
$$p\Delta N = igK \tag{2}$$
$$G = vgK - igK.$$

Hence[1] $$s_w W - c(vgK - igK) = igK. \tag{3}$$

There is in addition the savings = investment equation

$$s_w W - c(vgK - igK) + s_c P = gK. \tag{4}$$

Since $W = Y - P$, $P = \rho K$ (P = profits, ρ = the rate of profit), the above can be written

$$s_w Y - s_w \rho K - cvgK + cigK = igK \tag{3a}$$

and $$s_w Y + (s_c - s_w)\rho K - cvgK + cigK = gK. \tag{4a}$$

After rearranging the terms and dividing through by gK we get

$$\frac{s_w}{g}\frac{Y}{K} - \frac{s_w \rho}{g} - cv + ci = i \tag{3b}$$

$$\frac{s_w}{g}\frac{Y}{K} + \frac{(s_c - s_w)\rho}{g} - cv + ci = 1. \tag{4b}$$

Solving for v and ρ we get

$$v = \frac{1}{c}\left[\frac{s_w}{g}\frac{Y}{K} - \frac{s_w}{s_c}(1 - i) - i(1 - c)\right] \tag{5}$$

and

$$\rho = \frac{g(1 - i)}{s_c}. \tag{6}$$

The interpretation of these equations is as follows. Given the savings-coefficients and the capital-gains-consumption coefficient, there will be a certain valuation ratio which will secure just enough savings by the personal sector to take up the new securities issued by corporations. Hence the *net* savings of the personal sector (available for investment by the business sector) will depend, not only on the savings propensities of individuals, but on the policies of the corporations towards new issues. In the absence of new issues the level of security prices will be

---

[1] We subsume in the definition of c a constant share of assets owned by shareholders, for reasons explained below.

established at the point at which the purchases of securities by the savers will be just balanced by the sale of securities of the dis-savers, making the net savings of the personal sector zero. The issue of new securities by corporations will depress security prices (i.e. the valuation ratio) just enough to reduce the sale of securities by the dis-savers sufficiently to induce the net savings required to take up the new issues. If i were negative and the corporations were net *purchasers* of securities from the personal sector (which they could be through the redemption of past securities, or purchasing shares from the personal sector for the acquisition of subsidiaries) the valuation ratio would be driven up to the point at which net personal savings would be negative to the extent necessary to match the sale of securities to the corporate sector.[1]

In a state of Golden Age equilibrium (given a constant g, and a constant K/Y, however determined), v will be constant, with a value that can be $\gtreqless 1$, depending on the values of s_c, s_w, c and i. (All that one can assert is that, given the Pasinetti in-equality, $gK > s_w Y$, $v < 1$ when $c = (1 - s_w)$, $i = 0$; with $i > 0$ this will be true *a fortiori*.[2]

---

[1] The above equations assume that savings out of dividends are zero; cG is intended as the net excess of shareholders' consumption over dividend income. It would be possible to assume that there is only a single savings propensity for the household sector which applies equally to wages, dividends and capital gains. If we denote this by s_h, equations (3) and (4) above become

$$s_c P + s_h (W + (1 - s_c)P) - (1 - s_h)gK(v - i) = gK$$

and

$$s_h(W + (1 - s_c)P) - (1 - s_h)gK(v - i) = igK.$$

From this we obtain

$$\rho = \frac{g(1 - i)}{s_c}$$

as before and

$$v = 1 - \frac{1 - s_h \dfrac{Y}{gK}}{1 - s_h}$$

in place of equation (5) above. This implies that $v < 1$, when $s_h Y < gK$ (since $Y > gK$, in all cases).

[2] Assuming $g - s_w Y/K > 0$, it follows from (5) that $v < 1$ provided that

$$\frac{s_c - s_w}{cs_c}(1 - i) + i \lesseqgtr 1. \tag{i}$$

When $c = 1 - s_w$; (i) will hold if

$$\frac{s_c - s_w}{(1 - s_w)s_c} \lesseqgtr 0$$

or

$$s_c - s_w \lesseqgtr s_c - s_w s_c. \tag{ii}$$

Since $s_c < 1$, (ii) must hold.

The rate of profit in a Golden Age equilibrium (as given by equation (6)) will depend only on g, s_c and i, and will then be independent of the "personal" savings propensities, s_w and c. In this way it is similar to the Pasinetti theorem in that the rate of profit will be independent of s_w (and also of c) but it is reached by a different route; it will hold in any steady growth state, and not only in a "long-run" Golden Age; it does not postulate a class of hereditary capitalists with a special high-saving propensity. In the special case $i = 0$, it reduces to the simple Pasinetti formula, $\rho = g/s_c$.

The assumption that corporations issue securities which are a constant fraction, i, of their investment, irrespective of anything else (in particular, irrespective of v) is of course arbitrary. It is possible to conceive of numerous other assumptions to characterise the corporations' collective behaviour with regard to the issue of new securities. For example it would be possible to assume that the corporations' issue of new securities will depend on the *ex-post* difference between their savings ($s_c P$) and their investment (gK) and that such *ex-post* differences are only "recognised" at the end of certain intervals of time (of the accounting periods); any intervening difference being met by a depletion (or accretion) of their cash reserves. In other words, they issue securities periodically, to make good any past depletion of their liquid reserves; in the converse case, they respond *ex-post* to an accretion of cash reserves by redeeming securities (such as debenture issues or preference shares). Assuming that these accounting intervals are long enough, v and s will establish themselves at values corresponding to $i = 0$; this means that net personal savings will be zero, and the *ex-post* difference between $s_c P$ and gK will be zero: *no* new securities will, in fact, be issued (or redeemed) because there will be no occasion to. This kind of behaviour will thus lead to the simple Pasinetti formula $\rho = g/s_c$.

Has this "neo-Pasinetti theorem" any very-long-run "Pasinetti" or "anti-Pasinetti" solution? So far we have not taken any account of the change in the distribution of assets between "workers" (i.e. pension funds) and "capitalists"—indeed we assumed it to be constant. However since the capitalists are *selling* shares (if $c > 0$) and the pension funds are buying them, one could suppose that the *share* of total assets in the hands of capitalists would diminish continually, whereas the share of assets in the hands of the workers' funds would increase continually until, at some distant day, the capitalists have no shares left; the pension funds and insurance companies would own them all!

But this view ignores that the ranks of the capitalist class are constantly renewed by the sons and daughters of the new Captains of Industry, replacing the grandsons and granddaughters of the older Captains who gradually dissipate their inheritance through living beyond their dividend income. It is reasonable to assume that the value of the shares of the newly formed and growing companies grows at a higher rate than the average, whilst those of older companies (which decline in relative importance) grow at a lower rate. This means that the rate of capital appreciation of the shares in the hands of the capitalist group as a whole, for the reasons given above, is greater than the rate of appreciation of the assets in the hands of pension funds, etc. Given the difference in the rates of appreciation of the two funds of securities —and this depends on the rate at which new corporations emerge and replace older ones—I think it can be shown that there will be, for any given constellation of the value of the parameters, a long-run equilibrium distribution of the assets between capitalists and pension funds which will remain constant. But it would require further investigation that goes beyond the limits of this Appendix to demonstrate this formally.

E

RASMUSON LIBRARY
UNIVERSITY OF ALASKA-FAIRBANKS

4

CAUSES OF THE SLOW RATE OF ECONOMIC GROWTH IN THE UNITED KINGDOM[1]

I

One of the basic economic facts which has increasingly entered into national consciousness is the relatively slow rate of economic growth of Britain. Thanks to the work of various international organisations, there is now ample material on the comparative growth records of different countries, and in such comparisons Britain appears almost invariably near the bottom of the league-tables. Thus if we take the decade 1953–4 to 1963–4, the rate of growth of our gross domestic product is estimated to have been 2·7 per cent a year, as against 4·9 per cent in France, 5·6 in Italy, 6 per cent in Germany, and no less than 9·6 per cent in Japan. If we take a more recent period, say the five years 1960–5, our rate of economic growth at 3·3 per cent a year looks distinctly better, but our inferiority, in relation to the other advanced countries, appears even more pronounced, since some countries, such as the United States, Canada or Belgium, which previously grew at around 3–3½ per cent a year have all shown much higher growth rates in the more recent period. Indeed every other member of the "Paris Club" of advanced countries has chalked up a growth rate of at least 4½ per cent in the last five years; Japan remained outstanding with a rate of growth of almost 10 per cent a year.

As these facts became more generally known, the minds of our economists and men of affairs, and the public generally, have become increasingly preoccupied with finding the basic cause, or causes, of this phenomenon. There has been no shortage of

[1] Originally delivered as an Inaugural Lecture at the University of Cambridge, November 2nd 1966, and published by Cambridge University Press in 1966.

explanations. Some put the blame on the inefficiency of our business management; some on the nature of our education giving too little emphasis to science and technology, and too much to the humanities; some on the general social milieu which deprecates aggressive competitiveness and looks down on mere money-making as a career; some on over-manning and other restrictive practices of trade unions; some on the alleged national dislike of hard work; some on the insufficiency of investment, or of the right kind of investment; some on the economic policies of successive governments, being either too inflationary, or too deflationary, or both; and no doubt one could cite many other such "explanations".

There may be truth in some, if not all, of these contentions. The difficulty about them is that with one or two possible exceptions, they are not capable of being tested, and there is no way in which their individual role could in any way be quantified. Another basic difficulty with explanations of this kind is that while they may seem *plausible* in relation to some countries, they look implausible in relation to others, whose relatively poor performance equally calls for explanation. (Thus in the decade 1953–63, though *not* in the five years 1960–5, the rate of economic growth of the United States was almost as low as Britain's. Yet no one suggested that the same kind of factors— inefficiency of business management, slowness in introducing innovations, restrictive labour practices, etc.—were likely to have been the causes of *her* slow rate of progress.)

However, the purpose of my lecture today is not to dispute the possible validity of such explanations, nor to argue in favour of one or another, but to suggest an alternative approach which seeks to explain the recorded differences in growth rates in terms of the *stage* of economic development attained by different countries rather than in the realm of personal (or rather individual) abilities or incentives. Put briefly, the contention that I intend to examine is that fast rates of economic growth are associated with the fast rate of growth of the "secondary" sector of the economy—mainly the manufacturing sector—and that this is an attribute of an intermediate stage of economic development: it is the characteristic of the transition from "immaturity" to "maturity"; and that the trouble with the British economy is that it has reached a high stage of "maturity" *earlier* than others, with the result that it has exhausted the potential for fast growth before it had attained particularly high levels of productivity or real income per head. The meaning of the term "maturity" will, I hope, become evident in the course of this lecture; it is mainly intended to denote a state of affairs where real income per head has reached broadly the same level in the different sectors of the economy.

On this diagnosis the basic trouble with the British economy is that it suffers from "premature maturity". This may sound no less pessimistic a conclusion than the alternative view which attributes our failures to some basic deterioration in the national character—such as working too little, spending too much, too little initiative, vitality or incentive—but at least it has the advantage that if the diagnosis were correct, and if it came to be generally accepted, steps could be taken to ameliorate the situation through instruments more powerful than mere exhortation.

I shall begin by examining the empirical evidence in favour of my contention; I will then discuss the theoretical reasons to justify it; and finally its implication in terms of potential growth rates of Britain and other advanced countries.

II

Let us then begin with the evidence. If we take the twelve industrially advanced countries for which figures are available, as shown in Table 1 (there are a few countries, such as Sweden and Switzerland, which had to be omitted for lack of comparable data), we find that there is a very high correlation between the rate of growth of the gross domestic product and the rate of growth of manufacturing production, and what is more significant, we find that the faster the overall rate of growth, the greater is the *excess* of the rate of growth of manufacturing production over the rate of growth of the economy as a whole.

This is indicated by the regression equation shown at the bottom of the table which, in terms of all the usual tests, shows a

Table 1

RATE OF GROWTH OF G.D.P. AND RATE OF GROWTH OF MANUFACTURING
PRODUCTION (TWELVE INDUSTRIAL COUNTRIES, AVERAGE 1953–4 TO
AVERAGE 1963–4): EXPONENTIAL GROWTH RATES

	Annual rate of growth of G.D.P.[1]	Annual rate of growth of manufacturing production[1]
Japan	9·6	13·6[2]
Italy	5·6	8·2
West Germany	6·0	7·3
Austria	5·4	6·2
France	4·9	5·6
Netherlands	4·5	5·5[3]
Belgium	3·6	5·1
Denmark	4·1	4·9
Norway	3·9	4·6
Canada	3·6	3·4
U.K.	2·7	3·2
U.S.A.	3·1	2·6

[1] Derived from National Accounts Data of G.D.P., and G.D.P. in manufacturing, at constant prices.

[2] Index of manufacturing production.

[3] G.D.P. in industrial production (including mining).

Sources. National Accounts Statistics, O.E.C.D.; National Accounts Yearbooks, U.N.

Regression. Growth of G.D.P. (Y) on growth of manufacturing output (X),
$$Y = 1·153 + 0·614X, \quad R^2 = 0·959.$$
$$(0·040)$$
Standard error of residuals as a proportion of mean value of $Y = 0·0825$.

highly significant relationship between the rate of growth of the G.D.P. and the rate of growth of manufacturing production. On the basis of this one can predict fairly accurately the rate of growth of an economy—at least over a run of years—if one knows the rate of growth of its manufacturing production.

Of course, the mere fact that the growth of manufacturing output correlates with the growth of the G.D.P. is not in itself surprising, since the manufacturing sector is a fairly large component of the latter—somewhere between 25–40 per cent for the countries considered. But the regression equation asserts more than this. The meaning of the positive constant in the equation and of the regression coefficient which is significantly less than unity is that rates of growth above 3 per cent a year are found only in cases where the rate of growth in manufacturing output is in excess of the overall rate of growth of the economy. In other words, there is a positive correlation between the overall rate of economic growth and the *excess* of the rate of growth of manufacturing output over the rate of growth of the non-manufacturing sectors. I have not investigated how far this has been true of earlier historical periods, but in a study on historical growth rates since the nineteenth century published some years ago, Miss Deborah Paige found the same kind of relationship.[1]

Assuming, for the moment, that this relationship exists, is there some general hypothesis which is capable of explaining it? We must beware of attributing causal significance to a statistical relationship unless it can be shown to be consistent with some general hypothesis, which can be supported by other evidence. Since the differences in growth rates are largely accounted for by differences in the rates of growth of productivity (and not of changes in the working population), the primary explanation must lie in the technological field—it must be related to the behaviour of productivity growth. Is there some general reason which makes the rate of increase of output-per-man, for the economy as a whole, dependent on the rate of growth of manufacturing production? It has been suggested that because the *level* of productivity in manufacturing activities is higher than in the rest of the economy, a faster expansion of the high-productivity manufacturing sectors pulls up the average; and also that the incidence of technical progress—as measured by the *rate of growth* of productivity—is higher in manufacturing activities than in the other fields, so that a greater concentration on manufacturing increases the overall rate of advance.

However, neither of these suppositions seems capable of explaining the facts. The differences in the level of output per head between different sectors, as Beckerman has recently shown,[2] are quite incapable of explaining more than a small part of the observed differences in productivity growth rates, in terms of inter-sectoral shifts. The second proposition, if it were factually correct, would relate the rate of economic growth to the *size* of the manufacturing sector (in relation to the whole economy)

---

[1] "Economic Growth: The Last Hundred Years", *National Institute Economic Review*, July 1961, p. 41.

[2] *The British Economy in 1975* (Cambridge University Press, 1965), pp. 23–5.

rather than to its rate of expansion: it would make the rate of economic growth the highest in those countries whose industrial sector, as measured by the proportion of total manpower engaged in it, is the largest. On this test, therefore, Britain ought to come out near the top, not at the bottom of the league-table. But quite apart from this, the proposition is factually incorrect: technological progress and productivity growth is by no means confined to manufacturing; in many of the countries examined, productivity growth in agriculture and mining has been higher than in manufacturing, or in industrial activities taken as a whole.

There is, however, a third possible explanation—the existence of economies of scale, or increasing returns, which causes productivity to increase in response to, or as a by-product of, the increase in total output. That manufacturing activities are subject to the "law of increasing returns" was of course a well-known contention of the classical economists. One finds the origin of this doctrine in the first three chapters of the *Wealth of Nations*. Here Adam Smith argued that the *return* per unit of labour—what we now call productivity—depends on the division of labour: on the extent of specialisation and the division of production into so many different processes, as exemplified by his famous example of pin-making. As Smith explained, the division of labour depends on the extent of the market: the greater the market, the greater the extent to which differentiation and specialisation is carried, the higher the productivity. Neo-classical writers, with one or two famous exceptions, like Marshall and Allyn Young, tended to ignore, or to underplay, this phenomenon. As Hahn and Matthews remarked in a recent article "the reason for the neglect is no doubt the difficulty of fitting increasing returns into the prevailing framework of perfect competition and marginal productivity factor pricing".[1]

However, Adam Smith, like both Marshall and Allyn Young after him, emphasised the interplay of static and dynamic factors in causing returns to increase with an increase in the scale of industrial activities. A greater division of labour is more pro-

[1] "The Theory of Economic Growth: A Survey", *Economic Journal* December, 1964, p. 833.

ductive, partly because it generates more skill and know-how; more expertise in turn yields more innovations and design improvements. We cannot isolate the influence of the economies of large-scale production due to indivisibilities of various kinds, and which are in principle reversible, from such changes in technology associated with a process of expansion which are not reversible. Learning is the product of experience—which means, as Arrow has shown,[1] that productivity tends to grow the faster, the faster output expands; it also means that the *level* of productivity is a function of cumulative output (from the beginning) rather than of the rate of production per unit of time.

In addition, as Allyn Young emphasised, increasing returns is a "macro-phenomenon"—just because so much of the economies of scale emerge as a result of increased differentiation, the emergence of new processes and new subsidiary industries, they cannot be "discerned adequately by observing the effects of variations in the size of an individual firm or of a particular industry". At any one time, there are industries in which economies of scale may have ceased to be important. They may nevertheless benefit from a general industrial expansion which, as Young said, should be "seen as an interrelated whole". With the extension of the division of labour "the representative firm, like the industry of which it is a part, loses its identity".[2]

III

This, in my view, is the basic reason for the empirical relationship between the growth of productivity and the growth of production which has recently come to be known as the "Verdoorn Law", in recognition of P. J. Verdoorn's early investigations, published in 1949.[3] It is a dynamic rather than a static relationship—between the rates of change of productivity and of output, rather than between the *level* of productivity and the *scale* of output—primarily because technological progress enters into it, and is not just a reflection of the economies of large-scale pro-

[1] "The Economic Implications of Learning by Doing", *Review of Economic Studies*, June 1962, pp. 155–73.
[2] "Increasing Returns and Economic Progress", *Economic Journal*, December 1928, pp. 538–9.
[3] "Fattori che regolano lo sviluppo della produttivitá del lavoro", *L'Industria*, 1949.

duction. Since Verdoorn's work it has been investigated by many others, among them Salter,[1] and more recently by Beckerman,[2] though none of these authors (to my knowledge) has given sufficient emphasis to the fact that it is a phenomenon peculiarly associated with the so-called "secondary" activities—with industrial production, including public utilities, construction, as well as manufacturing—rather than with the primary or tertiary sectors of the economy.

Table 2

RATES OF GROWTH OF PRODUCTION, EMPLOYMENT AND PRODUCTIVITY IN MANUFACTURING INDUSTRY (TWELVE COUNTRIES, AVERAGE 1953–4 TO AVERAGE 1963–4): ANNUAL EXPONENTIAL GROWTH RATES

	Production[1]	Employment[2]	Productivity[3]
Japan	19·6	5·8	7·8
Italy[4]	8·1	3·9[5]	4·2
West Germany	7·4	2·8	4·5
Austria[7]	6·4	2·2	4·2
France[6]	5·7	1·8	3·8
Denmark[6]	5·7	2·5[5]	3·2
Netherlands[8]	5·5	1·4	4·1
Belgium	5·1	1·2[5]	3·9
Norway	4·6	0·2	4·4
Canada	3·4	2·1	1·3
U.K.	3·2	0·4	2·8
U.S.A.[7]	2·6	0·0	2·6

[1] Gross domestic product in manufacturing, at constant prices.
[2] Wage and salary earners adjusted for changes in weekly manhours.
[3] Output per manhour, derived from first two columns.
[4] 1954–5 to 1963–4.
[5] Incorporates estimated change in weekly manhours.
[6] 1955–6 to 1963–4.
[7] 1953–4 to 1962–3.
[8] Industrial production and employment (including mining).

Sources. National Account and Manpower Statistics, O.E.C.D. Statistical Yearbook, U.N.

Regressions.
(1) Rate of growth of productivity (P) on the rate of growth of manufacturing production (X),

$$P = 1·035 + 0·484X, \quad R^2 = 0·826.$$
$$(0·070)$$

(2) Rate of growth of employment (E) on rate of growth of manufacturing production (X),

$$E = -1·028 + 0·516X, \quad R^2 = 0·844.$$
$$(0·070)$$

Its application to the case of the manufacturing industries of the twelve countries in the period 1953–4 to 1963–4 is given in Table 2, which shows for each country the growth rates of pro-

[1] *Productivity and Technical Change* (Cambridge University Press, 1960).
[2] *Ibid.* pp. 221–8.

duction, productivity and employment. The results are summarised in two regression equations, productivity on output, and
employment on output—which are two different ways of looking
at the same relationship[1]—and which suggest that the growth of
output must have played a major role in the determination of
productivity growth rates. Again, the relationships by the usual
tests are shown to be highly significant and they suggest that
apart from an "autonomous" rate of productivity growth of
around 1 per cent a year, the latter is a function of the growth
in total output: each percentage addition to the growth of
output requires a 0·5 per cent increase in the growth of employment in terms of manhours, and is associated with a 0·5 per
cent increase in the growth of productivity. These coefficients
are very close to those found by Verdoorn and other investi-
gators.

There are some economists who, whilst admitting the statistical
relationship between productivity growth and production growth,
argue that it says nothing about cause and effect: the Verdoorn
Law, according to this view, may simply reflect the fact that
faster growth rates in productivity induce, via their effects on
relative costs and prices, a faster rate of growth of demand, and
not the other way round.

This alternative hypothesis is not, however, fully specified—
if it were, its logical shortcomings would at once be apparent.
If the rate of growth of productivity in each industry and in
each country was a fully autonomous factor, we need some
hypothesis to explain it. The usual hypothesis is that the growth
of productivity is mainly to be explained by the progress of
knowledge in science and technology. But in that case how is one
to explain the large differences in the *same* industry over the
same period in different countries? How can the progress of
knowledge account for the fact, for example, that in the period
1954–60, productivity in the German motor-car industry increased at 7 per cent a year and in Britain only 2·7 per cent a
year? Since large segments of the car industry in both countries

---

[1] One is a mirror-image of the other. The regression coefficients of the two equations
add up to unity and the two constants (but for a small discrepancy caused by rounding)
add up to zero.

were controlled by the same American firms, they must have had the same access to the improvements in knowledge and know-how. This alternative hypothesis is tantamount to a denial of the existence of increasing returns which are known to be an important feature of manufacturing industry, quite independently of the Verdoorn Law and one which is frequently emphasised in other contexts—as for example, in analysing the effects of economic integration.

Moreover, to establish this alternative hypothesis, it is not enough to postulate that productivity growth rates are auto-nomous. It is also necessary to assume that differences in produc-tivity growth rates between different industries and sectors are fully reflected in the movement of relative prices (and not in relative movements of wages and other earnings) and further, that the price-elasticity of demand for the products of any one industry, or for the products of manufacturing industry as a whole, is always greater than unity: none of this, as far as I know, has been submitted to econometric verification.

Once the relationship between productivity growth and pro-duction growth is recognised the large differences in the recorded productivity growth rates do not appear so remarkable, and we can take a rather different view of the "efficiency-ranking" of various countries. We can award marks to each country, not on the usual basis of simple productivity growth, but on a more sophisticated basis of the deviation of its productivity growth from the Verdoorn regression line: in other words, by relating its actual performance to what it could be expected to be, on the basis of the growth rate of total manufacturing production. On this test, we find that there was one outstandingly good performer—Norway—whose recorded productivity growth was one-third higher than could be expected; and there was one outstandingly bad performer—Canada—with a rate of productivity growth which was only one-half as high as the computed figure. There were two moderately poor performers—Italy and Denmark—with a deficiency of around 15 per cent, and three moderately good performers—Netherlands, Belgium and the United States—whose productivity record was 12–15 per cent above the average. As to the rest, four of them were strictly average—and this group comprises Japan, Germany, France and Austria—with deviations of less than 2 per cent from the regression line; and finally there was one *marginally* good performer, with a record that was 7 per cent better than the computed figure—the United Kingdom. If we award, as we must on this test, β to the strictly average performers and $\beta+$ to the moderately good performers, Britain, I think, must be rated $\beta?+$.

All this is subject of course to the statistical uncertainties inherent in all international comparisons, and many of these deviations are too small to be of much significance in judging a country's performance. But the interesting point about them is that with one notable exception—again Canada—they appear to be closely related to investment behaviour. The countries which invested a great deal in relation to their growth rate were the good performers, whilst the countries whose investment was small in relation to their growth rate were poor performers. If we measure investment behaviour by the incremental capital/output ratio (ICOR for short) we find that Norway, the best performer on the Verdoorn test, had the highest ICOR (over 5), all the good performers had over-average ICORs (over 3), all the average performers had average ICORs (around $2\frac{1}{2}$), and the poor performers had low ICORs (below 2).[1] (Canada was the one exception to this rule—a poor performer with a very high ICOR—but I am glad to be able to report that since the dates of this examination Canada has improved her showing quite considerably.) In other words, if we look for the effects of investment behaviour on growth, not in terms of the growth rate itself, but in terms of a country's performance according to the Verdoorn test, the figures make much more sense. But they also indicate that increasing returns is by far the more important cause of differences in productivity growth rates; differences in investment behaviour explain residual differences which are relatively less important.

I am not suggesting that the Verdoorn relationship applies *only* to manufacturing activities or that it applies to every manufacturing industry considered separately. But its application

---

[1] ICOR is defined here as the ratio between gross fixed investment in industry and the level of industrial production, divided by the growth rate of industrial production.

outside the industrial field is clearly far more limited. It certainly does not apply, on the evidence of the statistics, to agriculture and mining, where the growth of productivity has been much greater than the growth in production and where, in so far as any definite relation is shown, productivity growth and employment growth tend to be negatively related, not positively. This supports the classical contention that these are "diminishing returns" industries: the fact that this is overlaid by technological progress or the adoption of more capital-intensive methods may statistically conceal this, but it does not eliminate its significance. In some of the countries the relatively high rate of growth of productivity in agriculture is merely the passive consequence of the absorption of surplus labour in secondary and tertiary occupations, and not necessarily a reflection of true technological progress or of higher capital investment per unit of output.

There remains the tertiary sector, services, comprising such divergent items as transport, distribution, banking and insurance, catering and hotels, laundries and hairdressers, and professional services of the most varied kind, publicly and privately provided—which together account for 40–50 per cent or more of the total output and employment of the advanced countries. Over much of this field learning by experience must clearly play a role but economics of scale are not nearly so prominent and are exhausted more quickly. In the case of activities like research or education, the Adam-Smithian principle of the advantages of specialisation and of the division of labour must operate in the same sort of way as in industrial activities. But precisely in these fields it cannot be directly reflected in the estimates of productivity, since "output" cannot be measured independently of "input". In some fields in which output can be measured independently—as, for example, in transport and communications, statistical evidence shows no correlation between productivity growth and production growth. In yet others such as distribution, productivity—meaning sales per employee—tends to grow the faster the faster the rise in aggregate turnover; but in this case, it is merely a reflection of the changing incidence of excess capacity generated by imperfect competition, and not of true economies of scale. In other words, productivity may rise in automatic response to the rise in consumption caused by the growth of production in the primary or secondary sectors—just as the productivity of the milkman doubles, without any technological change, when he leaves two bottles of milk outside each door instead of one bottle.

It is the rate of growth of manufacturing production (together with the ancillary activities of public utilities and construction) which is likely to exert a dominating influence on the overall rate of economic growth: partly on account of its influence on the rate of growth of productivity in the industrial sector itself, and partly also because it will tend, indirectly, to raise the rate of productivity growth in other sectors. This will happen, or may happen, both in agriculture and in the distributive trades—in the first because it induces a faster rate of absorption of surplus labour; in the second because it secures a faster increase in the through-put of goods into consumption. And of course it is true more generally that industrialisation accelerates the rate of technological change throughout the economy.

IV

It remains to deal with the question of why it is that some countries manage to increase their rate of manufacturing production so much faster than others. The explanation, in my view, lies partly in demand factors and partly in supply factors, and both of these combine to make fast rates of growth the characteristic of an intermediate stage in economic development.

Economic growth is the result of a complex process of interaction between increases of demand induced by increases in supply and of increases in supply generated in response to increases in demand. Since in the market as a whole commodities are exchanged against commodities, the increase in demand for any commodity, or group of commodities, reflects the increase in supply of other commodities, and vice versa. The nature of this chain-reaction will be conditioned by both demand elasticities and supply constraints; by individual preferences or attitudes and by technological factors. The chain-reaction is likely to be the more rapid the more the demand increases are focused on commodities which have a *large* supply response, and the larger the demand response induced by increases in production—the latter is not just a matter of the marginal propensities in consumption but also of induced investment. Viewing this process from a particular angle—what determines the rate of growth of manufacturing output—it will be convenient to consider the problem in two stages: first, from the point of view of the sources of demand, and secondly from the point of view of the factors which govern potential supply.

Looking at the matter from the point of view of demand, this is fed mainly from three sources—from consumption, domestic investment and from net exports—by which I mean the net excess of exports over imports.

The behaviour of consumer demand depends on the changing structure of consumption associated with a rise in real incomes per head. It is well known that a *high* income elasticity for manufactured goods—as reflected in a growing proportion of consumer expenditure spent on manufactured products—is a characteristic of an intermediate zone in the levels of real income per head. At low levels of income a high proportion of both average and marginal incomes is spent on food. At very high levels of real income, the income elasticity of demand for manufacturers falls off, both absolutely and relatively to that of services: but for the continued appearance of new commodities, like washing machines or television sets, it would fall off more rapidly. In the middle zone in which this proportion is both large and growing, there is a double interaction making for faster economic growth: the expansion of the industrial sector enhances the rate of growth in real incomes; the rise in real incomes steps up the rate of growth of demand for industrial products.

This, however, is only part of the explanation. A more important source of growth in demand originates in capital investment. It is the peculiarity of a highly developed industrial sector that it largely provides the goods on which capital expenditure is spent, and thereby generates a demand for its own products in the very process of supplying them. Once a country attains the stage of industrialisation at which it largely provides for its own needs in plant and machinery and not just in consumer goods the rate of growth of demand for its products will tend to be stepped up very considerably, since the expansion of capacity in the investment sector by itself raises the rate of growth of demand for the products of its own sector, and thereby provides the incentives, and the means, for further expansion. Provided that entrepreneurial expectations are buoyant, and the process is not hampered by labour shortages, or shortages of basic materials, the very establishment of an investment goods sector makes for a built-in element of acceleration in the rate of growth of manufacturing output that could—theoretically—go on until technological constraints—the input/output relationships *within* the investment goods sector—impose a limit on further acceleration.

The third source of the rate of growth of demand arises from the changing structure of foreign trade. The early stages of industrialisation invariably involve reduced imports of manufactured consumer goods and increased imports of machinery and equipment. During this phase, therefore, the rate of growth of demand for domestic manufactures—which can be supposed to consist mainly of the so-called "light industries", generally textiles—rises faster than total consumption, on account of the substitution of home production for imports. But as the experience of many countries has shown, this phase of relatively rapid development tends to peter out as the process of import substitution of consumer goods is gradually completed. To maintain the rhythm of development it is necessary for the industrialising country to enter a second stage in which it becomes a growing net exporter of manufactured consumer goods. This is followed (or accompanied) by a third stage, marked by "import substitution" in capital goods, and for the reasons mentioned, it is likely to be associated with a fast growth rate, as the "heavy industries" develop out of relation to the growth of the rest of the economy. There is a fourth and final stage, at which a country becomes a growing net exporter of capital goods; it is at this last stage that "explosive growth" is likely to be encountered— when a fast rate of growth of external demand for the products of the "heavy industries" is combined with the self-generated growth of demand caused by their own expansion. It has been the passage into this fourth stage which I think mainly explains the phenomenal growth rates of post-war Japan. Fast though her growth of consumption has been, her growth due to the rise in the production of investment goods—both for home use and exports—was very much greater. But this again is a transitional stage: once the investment sector is fully developed, and once a country has acquired a reasonably large share of world trade in investment goods, the growth of demand is bound to slow down, as the broad historical experience of the older industrial countries has shown.

All this is looking at the matter from the demand side alone. The actual course of development may at any stage be slowed down, or interrupted by supply constraints; and as I shall argue presently, it is inevitable that sooner or later the rhythm of development should be slowed down on account of them.

Such supply constraints can take one of two forms: commodities or labour. As the industrial sector expands, it absorbs growing amounts of commodities (and services) produced outside the manufacturing sector: such as food and industrial materials produced by the primary sector (agriculture and mining); manufactured goods which it does not provide itself, or not in sufficient quantities and on which it is dependent on imports—this is probably relatively more important in the earlier stages of industrialisation, but as post-war experience has shown, there is a very large scope, even among the industrially highly developed countries, for trade in manufactured goods for industrial use, both finished goods and components. Finally, industrial growth generates demand for services of numerous kinds—like banking and insurance, lawyers, accountants and so on—and is thus responsible, in part at any rate, for the fast expansion of the "tertiary" sector. (Also, the growing use of durable consumer goods sets up a growing demand for repair and maintenance services.)

For an *individual* country—though not for the group of industrialised countries together—a commodity constraint generally takes the form of a balance of payments constraint: it arises because a particular rate of growth generates a rate of growth of imports which exceeds the rate of growth of exports. This is certainly true of countries in the early stages of industrialisation when the growth of industry, despite import-substitution, causes a substantial rise in *total* import requirements at a stage when the industrial development adds little, if anything, to the country's export potential. But it is also suggested that it may slow down the rate of growth of industrially advanced economies; and it is a widely held view that it has been a major constraint on the post-war economic growth of Britain.

It is certainly true that brief periods of relatively high growth during the last twenty years were invariably attended by a rapid growth of imports, resulting in balance of payments deficits; and it was the occurrence of these deficits, as much as the labour shortages and the resulting inflation, which forced the intro-duction of deflationary measures which brought these periods to an end. It is equally true that if the trend rates of growth in our exports had been higher, we could have sustained higher rates of growth of imports, and that if the rhythm of our develop-ment had been more even, imports would not have risen so fast as they did during the recovery phases. But this does not necessarily prove that the balance of payments was the *effective* constraint on our rate of economic growth. This would only follow if it could also be shown that with a faster rate of growth of exports, we could have achieved a higher rate of growth of manufacturing production, or else that we could have increased exports at a faster rate while keeping domestic investment and consumption rising at a lower rate. In the latter context it must be remembered that the volume of our exports has been pretty large in relation to the total volume of our manufacturing production; and while the share of our exports in world trade declined dramatically, the share of exports in our own manufacturing output remained remarkably steady. It is possible to interpret this by saying that it was the trend rate of growth of exports which governed the trend rate of growth of production, since any higher rate of growth of production would not have been compatible with keeping the balance of payments even, over a run of years. It is also possible to interpret this in the opposite way: that over a run of years it was the rate of growth of production of exportable goods which determined the rate of growth of our exports, and not the other way round.

The important question is whether, *apart* from balance of payments constraints, it would have been possible to increase our manufacturing output at a faster rate. Was the growth in production mainly governed by the growth in demand for manufactured products, or was it governed by supply-constraints, which would have frustrated a higher rate of growth of output, irrespective of the growth in demand?

V

And here we come back to the labour situation and to Verdoorn's Law. This as we have seen, suggests that a higher rate of growth of manufacturing output breeds higher rates of productivity growth, but not enough to obviate the need for a faster rate of growth of employment. In post-war Britain periods of faster growth in manufacturing industry invariably led to severe labour shortages which slowed down the growth of output and which continued for some time after production reached its cyclical peak—in fact, on almost every occasion, employment continued to rise after output had begun to fall. All this suggests that a higher rate of growth could not have been maintained unless more manpower had been made available to the manufacturing industry.

Indeed all historical evidence suggests that a fast rate of industrial growth has invariably been associated with a fast rate of growth of employment in both the secondary and the tertiary sectors of the economy. The main source of this labour has not been the growth of the working population, nor even immigration, but the reservoir of surplus labour, or "disguised unemployment" on the land. In the course of industrialisation there has been a continuous transfer of labour from the countryside to the urban areas in the course of which the percentage of the labour force in agriculture diminishes in a dramatic fashion. But the *longer* this process proceeds, the *smaller* the labour force remaining, the *less* it yields in terms of manpower availabilities in the secondary and tertiary sectors. Moreover, the process of transfer is bound to come to a halt once the gap between agricultural and industrial productivity is eliminated, and this becomes fully reflected in relative earnings. The United Kingdom, almost alone among the advanced countries, has reached the position where net output per head in agriculture is as high as in industry; though there is still a wide gap in relative wages which, I think, is mainly due to the fact that the fall in the demand for agricultural labour, owing to mechanisation, has outrun, over the last ten years, the rate of diminution in the agricultural labour force.

Table 3 shows, for the twelve countries, the rate of growth in

Table 3

RATES OF GROWTH OF LABOUR FORCE, AND THE RATE OF CHANGE OF
EMPLOYMENT IN AGRICULTURE, MINING, INDUSTRY AND SERVICES
(TWELVE COUNTRIES 1954-64): EXPONENTIAL GROWTH RATES

	Rate of growth of labour force	Rate of growth of employment[1] in agriculture and mining	Rate of growth of employment[2] in industry and services		
			Total	Industry[3]	Services[4]
Japan	1·5	−2.6	5·4	5·8	5·1
Italy	−0·1	−4·5	3·9	4·4	3·2
West Germany[5] ..	1·4	−4·1	2·8	2·7	2·9
Austria	0·2[6]	−3·6[6]	2·3	2·0	2·6
France	0·2	−3·5	2·2	1·9	2·4
Denmark[7] ..	0·8	−2·8	2·2	2·5	1·9
Netherlands	1·3	−2·0	2·3	1·9	2·7
Belgium	0·3	−4·4	1·9	1·5	2·3
Norway	0·3	−2·5	1·3	0·5	2·0
Canada	2·3	−2·8	3·5	2·3	4·3
U.K.	0·6	−2·3	1·1	0·6	1·6
U.S.A.	1·3	−2·4	1·8	0·8	2·4

[1] Including self-employed and unpaid family workers.
[2] Wage and salary earners.
[3] Manufacturing, construction and public utilities.
[4] Transport, distributive trades, financial and other services, public administration, etc.
[5] 1957-64.
[6] 1951-63.
[7] 1955-64.

Source. O.E.C.D. Manpower Statistics.

the total labour force, and the rate of change in employment in agriculture and mining, industry and the services; Table 4 shows the percentage composition in total employment between the three sectors in 1962-3.

One of the remarkable features of Table 3 is the uniform fall in employment in agriculture and mining in all countries; it varied between 2 per cent and 4½ per cent a year. In countries in which the agricultural labour force was still large, as a percentage of total, this meant a substantial annual addition to the labour force in industry and services—substantial both absolutely and in relation to the growth of the working population, which was relatively modest, in most countries—whilst in the countries where the size of the labour force in primary occupations was small—as in the United Kingdom and the United States—the rate of increase in employment in secondary and tertiary occupations was much smaller. As is shown in Table 3, the United Kingdom had the smallest rate of increase in employment in industry and services taken together, despite the fact that the rate of growth of her total labour force over this period was higher than that of five of the other eleven countries. The explanation is found in Table 4, which shows that Britain had the smallest proportion of the labour force in agriculture and mining.

Table 3 also shows that whilst the absorption of labour in the tertiary sector was substantial in all countries—at least of the

Table 4

PERCENTAGE COMPOSITION OF TOTAL EMPLOYMENT BETWEEN PRIMARY,
SECONDARY AND TERTIARY OCCUPATIONS (TWELVE COUNTRIES,
1962–3 AVERAGE)

	Primary (Agriculture and mining)	Secondary (Manufacturing, construction and public utilities)	Tertiary (Services)[1]	Total
Japan	30·0	30·3	39·7	100
Italy	27·8	39·4	32·8	100
Austria[2]	23·8	40·6	35·6	100
France	21·1	37·0	41·9	100
Norway	20·0	35·5	44·5	100
Denmark	19·1	39·5	41·4	100
West Germany	14·1	47·9	38·0	100
Canada	12·9	32·7	54·4	100
Netherlands	12·0	42·3	45·7	100
Belgium	10·6	44·0	45·4	100
U.S.A.	8·9	30·7	60·4	100
U.K.	6·7	44·0	49·3	100

[1] Includes transport, distribution, financial and other services, public administration, etc.

[2] 1961.

Source. O.E.C.D. Manpower Statistics.

same order of magnitude as the increase in industrial employment—it tended to be relatively greater (in relation to the growth
of industrial employment) in the slow-growing countries than
in the fast-growing ones. This may be due to the fact that the
growth of labour requirements in services is less sensitive to
changes in the rate of economic growth than the growth of labour
requirements in industry. One could certainly think of several
reasons why this should be so—for example, the rise in the standard of educational and health services which tends to proceed
by its own momentum. It is also possible that the relatively high
rate of growth of employment in services is to some extent a
consequence of the instability in the demand for labour in manufacturing: in the case of Britain, it may have been a by-product of
the stop-and-go cycle. Since employment opportunities in services are less sensitive to short-period variations in demand than
manufacturing employment, it is possible that a kind of ratchet
effect has been in operation: there may have been a drift of labour
into services as a result of a fall in employment in manufacturing
in the "stop" phase, which was not reversed in the subsequent
"go" phase.

However that may be, it is clear that if our basic hypothesis is
correct, *all* countries will experience a slow-down in their growth
rates as their agricultural labour reserves become exhausted. It is
the existence of an elastic supply curve of labour to the secondary
and tertiary sectors which is the main pre-condition of a fast
rate of development. As Table 4 shows, some of the advanced
countries—such as Japan, Italy or France—still possess a large
agricultural labour force (of the order of 15–30 per cent) so that
they still have a considerable period of potentially fast growth
ahead of them. But the United States, Belgium and also Germany
are approaching the structural pattern of the United Kingdom.
In the case of Germany, the rate of growth of production and
employment in industry has already slowed down considerably
in the last few years. In the United States—which operated with
a high unemployment rate throughout the 'fifties—growth could
be accelerated quite considerably by the orthodox techniques of
Keynesian economics, but now that unemployment has fallen
to lower levels, the rate of growth is likely to slow down again,

though the United States is still far off from a situation of acute labour shortage.

Britain, having started the process of industrialisation earlier than any other country, has reached "maturity" much earlier—in the sense that it has attained a distribution of the labour force between the primary, secondary and tertiary sectors at which industry can no longer attract the labour it needs by drawing on the labour reserves of other sectors. There are disadvantages of an early start, as well as advantages—as is shown by the fact that some of the latecomers of industrialisation have attained higher levels of industrial efficiency even before they became fully industrialised.

But once it is recognised that manpower shortage is the main handicap from which we are suffering, and once our thinking becomes adjusted to this, we shall, I hope, tend to concentrate our efforts on a more rational use of manpower in *all* fields, and to limit the absorption of labour into those sectors in which—if I may use a Pigovian phrase—the marginal social product is likely to be appreciably below the marginal private product.

It is possible, looking further ahead, that the new technological revolution—electronics and automation—will so radically reduce the labour requirements in industry as to make it possible to combine fast growth with *falling* industrial employment. But there are no signs of this yet. If we take the technologically most advanced country, the United States, we find that her fast growth of manufacturing production over the last few years was associated with large increases in the volume of manufacturing employment—fully in line with what the Verdoorn equation would lead to us expect.[1]

Finally there is the question how far a mature economy could continue to reap the benefits of economies of scale, not through a fast growth in manufacturing industry as a whole, but through greater international specialisation. If the main hypothesis advanced in this lecture is correct, and economies of scale in industry are the main engine of fast growth, at least some of its

---

[1] In 1962–5 manufacturing output of the United States (as measured by the index of manufacturing production) increased by 6·7 per cent a year; the rate of growth of the volume of man hours of employment was 2·7 per cent. The regression equation at the bottom of Table 2 yields a computed figure of 2·4 per cent.

benefits could continue to be secured by concentrating our resources in fewer fields and abandoning others—in other words, by increasing the degree of interdependence of British industry with the industries of other countries.

APPENDIX A

THE ROLE OF MANUFACTURING IN ECONOMIC GROWTH

The significance of the relationship between the growth of manufacturing output and the growth of the G.D.P. shown in Table 1 has been tested (i) by reference to the relation of the growth of non-manufacturing output (i.e. G.D.P. *minus* G.D.P. in manufacturing) to the growth in manufacturing production; (ii) by relating the growth rate of G.D.P. to the *excess* of the growth rate of manufacturing production over the growth rate of the non-manufacturing sectors. The results are summarised in the following regression equations:[1]

(1) Rate of growth of non-manufacturing output (Y) on rate of growth of manufacturing production (X)

$$Y = 1 \cdot 142 + 0 \cdot 550X, \quad R^2 = 0 \cdot 824.$$
$$(0 \cdot 080)$$

(2) Rate of growth of G.D.P. (Y) on the excess of the rate of growth of manufacturing over the rate of growth of non-manufacturing production (X)

$$Y = 3 \cdot 351 + 0 \cdot 954X, \quad R^2 = 0 \cdot 562.$$
$$(0 \cdot 267)$$

Both of these are statistically significant at the 99 per cent level and thus confirm the generalisation derived from Table 1. A comparison of regression (1) above with the regression in Table 1 shows that the exclusion of manufacturing output from G.D.P. makes no appreciable difference to the structural relationship: both the constants and the coefficients in the two equations are very similar.

[1] The four regression equations in this section relate to the same group of countries, and the same periods, as indicated in Table 1.

The significance of these findings has been further tested by examining the relationship between the growth rate of G.D.P. and the growth rate of agricultural production, mining, and the output of services.[1] No correlation was found between the rate of growth of G.D.P. and the rate of growth of either agricultural production or mining. As between G.D.P. and G.D.P. originating in "services" there is a highly significant relationship but of a different character, as shown by the following equation:

(3) Rate of growth of G.D.P. (Y) on rate of growth of G.D.P. in services (X)

$$Y = -0.188 + 1.060X, \quad R^2 = 0.930.$$
$$(0.092)$$

The fact that the coefficient is so near to unity, and the constant is negligible suggests that the causal relationship here is the other way round—i.e. that it is the rate of G.D.P. which determines the rate of growth of the "output" of services. It also confirms recent American studies[2] which suggest that, contrary to general belief, the income-elasticity of demand for services is not significantly greater than unity; the fact that most countries (as indicated in Table 3) had a higher rate of employment growth in "services" than in "industry" is not due to a high income-elasticity of demand, but to a lower rate of productivity growth in services. This latter finding is further confirmed by relating the rate of growth of output in "services" to the rate of growth of industrial production (manufacturing, construction and public utilities):

(4) Rate of growth of output in services (Y) on the rate of growth of industrial production (X)

$$Y = 1.283 + 0.597X, \quad R^2 = 0.846.$$
$$(0.0805)$$

This shows that the "real" output of services—as measured

[1] The term "services" comprises transport and communications; wholesale and retail trade; banking, insurance and real estate; ownership of dwellings; public administration and defence; health and educational services and miscellaneous services.
[2] Cf. Victor R. Fuchs, *The Growing Importance of the Service Industries*, New York, National Bureau of Economic Research, Occasional Paper No. 96 (1965).

in the national accounts of each country at constant prices—grows less than in proportion to industrial output, even though employment grows (in most cases) more than in proportion.[1]

APPENDIX B

THE VERDOORN LAW

The "Verdoorn Law" asserts that with a higher rate of growth of output, both productivity and employment increase at a faster rate, the regression coefficients with respect to each being of the same order of magnitude. This relationship was also investigated with regard to other sectors of the economy for which comparable data could be found in the O.E.C.D. statistics—i.e. public utilities (gas, electricity and water) and construction; agriculture and mining; transport and communications and "commerce" (the latter term includes the distributive trades, banking, insurance and real estate).[2] Owing to the lack of data, some countries had to be omitted in some of the estimates, and a somewhat shorter period taken; also, it was not possible to adjust the employment figures for changes in man hours outside the manufacturing sector. The results for each sector (including the manufacturing sector, already shown in Table 2) are summarised in the following set of regression equations:

Annual rates of growth of productivity (P) and of employment (E) on the rates of growth of output (X)[3]

---

[1] The only exceptions in the period considered (i.e. 1953–4 to 1963–4—though this would not be true of the more recent period, 1960–5) were the U.S.A. and Canada, where the output of services grew at a somewhat higher rate than industrial output.

[2] It was not possible to separate, on the employment statistics, the distributive trades from banking, insurance, etc. in more than a few cases; but the distributive trades account for much the greater part (around four-fifths or more) of the total output of this sector, and a similar proportion of employment.

[3] Since exponential growth rates have been used throughout, $P + E = X$, and hence the sum of the constants of the two equations should be zero, and the sum of the regression coefficients unity, irrespective of the nature of the correlations involved. However, since estimates of employment growth and of productivity growth have been separately rounded, the sum of these can vary from the total by one decimal point, which explains small deviations from the correct result in some of the pairs of regression equations.

Industry

(1) *Manufacturing*

$$P = 1 \cdot 035 + 0 \cdot 484X, \quad R^2 = 0 \cdot 826,$$
$$(0 \cdot 070)$$

$$E = -1 \cdot 028 + 0 \cdot 516X, \quad R^2 = 0 \cdot 844.$$
$$(0 \cdot 070)$$

(2) *Public utilities* (11 countries, 1953–63)[1]

$$P = 2 \cdot 707 + 0 \cdot 419X, \quad R^2 = 0 \cdot 451,$$
$$(0 \cdot 154)$$

$$E = -2 \cdot 690 + 0 \cdot 577X, \quad R^2 = 0 \cdot 609.$$
$$(0 \cdot 154)$$

(3) *Construction* (11 countries, 1953–63)[1]

$$P = -0 \cdot 543 + 0 \cdot 572X, \quad R^2 = 0 \cdot 810,$$
$$(0 \cdot 092)$$

$$E = 0 \cdot 552 + 0 \cdot 428X, \quad R^2 = 0 \cdot 702.$$
$$(0 \cdot 092)$$

Primary sector

(4) *Agriculture* (12 countries, 1953–63)[1]

$$P = 2 \cdot 700 + 1 \cdot 041X, \quad R^2 = 0 \cdot 812,$$
$$(0 \cdot 155)$$

$$E = -2 \cdot 684 - 0 \cdot 056X, \quad R^2 = 0 \cdot 013.$$
$$(0 \cdot 155)$$

(5) *Mining* (10 countries, 1955–64)[1]

$$P = 4 \cdot 0714 + 0 \cdot 671X, \quad R^2 = 0 \cdot 705,$$
$$(0 \cdot 153)$$

---

[1] For *public utilities* and *construction,* the equations relate to all countries listed in Table 2, except the Netherlands; the data relate to 1953–63, except for Austria (1951–61), Italy and France (1954–63), Denmark and Canada (1955–63). The same holds for *agriculture,* except that here the Netherlands (1953–63) is also included. The estimates on *mining* exclude Austria and Denmark; they relate to 1955–64, except for Netherlands where they relate to 1955–61.

$$E = -4.0714 + 0.329X, \quad R^2 = 0.365.$$
$$(0.153)$$

Tertiary sector

(6) *Transport and communications* (9 countries, 1955–64)[1]

$$P = 2.314 + 0.224X, \quad R^2 = 0.102,$$
$$(0.252)$$

$$E = -2.314 + 0.776X, \quad R^2 = 0.576.$$
$$(0.252)$$

(7) *Commerce* (9 countries, 1955–64)[2]

$$P = -1.751 + 0.953X, \quad R^2 = 0.932,$$
$$(0.098)$$

$$E = 1.744 + 0.056X, \quad R^2 = 0.044.$$
$$(0.098)$$

The regressions reveal an interesting pattern. In the case of construction and public utilities, the equations relating to both productivity and employment are similar to those in manufacturing, except that in the case of public utilities the constant term of the equations is much larger, and hence the significance of the relationship is less, than in the case of either manufacturing or construction.[3] One can thus conclude that the effects of economies of scale on the growth of productivity are significant not only for manufacturing industry, but for the industrial sector generally.

Agriculture and mining reveal a different picture. In each case, productivity growth shows a large trend factor which is

[1] In the case of *transport and communications*, the estimate excludes Austria, Denmark and Japan; the data relate to 1955–64, except for the U.S.A. (1955–63), France (1956–64) and West Germany (1957–64).

[2] *Commerce* includes G.D.P. originating in wholesale and retail trade, banking, insurance, real estate, at constant prices, and employment relating to the same category, except for Japan where the data on output and employment relate to wholesale and retail trade only. The estimate excludes Austria, Denmark and the Netherlands; it relates to 1955–64, except for Canada (1955–61), U.S.A. (1955–63), West Germany (1957–64) and France (1958–64).

[3] However, in the case of the construction sector there is a *negative* constant term of 0.5 per cent a year in the productivity equation, in contrast to manufacturing which shows a positive constant term of 1 per cent a year. The reasons for this are likely to be similar to those given below in the discussion of the equations for commerce.

independent of the growth in total output; the regression co-efficient of productivity is not significantly different from unity (except possibly for mining) whilst the regression for employment is not significantly different from zero for agriculture, and barely significant for mining. In both of these cases productivity growth has exceeded the growth of production for every single country, and the growth in productivity has owed nothing to increasing returns to scale.[1]

In the case of transport and communications, there is no correlation whatever between productivity growth and output growth; productivity increased at an independent rate of some 2·3 per cent a year (for the average of the nine countries considered) but beyond this any higher rate of growth of output required a corresponding increase in employment (as shown by the regression coefficient of employment on output which is not significantly different from unity). In this case, therefore, productivity growth appears to have been fully autonomous, and owed nothing to economies of scale.

Finally, in the case of commerce, there is a high correlation between productivity growth and output growth (with a regression coefficient not significantly different from unity) but no relation whatever between the growth of employment and of production. The regressions for commerce are remarkably similar to those of agriculture, except for one very important difference: in the case of agriculture there is a large positive constant, showing a trend-rate of increasing productivity, whereas in the case of commerce the trend-rate of growth of productivity is *negative*. This negative trend-rate has nothing to do with technological factors (which operate in the same sort of way in the distributive trades and banking as elsewhere—as, for example, the development of supermarkets or mechanisation) but is mainly a reflection of the peculiar manner in which competition operates in this field, tending constantly to eliminate

[1] In the case of agriculture the growth of output, for most of the countries considered, has probably been more a reflection of the effects of technological progress and capital investment in raising *yields per acre*, than of the rate of growth of consumer demand. The fact that employment was diminishing in all countries—at a fairly uniform rate of around 2–3½ per cent a year—may have simply been the result of the absorption of disguised unemployment, or the reflection of the fact that technological progress has, on the whole, been more labour-saving than land-saving.

abnormal profits through a multiplication of units, rather than through a reduction of prices or distributive margins. These estimates confirm the view that whilst an increase in the total turnover of banking or the distributive trades automatically raises productivity (i.e. turnover per employee) the inflow of labour into these trades is not directly connected with the rise in turnover.

APPENDIX C

THE ROLE OF INVESTMENT IN PRODUCTIVITY GROWTH[1]

It was suggested in the text that deviations from the "Verdoorn Law" in the industrial sector were correlated with investment behaviour. This hypothesis has been tested by means of multiple regressions which include the gross investment/output ratio (expressed as a percentage) as a measure of investment behaviour.

Because data on gross asset formation in the manufacturing sector were not obtainable for all countries, these estimates refer to the industrial sector, which is defined as manufacturing plus construction plus public utilities. For this sector the "Verdoorn equations" as shown in equation (4) above are:

Industrial Sector (12 countries, 1953-4–1963-4)

$$(1) \quad P = 0.888 + 0.446X, \quad R^2 = 0.847,$$
$$(0.060)$$

$$(2) \quad E = -0.888 + 0.554X, \quad R^2 = 0.893,$$
$$(0.060)$$

where X, E, and P are the rates of growth of output, employment, and productivity, respectively.

If the gross investment/output ratio is included as a second variable in the equation the following result is obtained:

[1] This Appendix was written later for the (extended) American edition of this lecture referred to on page 131 below.

Industrial Sector (12 countries, 1953-4–1963-4)

$$(3) \quad P = 0.527 + 0.356X + 0.048I, \quad R^2 = 0.880,$$
$$(0.079) \quad (0.029)$$

> where I is the gross investment/output ratio in industry, expressed as a percentage.

In this equation, the coefficient of I is not statistically significant. However, as stated in the text, Canada, in the period considered, showed abnormal behaviour in that she invested very heavily and yet had a very high negative residual calculated from the Verdoorn line. If Canada is excluded from the regression, the following is obtained:

Industrial Sector (11 countries, 1953-4–1963-4)

$$(4) \quad P = 0.709 + 0.268X + 0.073I, \quad R^2 = 0.960,$$
$$(0.047) \quad (0.017)$$

which shows that the investment/output ratio has been a significant factor in determining the rate of growth of productivity, for these countries.

The influence of the rate of growth of employment and of the investment/output ratio has been further investigated using a somewhat different approach—i.e. by regarding the rate of growth of output as the dependent variable, and the rate of growth of employment and the investment/output ratio as the independent variables.[1] The implication of the Verdoorn Law in this case is that the regression coefficient on the rate of growth of employment is significantly greater than unity. As is shown below, this remains true even if a multiple regression is used, allowing for the influence of investment as well as employment, on output.

For the twelve countries, a simple regression gives the following

---

[1] This was done to show that on the "production function" approach, the data reveal increasing returns to scale even when the influence of changes in the capital stock are allowed for. Since $I = Gv$, G_K, the rate of growth of the capital stock, is I/v, where v is the capital/output ratio. Hence assuming, say, $v=3$, equation (7) below implies a capital coefficient of 0.315 which, together with the employment coefficient of 1.320, shows a scale elasticity of output with respect to labour and capital input of 1.635.

result (which is of course implied by the Verdoorn equations above):

Industrial Sector (12 countries 1953-4–1963-4)

$$(5)\quad X = 2 \cdot 06 + 1 \cdot 614E, \quad R^2 = 0 \cdot 893.$$
$$(0 \cdot 176)$$

In a simple regression the value of R^2 is unaffected by an interchange of the independent and dependent variables, and for high values of R^2 the estimates of the regression coefficients are not significantly altered (the coefficient of X on E obtained algebraically from regression (2) above comes to $1 \cdot 80$).

A multiple regression of the rate of growth of output on the rate of growth of employment and the gross investment/output ratio gives the following equation for the full sample of twelve countries:

Industrial Sector (12 countries, 1953-4–1963-4)

$$(6)\quad X = 0 \cdot 835 + 1 \cdot 367E + 0 \cdot 097I, \quad R^2 = 0 \cdot 940.$$
$$(0 \cdot 168) \quad (0 \cdot 037)$$

and if Canada is excluded:

$$(7)\quad X = 0 \cdot 937 + 1 \cdot 320E + 0 \cdot 105I, \quad R^2 = 0 \cdot 986.$$
$$(0 \cdot 085) \quad (0 \cdot 018)$$

Both these regressions show that there is a significant partial correlation between the rate of growth of output and the gross investment/output ratio. It should be noted that the inclusion of the investment/output ratio, while it decreases the coefficient on the rate of growth of employment, does not alter the conclusion that this coefficient is significantly greater than unity; which implies that the rate of growth of productivity is positively correlated with the rate of growth of output and also with the rate of growth of employment.

APPENDIX D

PRODUCTIVITY AND GROWTH IN MANUFACTURING
INDUSTRY: A REPLY[1]

Professor Wolfe attacks me (in the May, 1968 issue of *Economica*) for being obscure and unconvincing in the inaugural lecture which I gave at Cambridge.[2] In this lecture I attempted to put forward a complex thesis concerning the causes of high and low rates of economic growth under capitalism, and this was necessarily somewhat scanty; there is a limit to the material one can pack into a single lecture. Such a treatment could only be successful if received with imagination and some goodwill; Professor Wolfe has picked on a large number of individual points (many of them trivial in substance) without attempting to come to grips with the thesis as a whole. I propose to publish a more comprehensive statement of the theory in due course.[3] Meanwhile rather than follow the negative approach of answering each point in turn—which would be both tedious and unconstructive—I shall concentrate on the main points which have clearly not been understood.

Foremost among these is my notion of "economic maturity". This is not some vague notion which can be defined in terms of "a situation in which there is relatively small employment in agriculture". In my lecture I defined it explicitly "as a state of affairs where real income per head had reached broadly the same level in the different sectors of the economy". I could have added, to convey its significance better, that "economic maturity" could also be defined as "the end of the dual economy"; or a situation in which "surplus labour" is exhausted; or one in which "growth with unlimited supplies of labour" (to use Arthur Lewis' phrase) is no longer possible.

The neo-classical framework of thought cannot accommodate

[1] Originally published in *Economica*, November 1968.
[2] J. N. Wolfe, "Productivity and Growth in Manufacturing Industry: Some Reflections on Professor Kaldor's Inaugural Lecture", *Economica*, vol. xxxv (1968), pp. 117-26.
[3] A somewhat more extended exposition was given in three lectures (subsequently published) at Cornell University: cf. *Strategic Factors in Economic Development*, Ithaca, New York, 1967.

F

notions like "disguised unemployment", the "dual economy", or the distinction between "capitalist" and "pre-capitalist" enterprise. For neo-classical theory *assumes* that the structure of demand determines the distribution of resources between different uses; that competition and mobility assures that "factor prices" tend to equality in all employments; that profit maximisation ensures equality of factor prices with the value of the marginal products of factors; subject only to friction etc., each "factor" will tend to be used where it makes the greatest contribution to the national product.

It would be generally agreed that these assumptions are at their most inappropriate in the case of an under-developed country, or a country in the earlier stages of industrialisation. In such countries high and low earnings sectors exist side by side; there are vast amounts of "surplus labour" or "disguised unemployment" in the low-productivity sectors, so that labour can be withdrawn from them without adverse effects on the output of those sectors; and the supply of labour in the high-productivity, high-earnings sector is continually in excess of the demand, so that the rate of labour-transference from the low- to the high-productivity sectors is governed only by the rate of growth of the demand for labour in the latter. In fact the size of the labour force in the non-industrial sector is a residual—entirely determined by the total supply of labour on the one hand and the requirements for labour in the industrial sector on the other hand. The best definition I could suggest for the existence of "labour surplus" in this sense is one which is analogous to Keynes' definition of "involuntary unemployment": a situation of "labour surplus" exists when a faster rate of increase in the demand for labour in the high-productivity sectors induces a faster rate of labour-transference even when it is attended by a *reduction, and not an increase, in the earnings-differential between the different sectors.*

For reasons that I explained in my lecture, the rate of growth of industrialisation fundamentally depends on the exogenous components of demand (a set of forces extending far beyond the income elasticities of demand for manufactured goods). The higher the rate of growth of industrial output which these demand conditions permit, the faster will be the rate at which labour is transferred from the surplus-sectors to the high-productivity sectors. It is my contention that it is the rate at which this transfer takes place which determines the growth rate of productivity of the economy as a whole. The mechanism by which this happens is only to a minor extent dependent on the *absolute* differences in the levels of output per head between the labour-absorbing sectors and the surplus-labour sectors. The major part of the mechanism consists of the fact that the *growth* of productivity is accelerated as a result of the transfer at both ends—both at the gaining-end and at the losing-end; in the first, because, as a result of increasing returns, productivity in industry will increase faster, the faster output expands; in the second because when the surplus-sectors lose labour, the productivity of the remainder of the working population is bound to rise.[1]

In the literature, the "surplus labour sector" is generally thought of as agriculture. This is because in the early stages of capitalist development much the greater part of the population draws its living from agriculture. However, disguised unemployment in "services" had been just as prevalent—in Victorian England (as in present-day India or Latin America) there were vast numbers of people who eked out a living in urban areas as hawkers, petty tradesmen, servants, etc. on very low earnings.[2] In the field of services however (unlike in agriculture) there are two contrary processes at work: on the one hand industrialisation absorbs labour from services on a large scale; on the other hand, the growth of industry itself gives rise to the growth of services of various kinds which are both complementary and ancillary to industrial activities (by "ancillary" I mean that the demand

---

[1] Indeed, the existence of disguised unemployment is by itself capable of explaining these results, even in the absence of increasing returns, since the increase in industrial output, brought about by transference, will be a net addition to the G.N.P.—there will be no compensating reduction in output elsewhere. As a matter of historical fact, I am convinced, however, that the growth of productivity resulting from increasing returns (both internal and external) has been a very important part of the picture. (On this see below.)

[2] This relates to both "self-employed" and employees alike. In the population Census of 1891, 15·8 per cent of the occupied population of Britain were classified as domestic servants. In the Census of 1961 the figure was 1·4 per cent. This reduction cannot be explained in terms of a shift in consumer preferences or by the assumption that domestic service is an "inferior good" with a negative income-elasticity of demand; it can only be explained by the growing absorption of surplus labour in the economy which resulted in a rise in wages in domestic service which was much in excess of the general rise in wages.

for these services, e.g. transport, distribution, accountancy, banking services, etc. is derived from, but cannot generate, industrial activities). As a result the total employment in services tends to rise during the process of industrialisation though less (in relation to the growth of total output) when the growth in total output is relatively fast.

While it has long been known that labour has no "opportunity cost" in an under-developed country—the absorption of labour through the growth of industry involving no reduction in output elsewhere—it has not been generally recognised that the same applies to most of the so-called "advanced countries" with relatively high incomes per head.

The view that growth rates, even in advanced countries, are dependent on the rate at which labour is transferred into manufacturing from other sectors would find confirmation, in the first place, if over-all growth rates are positively associated with rates of increase in employment in manufacturing.

This is shown for the group of twelve advanced countries given in Table 3 of my lecture for the period 1953-4–1963-4 by the following:[1]

$$(1) \quad \dot{G} = 2 \cdot 665 + 1 \cdot 066 \dot{E}_M \quad R^2 = 0 \cdot 828$$
$$(0 \cdot 15)$$

where $\dot{G}$ is the rate of growth of G.D.P. and $\dot{E}_M$ is the rate of growth of employment in manufacturing.

This result confirms my general hypothesis unless it could be shown that growth rates in manufacturing employment are themselves closely related to growth rates of total employment so that the former could be regarded as a proxy for the latter. Such positive association seems ruled out, however, by the fact that there is *no association at all* between rates of growth of G.D.P. and rates of growth of *total* employment:

$$(2) \quad \dot{G} = 4 \cdot 421 + 0 \cdot 431 \dot{E}_g \quad R^2 = 0 \cdot 018$$
$$(0 \cdot 994)$$

where $\dot{E}_g$ is the rate of growth of total employment.

[1] The sources for this and the following equations are given in the statistical tables of my lecture.

The positive correlation in Eq. (1) could only be consistent with the absence of any correlation in Eq. (2) if rates of growth in over-all productivity are *positively* associated with rates of growth of employment in manufacturing and *negatively* associated with rates of growth of employment outside manufacturing. This is duly confirmed by the following three equations:

$$(3) \quad \dot{P}_g = 1 \cdot 868 + 0 \cdot 991 \dot{E}_M \qquad\qquad R^2 = 0 \cdot 677$$
$$(0 \cdot 216)$$

$$(4) \quad \dot{P}_g = 4 \cdot 924 - 1 \cdot 800 \dot{E}_{NM} \qquad\qquad R^2 = 0 \cdot 427$$
$$(0 \cdot 660)$$

$$(5) \quad \dot{P}_g = 2 \cdot 899 + 0 \cdot 821 \dot{E}_M - 1 \cdot 183 \dot{E}_{NM} \quad R^2 = 0 \cdot 842$$
$$(0 \cdot 169) \qquad (0 \cdot 387)$$

where $\dot{P}_g$ denotes growth rates of G.D.P. per person in civilian employment, and $\dot{E}_M$ and $\dot{E}_{NM}$ denote growth rates of employment in manufacturing and non-manufacturing respectively.

It follows from the above also that in a mature economy it would be idle to look for evidence of a labour constraint in manufacturing either in terms of a differential rise in wages in manufacturing or in the relative incidence of unemployment and unfilled vacancies in the different sectors. Since the supply of labour to industry does not become inelastic until wages in the rest of the economy have risen to levels comparable to those in industry, an effective labour constraint in manufacturing would manifest itself in a *general* increase in wages throughout the economy, and in low levels of unemployment in *all* sectors. In a situation of *approaching* labour shortage one would expect the unemployment rate to be falling, and wages to rise faster in the non-manufacturing sectors than in manufacturing.[1]

One would expect, furthermore, that in a "mature" economy

---

[1] This has characterised the recent situation in the United States where, *pari passu* with a large increase in employment in the manufacturing sector (of 2·8 per cent a year in the last five years), wages rose faster in the low-paid sectors (wholesale and retail distribution and agriculture) than in manufacturing. (Cf. *Annual Report of the Council of Economic Advisers*, Washington, D.C., 1968, pp. 109–10.) It should also be pointed out that in the United States (where the level of unemployment has been much greater than in the United Kingdom throughout the post-war period) earnings in manufacturing are much higher in relation to the national average (and particularly in relation to agriculture and the distributive trades) than in the United Kingdom.

constrained by a labour shortage, the average level of unemployment would be *higher* in the manufacturing sector than in the rest of the economy, and not lower. This is because such an economy is almost inevitably subject to a "stop-and-go" cycle; variations in the pressure of demand induced by fiscal and monetary policies affect demand and employment in industry far more than in the non-industrial sectors.

There is finally the question of the existence of increasing returns to scale in manufacturing industries. I emphasised in my lecture that this is a "macro-phenomenon" which (in the words of Allyn Young) "cannot be discerned adequately by observing the effects of variations in the size of a particular firm or of a particular industry". Studies relating to the cost and size of individual plants are not therefore necessarily relevant; though there is a growing body of empirical evidence relating to individual industries which tends to confirm its importance.[1]

Nor do recent studies which fit production functions by means of linear multiple regressions lead to any confirmation that the parameters of a Cobb-Douglas function conveniently add up to unity. Indeed in all recent studies the Cobb-Douglas function was assumed to be a constantly shifting one, of the form $Ae^{ct}K^aL^b$ and not AK^aL^b, as indicated by Wolfe; and in many of these studies the result $a + b = 1$ is a tautological one which gives no indication whatever of the presence or absence of economies of scale.[2]

Wolfe was mistaken in suggesting that the constant in the regression equation of output on employment is an "error term". It is a constant term, which reflects explanatory variables that were excluded, one of which may be an autonomous time trend. It does not follow, therefore, that the introduction of further explanatory variables (such as capital investment) would necessarily reduce the value of the regression coefficient on employ-

[1] See, for example, J. S. Bain, *Barriers to New Competition*; C. Pratten and R. M. Dean, *The Economies of Large Scale Production in British Industry—an Introductory Study*; J. W. Kendrick, *Productivity Trends in the United States*; as well as the sources quoted in E. F. Denison, *Why Growth Rates Differ*, chapter on Economies of Scale.

[2] The existence of a linear homogeneous production function is derived not from observations but from *a priori* reasoning (i.e. profit maximisation under conditions of perfect competition) and the parameters are either "restricted" so as to add up to unity, or else are directly estimated from factor shares which by definition add up to unity.

ment—if the two variables are not inter-correlated, the introduction of a capital term should reduce the constant term, and not the regression coefficient on employment. Since owing to the acceleration principle there is always some inter-correlation between the rate of growth of employment and investment activity, one would expect a multiple regression of output on employment and capital investment to show lower coefficients on employment than a simple regression: but there is no reason to expect that the sum of the two coefficients in the one case should be *lower* than the single coefficient in the other case. I have indeed computed multiple regressions of output on employment and investment, and they show that even when the rôle of capital is taken into account, the regression coefficient of output on employment remains significantly greater than one.[1]

It would be wrong to suppose that the regression between output and employment showing a coefficient that is significantly greater than unity is a reflection of short-term or "cyclical" influences. The figures in my inter-country studies related to averages of ten-yearly periods, taking two-year averages for both the base-year and the end-year. This virtually eliminates short-period or cyclical influences. The short-period relationship between output and employment—showing in some cases a 5:1 relationship—largely reflects changes in the degree of utilisation of capacity. But the fact that there is short-period relationship of 5:1 does not exclude a long-period relationship of 1·5:1. It certainly provides no support for assuming that the long-period relationship must be smaller than 1:1.

Nor is it correct to suppose that more than a small part of the "Verdoorn Law" can be explained by "embodied" technical progress coupled with the association of a relatively high level of investment in fast-growing industries, in the absence of increasing returns. Unless one assumes that the rate of technical progress on successive vintages is itself accelerated as a result of a larger volume of investment (as in Arrow's "learning function", which comes to the same thing as increasing returns) the mere postulate of embodied technical progress does not entail that the average

[1] See Appendix C above.

rate of growth of productivity should be significantly faster in the faster-growing industries.

Differences in "saving propensities" (as measured by differences in the investment/output ratio) cannot account for more than a small proportion of the observed differences in growth rates. Wolfe is correct in saying that I do not regard "the supply of capital as a serious limitation on economic growth". This is because savings and capital accumulation in a capitalist economy do not represent an independent variable—a faster rate of growth induces a higher rate of investment; it also brings about a higher share of savings to finance that investment, through its effect on the share of profits. It is therefore more correct to say that a fast rate of capital accumulation is a *symptom* of a fast rate of growth than a *cause* of it.

5

THE CASE FOR REGIONAL POLICIES[1]

In Britain, as in other countries, we have become acutely aware in recent years of the existence of a "regional" problem—the problem, that is, of different regions growing at uneven rates; with some regions developing relatively fast and others tending to be left behind. In some ways this problem of fast and slow growing regions has not led to the same kind of inequalities in regional standards of living, in culture or in social structure, in the case of Britain as in some other countries—such as Italy, the United States or France. And in general, the problem of regional inequalities within countries is not nearly so acute as that between the rich and poor countries of the world—with differences in living standards in the ratio of 20:1, or even 50:1, as between the so-called "advanced" countries and the "developing" countries. Yet, as investigations by Kuznets and others have shown, the tremendous differences that now divide the rich and poor nations are comparatively recent in origin. They are the cumulative result of persistent differences in growth rates that went on over periods that may appear long in terms of a life-span, but which are relatively short in terms of recorded human history—not more than a few centuries, in fact. Two hundred, or two-hundred-and-fifty years ago, the differences in living standards, or in the "stage" of both economic and cultural development of different countries, or parts of the globe, were very much smaller than they are today.

The primary question that needs to be considered is what *causes* these differences in "regional" growth rates—whether the

[1] Originally delivered as the Fifth Annual Scottish Economic Society Lecture in the University of Aberdeen, February 1970 and published in *Scottish Journal of Political Economy*, vol. XVII no. 3, November 1970.

term "regional" is applied to different countries (or even groups of countries) or different areas within the same country. The two questions are not, of course, identical; but up to a point, it is illuminating to consider them as if they were, and to apply the same analytical technique to both.

In some ways an analysis of the strictly "regional" problem (within a common political area) is more difficult. There is first of all the question of how to define a "region" within a political area—a problem that does not arise when political boundaries, however arbitrary they may be from an economic or social point of view, are treated as a given fact one need not enquire about. There is in fact no unique way of defining what constitutes a "region"—there are innumerable ways; the most that one can say is that some ways of drawing such boundary lines are more sensible than others; and given the fact that this is so, the exact demarcation of a "region" may not make too much difference to the subsequent analysis.

Another aspect in which the analysis of "region" within a country is more difficult is in terms of the identification of the fate of an area with the fate of its inhabitants. The mobility of both labour and capital within countries tends to be considerably greater than between countries—even though economists, in their desire for clear-cut assumptions on which to build, tended to over-estimate the one and to under-estimate the other. (There is only an imperfect mobility within countries, and there is also some mobility between them.)

Finally, a region which is part of a "nation" or a "country" tends to have common political institutions, a common taxing and spending authority and a common currency—all of which have important implications on the manner in which its external economic relations are conducted.

THE ROLE OF "RESOURCE ENDOWMENT"

But subject to these differences, what can we say about the causes of divergent regional growth rates—whether inter-nationally or intra-nationally? If one refers to classical or neo-classical economic theory, the common explanation is in terms of

various factors—summed up under the term "resource endowment"—which are themselves unexplained. Some areas are
favoured by climate or geology; by the ability, vitality, in-
genuity of their inhabitants, and by their thriftiness, and these
innate advantages may be enhanced by good political and
social institutions. Beyond suggesting that the right kind of
human material is fostered by a temperate climate—in zones
which are neither too hot nor too cold—and all of this owes a
great deal to historical accidents and to luck, the theories which
explain riches or poverty in terms of "resource endowment" do
not really have anything much to offer by way of explanation.

Nevertheless one must agree that they go as far as it is possible
to go in explaining that part of economic growth—and until
fairly recently this was much the most important part—which
consisted of "land based" economic activities, such as agriculture
or mineral exploitation. These are clearly conditioned by climatic
and geologic factors—the suitability of soil, rainfall, the availability
of minerals, and so on. These provide the natural explanation
why some areas are more densely settled than others; and why
the comparative advantage in procuring different products (and
which settles the nature of their external trading relations) should
differ as between one area and another. No sophisticated explanation is needed why it is better for some areas to grow wheat
and for others bananas; or why some areas which are lucky in
possessing things with a fast-growing demand (such as oil or
uranium) are fortunate, from the point of view of their growth-
potential, in relation to others which possess minerals with a slow-
growing or declining demand—coal, for example. We would
all agree that some part of the interregional specialisation and the
division of labour can be adequately accounted for by such
factors.

It is when we come to comparative advantages in relation to
processing activities (as distinct from land-based activities)
that this kind of approach is likely to yield question-begging
results. The prevailing distribution of real income in the world—
the comparative riches or poverty of nations, or regions—is
largely to be explained, not by "natural" factors, but by the
unequal incidence of development in industrial activities. The

"advanced", high-income areas are invariably those which possess a highly developed modern industry. In relation to differences in industrial development, explanations in terms of "resource endowment" do not get us very far. One can, and does, say that industrial production requires a great deal of capital—both in terms of plant and machinery, and of human skills, resulting from education—but in explaining such differences in "capital endowment" it is difficult to separate cause from effect. It is as sensible—or perhaps more sensible—to say that capital accumulation results from economic development as that it is a cause of development. Anyhow, the two proceed side by side. Accumulation is largely financed out of business profits; the growth of demand in turn is largely responsible for providing both the inducements to invest capital in industry and also the means of financing it.

We cannot therefore say that industries will be located in regions which are "well endowed" with capital resources for reasons other than industrial development itself. It was not the result of the peculiar thriftiness of the inhabitants of a region, or of a particularly high degree of initial inequality in the distribution of income which "induced" a high savings-ratio, that some regions became rich while others remained poor. The capital needed for industrialisation was largely provided by the very same individuals who acquired wealth as a result of the process of development, and not prior to it. The great captains of industry, like Henry Ford or Nuffield, were not recruited from the wealthy classes—they started as "small men".

Nor is there a satisfactory "location theory" which is capable of explaining the geographic distribution of industrial activities. The only relevant factor which is considered in this connection is that of transport costs. But transport cost advantages can help to explain location only in those particular activities which convert bulky goods—where transport costs are an important element, and where processing itself greatly reduces the weight of the materials processed. If say, two tons of coal and four tons of iron are needed to make a ton of steel, it is better to locate steel plants near the coal mines and the iron ore deposits; and if these are themselves situated at some distance from each other, it is best to locate the steel plants near both places, in proportions determined by the relative weight of the two materials per unit of finished product—i.e., in this example, two-thirds of the plants near the iron ore, and one-third near the coal mines— since this arrangement alone would ensure full utilisation of transport capacity in both directions.

But where the effect of processing in reducing bulk is not so important, the location of the processing activity may be a matter of indifference—whether it is near the source of the materials, near the market for the products, or anywhere in between. It is often suggested that such "footloose" industries tend naturally to develop near the market for their products. But this again is a question-begging proposition. Great urban conurbations are normally large centres of industrial activity—the "markets" are there where the "industry" is. The engineering industry in this country is highly concentrated in and around Birmingham— it is also a great "market" for engineering goods of various kinds. But it does not explain why either of these should be located there, rather than in some other place, say Leeds or Sheffield.

THE PRINCIPLE OF "CUMULATIVE CAUSATION"

To explain why certain regions have become highly industrialised, while others have not we must introduce quite different kinds of considerations what Mydral[1] called the principle of "circular and cumulative causation". This is nothing else but the existence of increasing returns to scale—using that term in the broadest sense—in processing activities. These are not just the economies of large-scale production, commonly considered, but the cumulative advantages accruing from the growth of industry itself—the development of skill and know-how; the opportunities for easy communication of ideas and experience; the opportunity of ever-increasing differentiation of processes and of specialisation in human activities. As Allyn Young[2] pointed out

---

[1] *Economic Theory and Underdeveloped Regions*, London, Duckworth, 1957.
[2] "Increasing Returns and Economic Progress", *Economic Journal*, vol. xxxviii, December 1928.

in a famous paper, Adam Smith's principle of the "division of labour" operates through the constant sub-division of industries, the emergence of new kinds of specialised firms, of steadily increasing differentiation—more than through the expansion in the size of the individual plant or the individual firm.

Thus the fact that in all known historical cases the development of manufacturing industries was closely associated with urbanisation must have deep-seated causes which are unlikely to be rendered inoperative by the invention of some new technology or new source of power. Their broad effect is a strong positive association between the growth of productivity and efficiency and the rate of growth in the scale of activities—the so-called Verdoorn Law. One aspect of this is that as communication between different regions becomes more intensified (with improvements in transport and in marketing organisation), the region that is initially more developed industrially may gain from the progressive opening of trade at the expense of the less developed region whose development will be inhibited by it. Whereas in the classical case—which abstracts from increasing returns—the opening of trade between two regions will necessarily be beneficial to both (even though the gains may not be equally divided between them) and specialisation through trade will necessarily serve to reduce the differences in comparative costs in the two areas, in the case of the "opening of trade" in industrial products the differences in comparative costs may be enlarged, and not reduced, as a result of trade; and the trade may injure one region to the greater benefit of the other. This will be so if one assumes two regions, initially isolated from one another, with each having both an agricultural area and an industrial and market centre; with the size of agricultural production being mainly determined by soil and climate, and the state of technology; and the size of industrial production mainly depending on the demand for industrial products derived from the agricultural sector. When trade is opened up between them, the region with the more developed industry will be able to supply the needs of the agricultural area of the other region on more favourable terms: with the result that the industrial centre of the second region will lose its market, and will tend to be eliminated—

without any compensating advantage to the inhabitants of that region in terms of increased agricultural output.

Another aspect of assymetry between "land-based" and "processing" activities (which is basically due to economies of large-scale production) is that in industrial production, contractual costs form an important independent element in price-formation: competition is necessarily imperfect; the sellers are price-makers, rather than price-takers. Whereas in agricultural production incomes are derived from prices, in industrial production it is prices that are derived from, or dependent on, contractual incomes (i.e. on the level of wages).

As a result, the "exchange process"—the nature of the adjustment mechanism in inter-regional trade flows and money flows—operates differently in the two cases. In the case of trade between agricultural regions, the classical theory of the adjustment process is more nearly applicable. The price of agricultural commodities rises or falls automatically with changes in the balance of supply and demand; these price changes in individual markets will automatically tend to maintain the balance in trade flows between areas, both through the income effects and the substitution effects of price changes. Where the goods produced by the different regions are fairly close substitutes for one another, a relatively modest change in price—in the "terms of trade"—will be sufficient to offset the effects of changes in either supply or demand schedules as may result from crop failures, the uneven incidence of technological improvements, or any other "exogenous" cause. If the goods produced by the different regions are complements to rather than substitutes for each other, the adjustment process may involve far greater changes in the terms of trade of the two areas, and would thus operate mainly through the "income effects". But in either case, the very process which secures an equilibrium between the supply and demand in each individual market through the medium of price changes will also ensure balance between sales and purchases of each region.

In the case of industrial activities ("manufactures") the impact effect of exogenous changes in demand will be on production rather than on prices. "Supply", at any rate long-run supply, is normally in excess of demand—in the sense that producers would be willing to produce more, and to sell more, at the prevailing price (or even at a lower price) in response to an increased flow of orders. In this situation the adjustment process operates in a different manner—through the so-called "foreign trade multiplier". Any exogenous change in the demand for the products of a region from outside will set up multiplier effects in terms of local production and employment which in turn will adjust imports to the change in exports; on certain assumptions, this adjustment will alone suffice to keep the trade flows in balance.[1]

Some time ago Hicks[2] coined the phrase "super-multiplier" to cover the effects of changes of demand on investment, as well as on consumption; and he showed that on certain assumptions, both the rate of growth of induced investment, and the rate of growth of consumption, become attuned to the rate of growth of the autonomous component of demand, so that the growth in an autonomous demand-factor will govern the rate of growth of the economy as a whole.

From the point of view of any particular region, the "autonomous component of demand" is the demand emanating from *outside* the region; and Hicks' notion of the "super-multiplier" can be applied so as to express the doctrine of the foreign trade multiplier in a dynamic setting. So expressed, the doctrine asserts that the rate of economic development of a region is fundamentally governed by the rate of growth of its exports. For the growth of exports, via the "accelerator", will govern the rate of growth of industrial capacity, as well as the rate of growth of consumption; it will also serve to adjust (again under rather severe simplifying assumptions) both the level, and the rate of growth, of imports to that of exports.

The behaviour of exports on the other hand will depend both on an exogenous factor—the rate of growth of world demand for the products of the region; and on an "endogenous" or quasi-endogenous factor—on the movement of the "efficiency wages"

---

[1] The necessary assumptions are that all other sources of demand except exports are endogenous, rather than exogenous—i.e., that both Government expenditure and business investment play a passive rôle, the former being confined by revenue from taxation, and the latter by savings out of business profits.

[2] *A Contribution to the Theory of the Trade Cycle,* Oxford, 1950.

in the region relative to other producing regions, which will determine whether the region's share in the total (overall) market is increasing or diminishing. The movement of "efficiency wages" (a phrase coined by Keynes) is the resultant of two elements—the relative movement of money wages and that of productivity. If this relationship (the index of money wages divided by the index of productivity) moves in favour of an area it will gain in "competitiveness" and vice versa.

As regards the movement of money wages the one uncontroversial proposition that one can advance is that given *some* mobility of labour, there is a limit to the differences in the levels of wages prevailing between industrial regions, or between different industries of a region. Indeed, it is a well known fact that whilst the general level of money wages may rise at highly variable rates at different times, the pay differentials between different types of workers, or between workers doing the same job in different areas, are remarkably constant. This may be the result partly of the mobility of labour but also of the strong pressures associated with collective bargaining for the maintenance of traditional comparabilities.[1] But this means that the rates of growth of money wages in different regions will tend to be much the same, even when the rates of growth in employment differ markedly. On the other hand, under the Verdoorn Law, the rates of growth of productivity will be the higher, the higher the rates of growth of output, and differences in the rates of productivity growth will tend to exceed the associated differences in the rates of growth of employment.[2] Hence differences in the rates of productivity growth are not likely to be compensated by equivalent differences in the rates of increase in money wages.

[1] It has also been true in an international context that the comparative differences in the rates of growth of money wages in the different industrial countries had been smaller (in the post-war period at any rate) than the differences in the rates of productivity growth in the manufacturing industries of those countries, though the reasons why this has been so are not as yet well understood (cf. e.g. Kaldor, *Monetary Policy, Economic Stability and Growth*, Memorandum submitted to the Committee on the Working of the Monetary System. Principal Memoranda of Evidence, Vol. 3, pp. 146–153, London, H.M.S.O., 1960, at paras 22–3 and Table 1, reprinted in *Essays on Economic Policy*, vol. I, pp. 128–53).

[2] Recent empirical analyses of productivity growth in manufacturing industry suggest that a 1 per cent increase in the growth of output is associated with a 0·6 per cent increase in productivity and a 0·4 per cent increase in employment (cf. e.g.: *Economic Survey for Europe*, 1969, U.N. Geneva, 1970).

In other words, "efficiency wages" will tend to fall in regions (and in the particular industries of regions) where productivity rises faster than the average. It is for this reason that relatively fast growing areas tend to acquire a cumulative competitive advantage over a relatively slow growing area; "efficiency wages" will, in the natural course of events, tend to fall in the former, relatively to the latter—even when they tend to rise in both areas in absolute terms.

It is through this mechanism that the process of "cumulative causation" works; and both comparative success and comparative failure have self-reinforcing effects in terms of industrial development. Just because the induced changes in wage increases are not sufficient to offset the differences in productivity increases, the comparative costs of production in fast growing areas tend to fall in time relatively to those in slow growing areas; and thereby enhance the competitive advantage of the former at the expense of the latter.

This principle of cumulative causation—which explains the unequal regional incidence of industrial development by endogenous factors resulting from the process of historical development itself rather than by exogenous differences in "resource endowment"—is an essential one for the understanding of the diverse trends of development as between different regions. In reality, the influences and cross-currents resulting from processes of development are far more complex. The intensification of trade resulting from technological improvements in transport or the reduction of artificial barriers (such as tariffs between regions) has important diffusion effects as well as important concentration effects. The increase in production and income in one region will, as such, stimulate the demand for "complementary" products of other regions; and just as, in terms of microeconomics, falling costs generally lead to oligopoly rather than monopoly, so the principle of cumulative causation leads to the concentration of industrial development in a number of successful regions and not of a single region. These "successful" regions in turn may hold each other in balance through increasing specialisation between them—some area becomes more prominent in some industries and another area in some other industries.

Actually, in terms of national areas, Kuznets found that different industrialised countries are remarkably similar in industrial structure, at similar stages of industrial development. The tremendous increase in international trade in industrial products between highly industrialised countries since the Second World War was more the reflection of specialisation within industries than that between industries: it was mainly in parts and components and machinery for industrial use. For example, in the case of the motor car industry, whilst most developed countries have a developed and highly competitive motor car industry (and are large net exporters) there has been a huge increase in international trade in motor car components—with some countries supplying some part of a carburetter to everybody, and some other country doing the same for some other part of the engine, or the carburetter.

There are also important dis-economies resulting from excessive rates of growth in industrial activities in particular areas: the growing areas will tend to have fast rates of population growth (mainly as a result of immigration) with the associated environmental problems in housing, public services, congestion, and so on, and these at some stage should serve to offset the technological economies resulting from faster growth. But as is well known, many of these dis-economies are external to the individual producer and may not therefore be adequately reflected in the movement of money costs and prices. A counterpart to this are external economics in the slow growing or declining regions—in terms of unemployment of labour, or an under-utilised social infrastructure, which again tend to be external to the firm and hence inadequately reflected in selling costs or prices. There is some presumption therefore for supposing that, if left to market processes alone, tendencies to regional concentration of industrial activities will proceed farther than they would have done if "private costs" were equal to "social cost" (in the Pigovian sense) and all economies and dis-economies of production were adequately reflected in the movement of money costs and prices.

REGIONS AND COUNTRIES

Now consider some of the basic differences in the mode of operation of this principle—i.e. of "cumulative causation" as between different regions of a single country and as between different political areas.

There is, first of all, the fact that the inter-regional mobility of labour is very much greater than the international mobility of labour. As a result differences in regional growth rates cannot cause differences in living standards of the same order as have emerged in the last few centuries between more distant regions, separated by political and cultural barriers. Real earnings no doubt improve faster in the areas of immigration rather than in areas of emigration, but the very fact of easy migration limits the extent to which differences in regional growth rates will be associated with divergent movements in earnings per head. The fact that trade unions are nation-wide and collective bargains in most countries are on a national basis, is a further reason why the movement of real earnings in various regions broadly tends to keep in step.

A second and even more important fact is that a region which forms part of a political community, with a common scale of public services and a common basis of taxation, automatically gets "aid" whenever its trading relations with the rest of the country deteriorate. There is an important built-in fiscal stabiliser which arrests the operation of the export-multiplier: since taxes paid to the Central Government vary with the level of local incomes and expenditure, whilst public expenditures do not (indeed they may vary in an offsetting direction through public works, unemployment benefit, etc.), any deterioration in the export-import balance tends to be retarded (and ultimately arrested) by the change in the region's fiscal balance—in the relation between what it contributes to the central Exchequer and what it receives from it.

This "built-in" fiscal stabiliser—i.e. that a fall in exogenous demand leads to an increase in the public sector deficit, and thereby moderates the effect of the former on employment and incomes—operates of course on the national level as much as on the regional level; and it is one of the main reasons why a fall in exports does not generate a sufficient fall in the level of incomes to maintain equilibrium in the balance of payments through the adjustment in imports. But the important difference is that in the case of the region the change in the local fiscal balance is externally financed; in the case of the nation the balance of payments deficit causes a fall in reserves, or requires "compensatory finance" from abroad, which is by no means "automatic".

This is probably the main reason why there appears to be no counterpart to the "balance-of-payments problem" on the regional level. It is often suggested by the "monetary school" that the reason why a country with a separate currency gets into balance of payments difficulties, whilst a region never does, is because in the one case the "local money supply" is reduced in consequence of an excess of imports over exports; in the other case the monetary authorities offset the effects of the adverse balance on current account by "domestic credit expansion"—by replacing the outflow of money (resulting from the excess of imports) with "new" money. In my view this way of looking at the problem is putting the cart before the horse. The "replacement of the money" is simply a facet of the fact that the foreign trade multiplier is arrested in its operation through the induced fiscal deficit —possibly aggravated also by the fall in private saving in relation to private domestic investment (though in practice the latter factor may be quantitatively of less importance, since the foreign-trade multiplier will tend to induce a reduction in local investment, and not only in local savings). But exactly the same thing happens at the regional level—with the outflowing money being (at least partially) replaced by a larger net inflow from the Exchequer, which is a direct consequence of the "outflow"; but since it happens automatically as part of the natural order of things nobody kicks up a fuss, or even takes notice of it.

In these ways "regions" are in a more favourable position than "countries". On the other hand sovereign political areas can take various measures to offset the effect of an unfavourable trend in their "efficiency wages" which is not open to a "region"— i.e. by diverting demand from foreign goods to home goods, through varying forms of protection (tariffs and non-tariff barriers, such as preferences given in public contracts) and occasionally also—though usually only very belatedly, in extremities—through adjustment of the exchange rate.

Of these two instruments for counteracting adverse trends in "efficiency wages"—protection and devaluation—the latter is undoubtedly greatly superior to the former. Devaluation, as has often been pointed out, is nothing else but a combination of a uniform *ad-valorem* duty on all imports and uniform *ad-valorem* subsidy on exports. The combination of the two allows the adjustment in "competitiveness" to take place under conditions which give the maximum scope for obtaining the advantages of economies of scale through international specialisation. Protection on the other hand tends to reduce international specialisation, and forces each region to spread its industrial activities over a wider range of activities on a smaller scale, instead of a narrower range on a larger scale. The effects of protection in inhibiting the growth of industrial efficiency is likely to be the greater the smaller the G.N.P. (or rather the gross industrial product) of the protected area. It is no accident that all the prosperous small countries of the world—such as the Scandinavian countries or Switzerland—are (comparatively speaking) "free traders". They have modest tariffs, and a very high ratio of trade in manufactures (both exports and imports) to their total output or consumption.

It has sometimes been suggested—not perhaps very seriously—that some of the development areas of the U.K.—such as Scotland or Northern Ireland—would be better off with a separate currency with an adjustable exchange rate vis-à-vis the rest of the U.K. For the reason mentioned earlier, I do not think this would be a suitable remedy. However, we have now introduced a new instrument in the U.K.—R.E.P.[1]—which potentially could give the same advantages as devaluation for counteracting any adverse trend in "efficiency wages", but with the added advantage that the cost of the consequent deterioration in the terms of trade (the cost of selling exports at lower prices in terms of imports) is not borne by the region, but by the U.K. taxpaying community as a whole.

[1] The Regional Employment Premium.

For this same reason, perhaps, the drawback of R.E.P. as an instrument is that it would be politically very difficult to introduce it on a scale that could make it really effective. The present R.E.P. is equivalent to a 5-6 per cent reduction in the "efficiency wages" in the manufacturing sector of the development areas. Since "value added by regional manufacturing" is no more than a quarter, or perhaps a third, of the total cost of regional export-commodities (the rest consist of goods and services embodied that are mainly produced outside the region) the effect of a 6 per cent R.E.P. is no more than that of a 2 per cent devaluation (for the U.K. as a whole). It thus could have only one-fifth of the effect on "regional competitiveness" which the recent U.K. devaluation had on the U.K.'s competitiveness in relation to the rest of the world.

Development Area policy comprises a host of other measures as well, of which the differential investment grant is the most costly and the most prominent. In my view investment grants as an instrument are less effective for the purpose of countering adverse trends in competitiveness than subsidies on wages (and not only because they stimulate the wrong kind of industries— those that are specially capital intensive) but I would agree that this is an issue that requires closer investigation than it has yet received.

One further possibility can be considered. Given the limitation on the scope of development expenditures by the natural disinclination of the Central Government (or the Parliament at Westminster) to spend huge sums in subsidising particular regions, there is a case for supplementing Central Government sources from local sources—through more local fiscal autonomy. For example, if it were found (and agreed) that R.E.P. is an efficacious way of subsidising regional exports (I suppose this is far from agreed at the moment) and that this might have dramatic effects in terms of enhanced regional development in the long run, it could well be in the interest of the regions to supplement the centrally financed R.E.P. by the proceeds, say, of a local sales tax. Perhaps this is a dangerous suggestion since in practice the growth of locally financed subsidies might simply be offset by lesser subsidies from the Centre. It would be less "dangerous" however, if it was the Central Government which offered to raise the level of such subsidies—R.E.P. or even investment grants—on condition that a proportion of the cost should be raised by local taxation. Clearly, far more could be spent for the benefit of particular areas, if the areas themselves would make a greater, or a more distinct, contribution to the cost of such benefits. But these are thoughts for the distant future; long before they become practical politics we shall be deeply involved in the same kind of issues in connection with our negotiations to enter the Common Market.

6

CONFLICTS IN NATIONAL ECONOMIC OBJECTIVES[1]

Economics, at least since Adam Smith, has been concerned with understanding how the economic system works in order to discover by what kind of policies it could be made to work better. More wealth, and a more even distribution of wealth, have always been regarded without question or argument as the main objectives of national economic policy. But up to fairly recently—up to the Second World War in fact—the tasks of economic policy were mainly thought of as the creation of a framework of laws and institutions which provided the best environment for the operation of market forces, and not as any direct manipulation of those forces.

THE FOUR MAJOR OBJECTIVES OF POST-WAR POLICY

Since that time the notion of "economic policy objectives" has acquired a new precision—one could almost say a new meaning— and governments have come to be judged by performance criteria which they would have strongly disclaimed in earlier days. The best evidence for this is that policy objectives have come to be expressed in quantitative terms—as "targets." Successive post-war Chancellors have announced a *full-employment* target, expressed in terms of an average percentage of unemployment which is not be to exceeded (3 per cent by Mr. Gaitskell in 1950): a *balance of payments* target, expressed in terms of a current surplus of so many millions (such as the £300 million put forward by Mr.—now Lord—Butler in 1952); a *growth*

---

[1] Originally delivered as Presidential Address to Section F of the British Association at Durham, September 1970, and printed in *Economic Journal*, vol. LXXXI March 1971.

target (4 per cent by Mr. Maudling in 1964 and in the National Plan of 1965) and a *wage-increase or incomes policy* target (by Sir Stafford Cripps in 1949; by Mr. Selwyn Lloyd in 1962; Mr. Maudling in 1964; Mr. Brown in 1965; by legislation in 1966, etc.).

Though the status of such official targets was never clearly defined, the very fact of their announcement was an outward manifestation of a deep-seated change in public attitudes in regard to the powers and responsibilities of Government in the economic sphere. It has come to be taken for granted—by the leaders of both of the major political parties, as well as by the public—that Governments can, and should, assume responsibility for the "management of the economy"; and that "successful management" comprises the simultaneous attainment of at least the four major objectives.

The fact that these have come to be accepted as mandatory objectives of policy—i.e., as ends that the public can legitimately expect from its Government—was the most important political result of the intellectual revolution engendered by the publication of Keynes' *General Theory of Employment*. The important message of that work was the idea that in a market economy the total amount of goods and services produced is not (or not normally) determined by the amount of scarce resources at its disposal, and the efficiency with which they are utilised, but on certain features of the process of income generation which tend to establish an equilibrium level of effective demand that will limit the amount produced, irrespective of potential supply.

Keynes' theory has shown how the economy can be managed so as to secure the full utilisation of resources, in particular the full employment of labour, mainly by Government action in the fiscal and monetary field, without any radical change in the framework of institutions of a market economy. This idea had a tremendous appeal, the more so since war-time experience has demonstrated how quickly, given sufficient demand, unemployment could be made to disappear; and the pressure of public opinion created by that experience was undoubtedly responsible for the famous declaration of the war-time Coalition Government which stated that "the Government accept as one of their primary aims and responsibilities the maintenance of a high and stable level of employment after the War."[1]

Once that responsibility had been assumed, it was quite inevitable that successive post-war Governments should also assume responsibility, or at least be *held* responsible, for the other vital aspects of the performance of the economy necessary to make a full-employment policy viable, in particular for ensuring a satisfactory balance of payments, and for ensuring a "reasonable stability of wages and prices." Both of these "associated requirements" figure quite prominently in the 1944 White Paper, which may be regarded—along with Beveridge's book on Full Employment, published in the same year[2]—as the original blueprint from which all post-war policies of economic management have evolved. In the matter of price stability, the White Paper states quite categorically that "increases in the general level of wages must be related to increased productivity." In the matter of the balance of payments it emphasised that "to avoid an unfavourable foreign balance we must export much more than we did before the war."

However, there was little understanding of the difficulties which were to arise in the attempt to achieve all these objectives simultaneously, or of how Government policy was to be conducted if they were not attained, or if the various objectives came into open conflict with one another.

On the question of the balance of payments, the White Paper stated, somewhat surprisingly, that "the state of our foreign balance depends very largely upon the behaviour of persons and Governments outside our jurisdiction" and suggested that the best way to make sure that we shall be able to export enough to pay for our imports is to ensure, by means of international agreements (of the type of Bretton Woods and G.A.T.T.—neither of which were then in existence), "conditions of international trade which will make it possible for all countries to pursue policies of full employment to their mutual advantage." There was no hint of a suggestion that the maintenance of full employment might prove incompatible with a continued equili-

---

[1] Cf. White Paper on *Employment Policy*, Cmnd. 6527, May 1944.
[2] W. H. Beveridge, *Full Employment in a Free Society* (London, 1944).

brium in the balance of payments under a regime of fixed exchange rates, even when prices and wages were kept "reasonably
stable" and when the world economy was expanding.

On the question of price and wage stability, the White Paper
stated that "it will be essential that employers and workers
should exercise moderation in wages matters," and "that condition can be realised only by the joint efforts of the Government,
employers and organised labour." But it offered no suggestion
of the kind of institutional arrangements that would be needed
if the determination of wages and prices were no longer to be
left to the impersonal forces of the market.

TARGETS AND INSTRUMENTS

In the language of present-day econometrics, the failure of
post-war Governments to pursue a policy consistent in terms of
its declared objectives could thus be primarily attributed to an
insufficient orchestration of instruments—of not having enough
separate policy instruments at hand to secure the simultaneous
attainment of the various objectives. It is a well-known principle
of the modern theory of economic policy, first put forward by
Professor Tinbergen,[1] that in order to secure a stated number of
objectives the Government needs to operate at least an equal
number of different policy instruments—it is only in exceptional
circumstances that the same instrument can secure the attainment of more than one "target" simultaneously. If demand
management (through fiscal policy) is used to secure the target
level of employment, another instrument—which can only
be thought of in terms of an incomes policy—is needed to secure
the target rate of wage increases; and yet a further instrument—a
flexible exchange rate—to secure the target balance of payments.
If in addition the Government wishes to secure a target rate of
productivity growth it needs yet further instruments to secure a
more effective utilisation of resources.

On a formal theoretical plane one could thus assert that the

---

[1] J. Tinbergen, *On the Theory of Economic Policy* (Amsterdam, 1952), Chapters IV
and V. Also J. E. Meade, *The Balance of Payments, Mathematical Supplement* (Oxford,
1951), pp. 28–9.

basic cause of our failures was that of trying to achieve too much with too little freedom of action—of failing to grasp the full implication of the principles of economic management. On a more realistic plane, I think one must recognise that the limits on the degrees of freedom of Governmental policy were set by political, social and ideological constraints which inhibited action in certain fields; the intellectual failure to recognise the need for them was a symptom, rather than the cause, of the inhibition. The tremendous resistance which Governments have invariably put up to devaluation—even in circumstances where such an adjustment was plainly in accord with both the letter and the spirit of the Bretton Woods agreement—has, I am sure, far more deep-seated causes than simply a failure by Ministers or officials to make a proper study of the writings of Professor Tinbergen. As recent events have shown, the resistance can be almost equally strong when the required adjustment involves revaluation (as in the German case) rather than devaluation. Equally, the resistance to an incomes policy by economists and politicians of both the right and the left had more to do with a refusal to accept its social and political implications than with the uncritical acceptance of the econometric studies of Professor Phillips which confirmed many of our economists in the more comfortable view that, provided monetary and fiscal policy is properly conducted and the pressure of demand is not allowed to exceed certain limits, wage and price inflation will automatically be contained by the forces of the market.

As a result of the extraordinary stresses and strains of the last few years—on an international plane, and not only in this country —there has been a distinct improvement, and there is now a much greater consensus of opinion on the need for such instruments than existed before. It is now more widely accepted that adjustments in the exchange rate are a legitimate, indeed an indispensable, part of the international "adjustment process"—for keeping the system of international payments in reasonable balance— and the I.M.F. has been charged with the task of putting forward suggestions for greater exchange-rate flexibility within the general framework of the system. It is also far more generally acknowledged—even by Conservative Prime Ministers—that the process of inflation is "cost-induced," not "demand-induced," with the evident implication that it can be tackled only by an incomes policy—though I must confess, I am no more clear than others by what kinds of institutional arrangements such an instrument could be effectively operated. Can it be based on anything less than the creation of a social consensus on what constitutes a fair system of pay differentials on a national scale, and if so, is there a way of bringing this about?

As the problem of an incomes policy raises sociological and political issues that are outside my competence, and as it is a problem that is common to all industrial countries, and not specific to Britain, I do not propose to consider it today in any detail. Instead I shall devote the rest of this address to the other major problem of economic management—the question of exchange-rate policy. Here my contention is not merely that we should have used this instrument more often and more readily to avoid the periodic interruptions to our economic growth on account of balance-of-payments crises, important and un-welcome though these have been. My basic contention, which I propose to develop at some length, is that by choosing the control of the pressure of demand through fiscal management as the centrepiece of action, we have opted, quite unintentionally, for the creation of an economic structure which has involved a slower rate of growth in our productive potential than was both possible and desirable.

My main criticism of the philosophy underlying the White Paper, and of the post-war policies of economic management that were built on it, is that it treated the problem of full employment and (implicitly) of growth as one of internal demand management, and not one of exports and of international competitiveness.

This was the result of the failure of the economists who were responsible for laying out the groundwork of the new policy to examine, or to appreciate, the true implications of the Keynesian model of under-employment equilibrium, elaborated in terms of a "closed economy," to an "open economy" such as Britain. As I was one of the economists engaged in laying out the groundwork—in a memorandum prepared for Sir William

Beveridge's working group in 1943[1]—I would like to state that I feel I am as much responsible for that failure as any other economist of the time. And by the word "failure" I do *not* mean—as will become evident in the concluding part of this address—that the policy was fundamentally wrong, in the sense that Britain would now be better off if it had never been invented or adopted. This is far from the case. What I do mean to suggest is that it was very much a policy of the "second best"; and that after twenty-five years of experience it is time to re-examine its foundations to see whether for the future we cannot replace it with something better.

A LOOK-BACK TO THE 1920S

As I have no time to develop the argument in terms of basic theoretical models, I propose to demonstrate my point by asking what would have happened if the principles of demand management, as laid down in the White Paper, had been applied to deal with the pre-war unemployment problem. For this purpose it is best to start with the 1920s, when the rest of the world was prosperous, and world trade expanding, whilst in Britain, starting from 1921, unemployment, except for brief periods, had never fallen below a million and a quarter, or 10 per cent of the labour force.

I propose to begin by quoting at some length from an internal Treasury minute that has recently come to light, written by Winston Churchill as Chancellor of the Exchequer in February 1925 in connection with the discussions that were going on inside the Government concerning the return to the Gold Standard. (It is worth quoting this document at some length, partly as a tribute to the intuition and intelligence—in hitherto unsuspected directions—of one of our greatest national leaders, but also because in analysing what would have been the right answer to Churchill's queries one comes to grips with what was wrong with our pre-war policies, and by implication, also with our post-war policies.) Churchill wrote:

[1] "The Quantitative Aspects of the Full Employment Problem in Britain", published as Appendix C to Beveridge's *Full Employment in a Free Society* (London, Allen and Unwin, 1944), pp. 344–401 and reproduced in *Essays on Economic Policy*, I, pp. 23–82.

"The Treasury have never, it seems to me, faced the profound significance of what Mr. Keynes calls 'the paradox of unemployment amidst dearth'. The Governor shows himself perfectly happy in the spectacle of Britain possessing the finest credit in the world simultaneously with a million and a quarter unemployed . . . *This is the only country in the world where this condition exists.* The Treasury and Bank of England policy has been the only policy consistently pursued. It is a terrible responsibility for those who have shaped it, unless they can be sure that there is no connection between the unique British phenomenon of chronic unemployment and the long, resolute consistency of a particular financial policy. . . . It may be of course that you will argue that the unemployment would have been much greater but for the financial policy pursued; that there is no sufficient demand for commodities, either internally or externally to require the services of this million and a quarter people; that there is nothing for them but to hang like a millstone round the neck of industry and on the public revenue until they become permanently demoralised. You may be right, but if so, it is one of the most sombre conclusions ever reached. On the other hand I do not pretend to see even 'through a glass darkly' how the financial and credit policy of the country could be handled so as to bridge the gap between a dearth of goods and a surplus of labour; and well I realise the danger of experiment to that end. The seas of history are full of famous wrecks. Still, if I could see a way, I would far rather follow it than any other. I would rather see Finance less proud and Industry more content."[1]

Today, with almost a half century of experience and of progress in economic theory behind us, we can see "through a glass darkly" rather better than either Churchill or his official advisers were able to do in 1925.

Most economists would now agree that fiscal policy, combined with credit policy, could have been so handled as to

[1] Minute of February 22, 1925, quoted in D. E. Moggridge, *The Return to Gold, 1925* (Cambridge University Press, 1969), p. 54. Italics not in the original.

eliminate (at least gradually, even if not immediately) unemployment, and that such a policy would *not* have involved a "vicious and cumulative inflation" that would have gone on until money "ceased to be acceptable as value."[1] On the other hand, any such policy which raised production and employment through a stimulus to domestic demand would have involved an increase in imports relative to exports; this would have brought a downward pressure on sterling on the exchanges, and would have made it quite impossible to return to the Gold Standard.

Indeed, there was no way of pursuing a full-employment policy in Britain in the 1920s consistently with a return to the Gold Standard at the pre-war parity of $4.86. As a result of the deflationary policies adopted on the recommendation of the Cunliffe Committee (which regarded the restoration of the Gold Standard as the most important national economic objective) and the rise in the sterling exchange rate, British exports failed to recover: in 1924 the volume of exports was only 72 per cent of pre-war, whilst imports had regained the pre-war level;[2] British exports performed very badly even in relation to continental European countries, who were only just recovering from the war.[3] Unemployment was largely concentrated in the traditional export industries—steel and engineering, shipbuilding, textiles and coal. The only possible way in which this heavy unemployment could have been absorbed would have been through higher exports, which in turn would have required abandoning the Gold Standard objective and opting instead for a floating rate—for the "managed currency" advocated by Keynes in 1924.[4]

The truth that was hidden from Churchill and his official advisers in 1925—and was evidently not perceived even by the authors of the White Paper twenty years later—is that the main autonomous factor governing both the level and the rate of

---

[1] Cf. the official reply to Churchill's minute quoted by Moggridge, *op. cit.*, p. 55.
[2] *The British Economy, Key Statistics* 1900–1966 Table B (London and Cambridge Economic Service).
[3] Cf. A. Maddison, "Growth and Fluctuations in the World Economy, 1870–1960", *Banca Nazionale del Lavoro, Quarterly Review*, June 1962, Tables 25 and 27.
[4] Keynes, J. M., *A Tract on Monetary Reform* (London, 1924), Chapters IV and V. Keynes' proposal was that the Bank of England should announce fixed buying and selling prices for gold (or dollars) every Thursday, but that it should have freedom to vary these rates up and down at weekly intervals, in the same way as the Bank rate.

growth of effective demand of an industrial country with a large share of exports in its total production and of imports in its consumption is the external demand for its exports;[1] and the main factor governing the latter is its international competitiveness, which in turn depends on the level of its industrial costs relatively to other industrial exporters. Since the level of money wages is bound to be sticky in a downward direction, and is not greatly influenced by world prices in an upward direction, the degree of competitiveness, given the relationship of wage-rates and productivity levels of different industrial countries, depends largely on the exchange rate.[2] Moreover, owing to the existence of increasing returns to scale in manufacturing industries, any initial advantage in terms of export competitiveness tends to have a cumulative effect, since the country which is able to increase its manufactured exports faster than the others also tends to have a faster rate of growth of productivity in its export industries, which enhances its competitive advantage still further. The task of maintaining competitiveness through the choice of a favourable exchange rate is therefore of the highest importance to an industrial country from the point of view of its long-run

---

[1] According to all recent evidence, external influences, operating through export demand, determined both the timing and the scale of fluctuations in the British economy throughout the nineteenth century; with the possible exception of the 1901–14 period (which has special features) the level of domestic investment has generally followed the movement of exports. Cf. Appendix A of W. H. Beveridge's *Full Employment in a Free Society* (prepared in collaboration with Mr. Harold Wilson), particularly pp. 294–305; Sayers, R. S., *The Vicissitudes of an Export Economy: Britain since 1880*, the Mills Memorial Lecture (Sydney, 1965); *A History of Economic Change in England, 1880–1934* (Oxford, 1967), part. Chapters 2 and 3; Ford, A. G., "British Economic Fluctuations, 1870–1914", *Manchester School*, June 1969, pp. 99–130.

[2] This is not to deny that the rate of increase in money wages—with or without an incomes policy—is influenced by the cost of living, so that money wages will tend to rise faster as a result of a falling exchange rate and rising import prices; if the movement of wages is controlled, or moderated, by an incomes policy a flexible exchange rate will put a greater strain on this instrument. But there is no reason for supposing that the "efficiency wages" of a country, in terms of international currency, cannot be permanently lowered by a downward adjustment of the exchange rate, even though the change in the exchange rate necessary to secure a given reduction in "efficiency wages" will be greater than it would be if money wages did not react to the change in the cost of living. It must also be borne in mind that the change in "efficiency wages", or in the terms of trade, that is necessary to achieve a given increase in the volume or the rate of growth of exports, comes to the same whether it is achieved by a change in internal costs (*i.e.*, in the level of wages), or a change in the exchange rate, or some combination of both. There is no net national cost in "devaluation" that is not equally involved in some alternative policy—such as "freezing" wages by incomes policy for long enough (relatively to other countries) while productivity is rising—which secures the same improvement in "efficiency wages" and in exports.

growth potential and not only on account of its short- or medium-term effect on the level of employment.

STATIC AND DYNAMIC ASPECTS

The "orthodox" Keynesian of the 1930s, in looking at the problem of the 1920s, would not have quarrelled with the view that a full-employment policy would have been incompatible with the return to the Gold Standard; he would have argued, however, that the adoption of a floating rate, or a "managed currency," would not have been sufficient in the absence of further measures to deal with the problem of insufficiency of demand due to excessive saving, unless the exchange rate were kept low enough to yield a large export surplus—that is to say, by generating sufficient overseas investment to make up for the lack of home investment.

However, this problem takes on an entirely different aspect if it is considered in a dynamic setting and not, as the original Keynesian models of the 1930s, in a purely static one. If we consider the problem in terms of the *growth rates* of demand, and not just in terms of the *levels* of demand, we can no longer treat the level of domestic investment as being autonomously determined; industrial investment will be all the greater the faster the demand for the products of industry is growing and the more fully its existing capacity is utilised. Professor Matthews has shown in a recent paper that the important difference between the full-employment level of effective demand of the post-war period and that of the under-employment situation of the pre-war period was mainly in the level of investment (particularly in industrial investment) in relation to full-employment output; it was not due to a more "expansionary" fiscal policy.[1] On Hicks' principle of the "super-multiplier,"[2] any given (exogenous) rate of growth of demand will generate a certain ratio of

---

[1] R. C. O. Matthews, "Why Has Britain Had Full Employment Since the War?", *Economic Journal*, September 1968, pp. 555–69. However, in my own view (as will be argued below) the true effects of Keynesian policies adopted since the war lay in the repercussions of maintaining a certain rate of *growth* of demand on the incentive to invest; they cannot be adequately discerned in terms of a "static" analysis which considers only the changes in the composition of the *sources* of demand.

[2] J. R. Hicks, *A Contribution to the Theory of the Trade Cycle* (Oxford, 1950), p. 62.

investment to output (including both "autonomous" and "induced" investment) that will be all the greater the higher the rate of growth of demand: for any given savings ratio, therefore, there is some rate of growth of export demand which, at any given fiscal balance, will generate sufficient domestic investment to balance full-employment savings. (This will be true even when account is taken of the fact that, under full-employment conditions, not only the volume of savings, but the ratio of savings to income, would have been higher, because a lower exchange rate would have secured higher profits in the export trades; it would also have brought about in the export trades, and, through the multiplier effects, in the economy generally, a higher degree of utilisation of capacity, and hence a higher share of profits in output.)

It is quite possible therefore that if we *had* adopted a "managed currency" in the 1920s (i.e., the system that was actually in operation in 1932–35, when the exchange rate was free to vary, but the actual movements of the rate were heavily influenced by official intervention) and if the exchange rate had been purposively managed with a view to maintaining an appropriate rate of growth of exports, we should thereby have secured both sufficient exports to give us a satisfactory balance of payments and sufficient domestic investment to secure both full employment and a satisfactory growth of capacity; and this could have been achieved without any drastic change in budgetary conventions and without producing any undue surplus in the balance of payments (because of the additional imports which would have been generated).

Since world trading conditions are constantly changing, and our own state of export competitiveness is much under the influence of the rise of new industrial exporters, it cannot, of course, be supposed that any constant exchange rate (in terms of gold or dollars) would have secured a steady rate of growth of exports over time—unless money wages had moved in the highly implausible manner (implicitly assumed by the then prevailing theory) so as to compensate for any net change in the demand for labour. The exchange rate would have had to be varied in the light of experience, though there is no reason to suppose that such adjustments would have been only in one direction. For reasons which I shall consider in more detail presently, our productivity growth would have been accelerated as well, and it might occasionally have been necessary to raise the exchange rate in order to prevent the demand for exports from rising faster than desirable.

The ideal rate of growth of exports, from a long-run point of view, is that which maximises the rate of growth of the real national income. What that rate is depends partly on the effects of a higher rate of growth of exports and of investment on the rate of productivity growth, and partly on its effects on the terms of trade. A higher rate of growth of exports (just as a higher volume of exports at any given time) necessarily involves *less* favourable terms of trade, at least in "commodity" terms (not necessarily in "factorial" terms); it also involves (up to a point at any rate) a higher "underlying" growth rate of the G.D.P.; the theoretically optimal target is therefore the one which secures that particular underlying growth rate of productivity at which the rate of growth of real income (taking into account the terms of trade) is the highest.[1]

It does not follow, of course, that this ideal, or "target," rate of growth of exports would be the same as the one required to secure the equality of domestic savings and domestic investment at full employment (or, what comes to the same thing, a zero balance on current account); nor is this necessarily a desirable condition, since a certain proportion of domestic savings will be required to finance overseas investment, and it is therefore desirable to aim at a *surplus* on current account. Hence reliance on exchange-rate policy to secure the desirable rate of growth of exports does not mean that fiscal policy will play a purely "neutral" rôle; the instrument of fiscal policy would still be required to secure that fiscal balance (which may be positive or

---

[1] I would hesitate to hazard a guess of what this "ideal" rate of growth of exports would have been in the circumstances of *post-war* Britain. It would almost certainly have been higher than the attained rate of growth of manufactured exports of $2\frac{1}{2}$ per cent a year in the period 1951–66; it would most probably also have been lower than the rate of growth of the volume of world trade in manufactures over the same period, which was 7 per cent a year. In other words, it would have involved a more gently falling trend in the United Kingdom share of world trade as compared with the recorded fall from 22·5 per cent in 1951 to 12·9 per cent in 1966.

negative) which reconciles, over a run of years, the optimal rate of growth of exports and of the G.D.P. with the maintenance of a "target surplus" in the current balance of payments.

CONSUMPTION-LED GROWTH AND EXPORT-LED GROWTH

I am not suggesting that in the circumstances of the war or the immediate post-war period this type of policy of "demand management" would have been a practicable alternative to the policies outlined in the 1944 White Paper—even if its advantages had been seen, which they clearly were not. First, though we had actual operational experience with floating exchange rates, we had, in effect, abandoned that system already in 1935 with the Tripartite Agreement, and the interval of time between that and the outbreak of the war was far too short for the ill consequences of its abandonment to be fully appreciated. Second, we were living in a world where trade was almost wholly regulated by quantitative controls, and where the world was hungry for goods—the problem was how to set aside enough resources for exports, not how to sell them. Third, as the White Paper emphasised, international agreements that would make it possible to dismantle controls and get the world economy expanding on the basis of free multilateral trade rightly appeared to be the major long-term interest of Britain as a trading nation. The Bretton Woods Agreement, which held out the hope for a return to this system on the basis of fixed exchange rates and currency convertibility, and which provided the finance (albeit on a rather meagre basis) to start it off, was an essential keystone of this policy; and although (as is clear from the Parliamentary debates) many people felt misgivings, in general, most people felt that the advantages of assuming the obligations of Bretton Woods greatly outweighed the risks.

Since then a quarter of a century has elapsed. We must be free to reconsider our future policies in the light of that experience, particularly our experience of the difficulty of getting an adequate growth of exports even in a period in which world trade was rapidly expanding. The actual policies of economic management that we have been operating up to now—which relied on internal demand management through fiscal measures and a system of fixed exchange rates, making use of exchange-rate adjustments only in extreme situations of severe crisis—can be seen to suffer from a number of disadvantages, both from the point of view of their operational efficiency in the short-term and from their structural effect on economic growth in the long-term.

Though the intention of the policy has been to give priority to the growth of exports and investment, the very fact that the policy aimed at regulating the pressure of demand by internal measures—by stimulating or restraining personal consumption—meant, in the circumstances of the United Kingdom, that personal consumption expenditure took over the rôle of the "prime mover" of the economy.[1] This is because in a capitalist economy private business investment is largely demand-in-duced: it responds little to direct incentives (such as interest rates, tax incentives or subsidies); it is far more effectively in-fluenced through the control of final demand. Hence both fiscal measures and monetary measures (credit control) operated on the economy primarily by controlling the *rate of change* of consumer expenditure.

This meant that as a result of demand management personal consumption has taken over the rôle of exports as the autonomous factor governing the rate of growth of demand; hence both the level of investment and the composition of investment have mainly been controlled by the growth in consumption; the growth of capacity in the various industries has been governed by the structure of demand of domestic consumers, and not (or not mainly) by the growth of world demand for different products. Since investment has not directly been induced by exports,

---

[1] I am not suggesting that the regulation of the pressure of demand by fiscal measures would in *all* circumstances lead to this result; one can conceive of the use of fiscal measures, the main effect of which was to accommodate an excessive rate of growth in exports which would otherwise have caused inflation through an excessive pressure of demand (as, e.g., in the case of Germany in recent years). But in those circumstances it was not fiscal policy but the growth of exports itself which was primarily res-ponsible for ensuring continued growth and full employment; fiscal policy made it possible to maintain a growth of exports that was in excess of the economy's growth potential (at the cost of an unwanted and growing export *surplus*); it was not an in-strument for ensuring growth in circumstances in which the exogenous growth in export demand lagged behind the growth potential.

the growth of exports itself mainly depended on the growth of capacity of the various industries, reflecting the growth, and the pattern, of domestic consumption.

In the case of an industrialised country which is an "open economy," such "consumption-led" growth has several disadvantages as against "export-led" growth.

First, the Government is bound to take a cautious line in deciding on the permissible rate of growth of consumer demand, since any large stimulus to demand would lead to a disproportionate rise in investment, which in the short run would overspill (both in the form of stockbuilding and investment-goods purchases) into imports and cause a sudden rise in the trade deficit. (In a closed economy, or an economy controlled by import licences, an investment boom is restrained by capacity shortages until it can be accommodated—hence the Government could take a less cautious line in deciding on the permissible rate of growth of demand.)

Second, the caution dictated by the first consideration will mean that the incentive to invest will be weak, and hence the level of investment, as a proportion of output, will be low; this in turn will mean that fiscal policy, though cautious on the rate of growth of demand, will nevertheless operate so as to permit consumption to take up a high share of total demand if full employment is to be maintained. Hence, as an unintended consequence of the policy of managing the pressure of demand, a structure of final demand will be generated in which consumption will take up a high proportion, and investment a relatively low proportion, of total output; this factor alone (on account of the effects of capital investment on the rate of technological progress) will make for a relatively low rate of growth of productivity and a low "underlying" growth rate.

The main structural weakness of "internal demand management" with a fixed exchange rate—in an economy in which the exogenous growth in export demand is insufficient to match the growth potential—is that it provides no effective instrument for transferring resources from consumption to investment. Reducing consumption through higher taxes or stricter control of consumer credit will release resources, but it will weaken the incentive to invest at the same time; and may result in *less* investment, not more. Post-war Governments have constantly been plagued with the dilemma whether to restrain consumption, so as to provide more resources for investment and exports, or to allow a relatively free rein to the growth of consumer demand, so as to ensure the growth of capacity (and the growth of efficiency) that is vital to exports. With export-led growth this dilemma does not arise—consumption can be restrained in order to release resources; the growth of foreign demand will provide the incentive to utilise them effectively—not only through higher exports but in increasing the capacity of the export industries.[1]

Third, the pattern of the rate of growth of output and output capacity will reflect the pattern of final consumer demand, which gives far less scope for realising the productivity gains resulting from increasing returns. There is now a very considerable body of evidence to show that manufacturing industries exhibit strongly increasing returns, while other economic activities (agriculture, mining or services) do not.[2] Hence the rate of growth of productivity in the manufacturing industries will be the greater, the higher the rate of growth of production; the overall rate of productivity growth in the economy will be the greater, the faster manufacturing output rises in relation to the rest of the economy, and the larger the share of productive resources (both labour and capital) engaged in manufacturing activities.

On the evidence of the latest input–output estimates of the National Income Blue Book, only about 30 per cent of personal consumption expenditure generates income in manufacturing industry; the corresponding figure in export demand (for goods and services) is 70 per cent. Hence consumption-led growth involves far less increase in the demand for manufactured goods than export-led growth; as a result, the growth in the manu-

[1] Special problems may arise from any large or sudden stimulus to exports in connection with the fact that the industries (such as engineering) which provide the most important source for higher exports are also those which produce the plant and machinery necessary for an expansion of their own capacity—if they are asked to do too much of the one they cannot do enough for the other. (The 1949 devaluation proved largely abortive in its effects, mainly because soon after the event the engineering industries became overloaded with rearmament orders, leaving little scope either for higher exports or faster growth of capacity.)

[2] For the latest published estimates cf. E.C.E. *Economic Survey for Europe for 1969*, Part 1 (Geneva, United Nations, 1970), Chapter III.

facturing sector will be smaller, relatively to the rest of the economy, at any given rate of growth; with the consequence that, at a given ratio of investment to output, the rate of productivity growth will be lower.[1]

For both of these latter reasons—a high investment ratio and a high share of manufacturing in the growth of output—export-led growth generates a higher "underlying growth rate" than consumption-led growth. Of these two, the latter factor may be of quantitatively far greater importance, and though some of its effect will be temporary—i.e., will be confined to the phase in which the structure of the economy is adjusted to a higher rate of growth of the autonomous component of demand, and in which therefore both exports and investment grow at a *faster* rate than the G.D.P. as a whole—some of it will be permanent. Owing to the indefinite scope for technological progress through a continual increase in specialisation, and the subdivision of productive processes—the main reasons for continued economic progress adduced by Allyn Young in his famous Presidential address to the British Association forty-two years ago[2]—the rate of productivity growth will remain relatively high in the manufacturing sector, even when all sectors grow at the same rate. Also the "temporary" phase during which productivity growth in the economy should rise at a still faster rate relates to a period of structural change which, judging by the experience of other countries, may extend over several decades.

Fourth, since with "consumption-led" growth the growth of exports will follow the growth of productive capacity rather than lead it, while the growth of imports will be simultaneous with the growth of domestic consumption and investment (and may even precede it), the policy of internal demand management is likely to create a situation of inherent precariousness in the balance of payments—with the growth of imports always tending to exceed the growth of exports. This makes the task of policy-makers far more difficult; the success of the policy is more critic-

[1] According to the findings of the E.C.E. (*op. cit.*), the United Kingdom has been the country with one of the largest "negative residuals" in the relationship between the growth of manufacturing production and the stage of development, as measured by the level of G.D.P. per head.

[2] "Increasing Returns and Economic Progress", Glasgow meeting, September 1928 (*Economic Journal*, December 1928).

ally dependent on the accuracy of short-term forecasts—on the likely movement of exports, imports, consumption and investment in the near future, resulting from *existing* policies—with the result that inevitable errors in short-term forecasting force the Government to sudden and unforeseen counter-measures of a far too violent character. With export-led growth, the Government has far more elbow room to allow the effects of such errors to be reflected in fluctuations in the export–import balance—which means spreading this effect on the world economy as a whole, rather than making the home economy bear the full brunt of the consequential adjustment. Hence when demand management is founded on exchange-rate policy, and not on fiscal policy, the success of the policy is likely to be less dependent on the accuracy of short-term forecasts, and the problem of successful economic management is less difficult.

Thus the main cause of our post-war difficulties can be traced to a mistaken orientation in our general policies of economic management which made success more difficult to achieve operationally and which also made the reward of successful management a relatively meagre one.

But in saying this I do not wish to imply that the post-war attempt at "managing the economy" was a failure in the sense that we would have been better off without it. On the contrary, I am convinced that in comparison to the restoration of the pre-war system of *non*-management—which would have meant operating under a system of fixed exchange rates combined with a "neutral" fiscal policy—we have achieved higher employment and also more stability of employment; a higher level of investment, a faster rate of economic growth and also a faster trend rate of growth of exports. The reason for this is that the managed growth of the domestic market ensured a *certain* rate of growth of industrial capacity, which also induced, as a by-product, a steady growth in our capacity to export. Without it we might well have had not only more unemployment but also far less investment and, in consequence, an even worse export performance. Consumption-led growth is clearly preferable to economic stagnation—which might well have been the alternative if the autonomous growth of exports had not in itself been sufficient to keep up an adequate level of investment. But while our post-war policies may have thus served to mitigate, not aggravate, the long-term adverse trends in our international competitiveness due to the continued emergence of new industrial rivals, they have failed to come to grips with the basic problem, and have failed to devise policies for countering these trends effectively.

If we enter the Common Market, and the Community proceeds with its plans for currency integration and not just customs integration, our economic dilemmas are likely to become much greater. For not only shall we be precluded from employing the instrument of a managed exchange rate but our existing instrument of ensuring a continued growth of domestic demand through fiscal policy will itself be far more difficult to operate. Unless we manage to become the fast-growing industrial centre of the Community—a difficult prospect, if we start off by being the slow-growing area—we may be faced with the same problem of declining total demand and employment as our development areas have had during the last twenty years, and with no more ability to counter it by local policies, without external assistance.

The obstacles to gaining international acceptance for a policy of a "managed floating rate" may not now be as great as they would have been a few years ago—particularly if it were accompanied by an assurance that the policy will be so operated as to keep the growth of exports to a target rate that is a reasonable one in the light of the rate of growth of world trade as a whole. But it would be dangerous to underestimate the serious internal problems which the adjustment from "consumption-led growth" to "export-led growth" would involve—a far more difficult problem than if one had started from a situation of heavy unemployment, as in the 1920s.[1] The adjustment to the 1967 devaluation had to be accompanied by severe increases in

---

[1] Most countries who have successfully followed "export-led" growth, and attained relatively fast rates of growth of manufacturing output, started from a position of heavy "disguised unemployment" (rather than open unemployment) in the form of vast labour reserves in agriculture and services, which made it possible for them, through the growth in total industrial employment, to provide more resources for exports and investment, without restraining the growth of domestic consumption. This is not possible in a "mature economy", with near-full-employment, such as Britain. I have discussed the manpower aspects of the growth process in an earlier paper, *Causes of the Slow Rate of Economic Growth in the United Kingdom* (reprinted on p. 100 above).

taxation (as well as cuts in the Government's expenditure programmes) in order to release resources; the share of exports in the G.D.P. rose (in terms of constant 1963 prices) from the pre-devaluation figure of about 21 to 25 per cent in 1969; with export-led growth, this ratio would have to rise still higher. And while, with a tremendous effort, we have managed to release resources for the turn-round in the balance of payments, we have not yet adjusted the economy for the rise in investment (particularly of manufacturing investment) required to sustain a higher rate of growth. The ratio of consumption to G.D.P. in Britain is still appreciably higher, and that of investment lower, than in all the industrialised countries with higher trend rates of growth. The adjustment to an export-led growth with a higher underlying growth rate would require therefore holding back the growth of consumption for a further period—with all the political unpopularity which such a policy entails.

7

THE IRRELEVANCE OF EQUILIBRIUM ECONOMICS[1]

The purpose of my lecture today is to explain why, in my view, the prevailing theory of value— what I called, in a shorthand way, "equilibrium economics"—is barren and irrelevant as an apparatus of thought to deal with the manner of operation of economic forces, or as an instrument for non-trivial predictions concerning the effects of economic changes, whether induced by political action or by other causes. I should go further and say that the powerful attraction of the habits of thought engendered by "equilibrium economics" has become a major obstacle to the development of economics as a *science*—meaning by the term "science" a body of theorems based on assumptions that are *empirically* derived (from observations) and which embody hypotheses that are capable of verification both in regard to the assumptions and the predictions.

The word "equilibrium" in economics is used, of course, in all kinds of contexts—in Keynesian economics for example, or in theory of the balance of payments, and so on. I should therefore make clear that the notion of equilibrium to which I refer is that of the general economic equilibrium originally formulated by Walras, and developed, with ever-increasing elegance, exactness, and logical precision by the mathematical economists of our own generation, of whom perhaps the French economist, Gerard Debreu, is now regarded as the most prominent exponent.[2]

Taken at its purest and most abstract level, the pretensions of this equilibrium theory are modest enough. Although Debreu describes the subject-matter of his book as "the *explanation* of the

[1] Originally delivered as the Goodricke Lecture at the University of York, May 10, 1972. First printed in the *Economic Journal*, Vol. 82, December 1972.
[2] *Theory of Value, An Axiomatic Analysis of Economic Equilibrium*, Cowles Foundation Monograph no. 17, New York, 1959.

price of commodities resulting from the interaction of the agents of a private ownership economy",[1] it is clear that the term "explanation" is not used in the ordinary everyday sense of the term. It is intended in a purely logical and not in a "scientific" sense; in the strict sense, as Debreu says, the theory is "logically entirely disconnected from its interpretation". It is not put forward as an explanation of how the actual prices of commodities are determined in particular economies or in the world economy as a whole. By the term "explanation" Debreu means a set of theorems that are *logically* deducible from precisely formulated assumptions; and the purpose of the exercise is to find the minimum "basic assumptions" necessary for establishing the existence of an "equilibrium" set of prices (and output/input matrixes) that is (*a*) unique, (*b*) stable, (*c*) satisfies the conditions of Pareto optimality. The whole progress of mathematical economics in the last thirty to fifty years lay in clarifying the minimum requirements in terms of "basic assumptions" more precisely: without any attempt at verifying the realism of those assumptions, and without any investigation of whether the resulting theory of "equilibrium prices" has any explanatory power or relevance in relation to actual prices.

I. AXIOMATIC THEORY AND SCIENTIFIC HYPOTHESIS

It would take me too long to enumerate all these basic assumptions; it would also lead me away from my main argument. But unlike any scientific theory, where the basic assumptions are chosen on the basis of direct observation of the phenomena the behaviour of which forms the subject-matter of the theory, the basic assumptions of economic theory are either of a kind that are unverifiable—such as that producers "maximise" their profits or consumers "maximise" their utility—or of a kind which are directly contradicted by observation—for example, perfect competition, perfect divisibility, linear-homogeneous and continuously differentiable production functions, wholly impersonal market relations, exclusive rôle of prices in information flows and perfect knowledge of all relevant prices by all agents and

[1] *Ibid.*, p. vii, italics mine.

perfect foresight. There is also the requirement of a constant and unchanging set of *products* (goods) and of a constant and unchanging set of *processes of production* (or production functions) over time—though neither category, goods nor processes, is *operationally* defined: in other words, no attempt is made to show how these axiomatic concepts are to be defined or recognised in relation to empirical material.

While this pure theory is not *intended* to describe reality, it is put forward as the necessary conceptual framework—the necessary starting point—for any attempt at explaining how a "decentralised" system works; how individuals guided entirely by the market, or rather by price information, sort themselves out between different activities and thereby secure the maximum satisfaction both to themselves and, in the specific Pareto-sense, to society as a whole.

Indeed it is the deep underlying belief, common to all economists of the so-called "neo-classical" school, that general equilibrium theory is the one and only starting point for any logically consistent explanation of the behaviour of de-centralised economic systems. This belief sustained the theory despite the increasing (*not* diminishing) arbitrariness of its basic assumptions—which was forced upon its practitioners by the ever more precise cognition of the needs of logical consistency. In terms of gradually converting an "intellectual experiment" (to use Professor Kornai's phrase)[1] into a scientific theory—in other words, into a set of theorems directly related to observable phenomena[2]—the

---

[1] J. Kornai, *Anti-Equilibrium. On economic systems theory and the tasks of research*, Amsterdam, North Holland Publishing Co., 1971, p. 11.

[2] The difference between a scientific theory and an "axiomatic" theorem has been well put by Einstein:

"Physics constitute a logical system of thought which is in a state of evolution, whose basis cannot be distilled, as it were from experience by an inductive method, but can only be arrived at by free invention. The justification (truth content) of the system rests in the verification of the derived propositions by sense experiences."

"The skeptic will say: 'it may well be true that this system of equations is reasonable from a logical standpoint. But it does not prove that it corresponds to nature'. You are right, dear skeptic. Experience alone can decide on truth."

A. Einstein, *Ideas and Opinions*, New York, 1960, pp. 322 and 355 (quoted by Kornai, *op. cit.*, pp. 9–10).

The difference mainly resides in this. In the case of physics, any fundamental reconsideration of the basic "axioms" of the system is the result of observations which could not be made consistent with existing hypotheses. Examples (chosen at random) are the observation that the amount of radiation emitted by Pitchblende was greater than could be accounted for by the absorption of sunlight; that a stream of light

development of theoretical economics was one of continual *de*gress, not *pro*gress: the ship appears to be much further away from the shore now than it appeared to its originators in the nineteenth century. The latest theoretical models, which attempt to construct an equilibrium path through time with all prices for all periods fully determined at the start under the assumption that everyone foresees future prices correctly to eternity, require far more fundamental "relaxations" for their applicability than was thought to be involved in the original Walrasian scheme. The process of removing the "scaffolding", as the saying goes—in other words of *relaxing* the unreal basic assumptions—has not yet started. Indeed, the scaffolding gets thicker and more impenetrable with every successive reformulation of the theory, with growing uncertainty as to whether there is a solid building underneath.

Yet the main lessons of these increasingly abstract and unreal theoretical constructions are also increasingly taken on trust—as if in the social sciences, unlike the natural sciences, the problem of verification could be passed over or simply ignored. It is generally taken for granted by the great majority of academic economists that the economy always approaches, or is near to, a state of "equilibrium"; that equilibrium, and hence the near-actual state of the world, provides goods and services to the maximum degree consistent with available resources; that there is full and efficient utilisation of every kind of "resource"; that the wage of every kind and quality of labour is a measure of the net contribution (per unit) of these varying kinds and qualities of labour to the total product; that the rate of profits reflects the net advantage of substituting capital for labour in production, etc., etc.—all propositions which the *pure* mathe-

---

which passed through a glass and was directed at a mirror at some particular angle is not reflected by the mirror; or that there is a "reddening" of the spectrum observed in distant stars. In economics, observations which contradict the basic hypotheses of prevailing theory are generally ignored: the "theorist" and the "empiricist" operate in two isolated compartments and the challenge of anomalous observations is ignored by the theorist—as something that could be taken into account at the stage of "second approximation" without affecting the basic hypotheses. And where empirical material is brought into conjunction with a theoretical model, as in econometrics, the rôle of empirical estimation is to "illustrate" or to "decorate" the theory, not to provide support to the basic hypothesis (as for example, in the case of numerous studies purporting to estimate the coefficients of production functions).

matical economist has shown to be valid only on assumptions that are manifestly unreal—that is to say, directly contrary to experience and not just "abstract". In fact, equilibrium theory has reached the stage where the pure theorist has successfully (though perhaps inadvertently) demonstrated that the main implications of this theory cannot possibly hold in reality, but has not yet managed to pass his message down the line to the textbook writer and to the classroom.

Yet without a major act of demolition—without destroying the basic conceptual framework—it is impossible to make any real progress. There is, I am sure, a vague sense of dissatisfaction, open or suppressed, with the current state of economics among most members of the economics profession—as is evidenced, for example, by recent Presidential addresses to the Royal Economic Society and to section F of the British Association.[1] On the one hand it is increasingly recognised that abstract mathematical models lead nowhere. On the other hand it is also recognised that "econometrics" leads nowhere—the careful accumulation and sifting of statistics and the development of refined methods of statistical inference cannot make up for the lack of any basic understanding of how the actual economy works. Each year new fashions sweep the "politico-economic complex" only to disappear again with equal suddenness—who can now recollect the great revival of the quantity theory of money of three years ago, or the more recent belief that frequent fiscal adjustments, guided by the best forecasting techniques, can maintain the steady growth of the economy at its pre-determined growth potential, not to speak of the Phillips Curve? These sudden bursts of fashion are a sure sign of the "pre-scientific" stage, where any crazy idea can get a hearing simply because nothing is known with sufficient confidence to rule it out.

---

[1] E. H. Phelps Brown, "The Underdevelopment of Economics"; G. D. N. Worswick, "Is Progress in Economic Science Possible?", *Economic Journal*, March 1972, pp. 9–20 and 73–86.

II. WHERE ECONOMIC THEORY WENT WRONG

The difficulty with a new start is to pinpoint the critical area where economic theory went astray. In my own view, it happened when the theory of value took over the centre of the stage—which meant focusing attention on the *allocative* functions of markets to the exclusion of their *creative* functions—as an instrument for transmitting impulses to economic change.

To locate the source of error with more precision, I would put it in the middle of the fourth chapter of Vol. I of the *Wealth of Nations*. The first three chapters are devoted to the principle of the Division of Labour. These explain that the larger the production, the lower real cost per unit tends to be, because the larger the production, the more efficient the modes of production that can be employed: the greater the specialisation and the sub-division into different processes. In the first chapter Smith gave numerous reasons for this basic law, beautifully illustrated by the example of pin-making. In the second chapter he explains the peculiarly human characteristic of the propensity to truck, barter and exchange one thing for another—"nobody ever saw a dog make a fair exchange of one bone for another with another dog"—which alone makes it possible to develop the division of labour through social co-operation. Indeed for Smith the existence of a "social economy" and the existence of increasing returns were closely related phenomena. And the third chapter, perhaps the most significant of them all, is devoted to the proposition "that the division of labour is limited by the extent of the market"—a theorem which Allyn Young, writing 150 years later (in a paper to which I shall refer more extensively presently), regarded as "one of the most illuminating and fruitful generalisations which can be found anywhere in the whole literature of economics".

But in the following chapter, after discussing the need for money in a social economy, Smith suddenly gets fascinated by the distinction between money price, real price and exchange value, and from then on, hey presto, his interest gets bogged down in the question of how values and prices for products and factors are determined. One can trace a more or less continuous development of price theory from the subsequent chapters of Smith through Ricardo, Walras, Marshall, right up to Debreu and the most sophisticated of present-day Americans.

The basic assumption of this theory is constant costs, or constant returns to scale. With Smith and Ricardo, this was implicit in the very notion of the "natural price" determined solely by costs of production (irrespective of demand). With the neo-classical school—in any rigorous formulation of it—it was explicit in the assumption of homogeneous and linear production functions which is one of the required "axioms" necessary to make the assumptions of perfect competition and profit-maxi-misation consistent with one another.[1] Though Marshall, through the notion of "external economies" and the use of the partial equilibrium technique, thought he could accommodate both increasing and decreasing returns to scale within the same analytical framework—an attempt which was shown to be logically faulty in Piero Sraffa's famous 1926 article on the Laws of Returns[2]—the general equilibrium school (as distinct from Marshall) has always fully recognised the *absence* of increasing returns as one of the basic "axioms" of the system. As a result, the existence of increasing returns and its consequences for the whole framework of economic theory have been completely neglected.

III. THE DOMINATING ROLE OF INCREASING RETURNS

Yet on an empirical level, nobody doubts that in any economic activity which involves the processing or transformation of basic materials—in other words, in industry—increasing returns dominate the picture for the very reasons given by Adam Smith in the first chapter of the *Wealth of Nations*: reasons that are

---

[1] This of course, embraces the classical case of increasing costs of production (in terms of labour and capital) due to the fixity of supply of land, provided the fixed factor earns its due rent. It is *not* consistent however with diminishing returns to scale—when *all* factors are increased in the same proportion, and the product increases in less than the same proportion—due, e.g., to "external diseconomies."

[2] "The Laws of Returns under Competitive Conditions", *Economic Journal*, December 1926, p. 535. To be fair, Sraffa's critique had more relevance to the "Marshallian school" at Cambridge (and particularly to Pigou) than to Marshall himself who always expressed considerable doubt about the applicability of the theory of "normal price" to the case of increasing returns. (See particularly Appendix H of the *Principles*.)

fundamental to the nature of technological processes and not to any particular technology.[1] One aspect of this is that *plant costs* per unit of output necessarily decrease with size in any integrated process of operation—such as a steel plant, a chemical plant, an electricity generator or an oil tanker—simply on account of the three-dimensional nature of space.[2] Provided the technical problems of construction can be solved, an increase in size is bound to bring further cost reductions since capacity is bound to increase faster than construction cost.[3] In the last decade, for example, there have been very large increases in the size of generating stations, of oil tankers and of the "optimal" steel plants, and there appears to be no reason why this process should come to a halt.

Another aspect, to which Allyn Young attributed major importance, is the break-up of complex processes into a series of simple processes, "some of which at least lend themselves to the use of machinery." He argued that the extent to which capital is used in relation to labour is predominantly a matter of the scale of operations—the capital/labour ratio in production is a function of the extent of the market rather than of relative factor prices.[4]

[1] As Smith emphasised in the first chapter, the opportunities for enrichment through a greater division of labour are far more important in manufactures than in agriculture: "The most opulent nations, indeed, excel all their neighbours in agriculture as well as in manufactures; but they are commonly more distinguished by their superiority in the latter than the former."

[2] For a discussion of this cf. G. C. Hufbauer, *Synthetic Materials and the Theory of International Trade*, Duckworth, London, 1966, pp. 46 ff. For a much earlier account of the same idea, cf. E. A. G. Robinson, *The Structure of Competitive Industry*, Cambridge, 1931, pp. 29–31.

[3] For example, the cost of construction of a cylinder (or a pipeline) may be assumed to vary with the size of the diameter, since $2r\pi$ will indicate the size of the surface to be covered per unit of length. The capacity of the cylinder will grow on the other hand as the square of the radius, $r^2\pi$. Since a larger cylinder will require a thicker steelplate, the material costs will increase more than in proportion, but the labour costs will increase less than in proportion. Assuming that labour and material costs *together* vary in linear proportion to r, and assuming that one wished to describe this relation in terms of a "production function" of the Cobb-Douglas type (i.e., with a constant elasticity of substitution of unity) the sum of the coefficients of the function would add up exactly to 2. See also Appendix on "Indivisibilities and Increasing Returns," below.

[4] "It would be wasteful to make a hammer to drive a single nail; it would be better to use whatever awkward implement lies conveniently at hand. It would be wasteful to furnish a factory with an elaborate equipment of specially constructed jigs, lathes, drills, presses and conveyors to build a hundred automobiles; it would be better to rely mostly upon tools and machines of standard types, *so as to make a relatively larger use of directly-applied and a relatively smaller use of indirectly-applied labour*. Mr. Ford's

Finally, there are the inventions and innovations induced by experience to which Adam Smith paid the main emphasis—what we now call "learning by doing," or "dynamic economies of scale". The advance in scientific knowledge in physics or in the science of engineering in the laboratory cannot by itself secure the innumerable design improvements that result from the repeated application of particular engineering principles. The optimum design for the steam engine or for the diesel engine or the sewing machine has only been achieved after many years or decades of experience: that for the nuclear power plant is still far away. The gain in design through experience is even more important in the making of plant and equipment; hence the *annual* gain of productivity due to "embodied technical progress" will tend to be all the greater the larger the number of plants constructed per year.[1]

It was left to Allyn Young to explore the main implications of Adam Smith's theorem on the manner of operation of economic forces in his famous article "Increasing Returns and Economic Progress", originally given as a Presidential address to Section F of the British Association in 1928.[2] On re-reading this paper after a lapse of many years, I feel convinced that it was so many years ahead of its time that the progress of economic thought has passed it by despite the attention it received at the time of its original publication. Economists ceased to take any notice of it long before they were able to grasp its full revolutionary implications. This was partly because Young was a man of exceptional

---

methods would be absurdly uneconomical if his output were very small, and would be unprofitable even if his output were what many other manufacturers of automobiles would call large." *Op. cit.*, below, p. 530, italics added.

[1] On all these aspects there is a rapidly growing volume of empirical evidence, which makes the neglect of increasing returns by the theoretical model-builders all the more surprising. Taking only more recent publications, there is, apart from the sources cited by Hufbauer, *op. cit.*, the Annex on "Industrial Profiles" to the *Manual of Industrial Project Analysis* issued by the O.E.C.D. Development Centre (the Manual, but *not* the Annex, was prepared by I. M. D. Little and J. A. Mirrlees) which shows very large scale-economies in every one of the 18 types of industrial activities, such as brick-making, sugar manufacture, meat packaging, ironfounding, etc. for which detailed estimates are given. C. F. Pratten found (*Economies of Scale in Manufacturing Industry* D.A.E. Occasional Paper No. 28, Cambridge University Press, 1971) that of 44 types of activities examined, the minimum efficient scale for a *single plant* is 100 per cent or more of total U.K. output in 7 cases, and in the range of 25–80 per cent in 10 other cases. (This does not take into account, of course, economies due to greater differentiation and subdivision of processes.)

[2] *Economic Journal*, December 1928, pp. 527–42.

modesty who underplayed, rather than emphasised, the full implication of what he was saying; his manner of exposition is suggestive, rather than compelling, and at times (as for example in the Appendix attached to the paper) obscure. It was partly also because its importance as a basic criticism of general equilibrium theory could not be appreciated at a time when that theory itself was not properly understood.

The consequences of abandoning the axiom of "linearity" and assuming that, in general, the production of any one commodity, or any one group of commodities, is subject to increasing returns to scale, are very far-reaching. The first and most important casualty is the notion of "general equilibrium" as such. The very notion of "general equilibrium" carries the implication that it is legitimate to assume that the operation of economic forces is constrained by a set of exogenous variables which are "given" from the outside and stable over time. It assumes that economic forces operate in an environment that is "imposed" on the system in a sense other than being just a heritage of the past—one could almost say an environment which, in its most significant characteristics, is independent of history. These critical exogenous features of the "environment" include Pareto's "tastes and obstacles"—the preferences of individuals as consumers, the transformation functions of factors into the products and the supply of resources—at any rate of "ultimate resources" —which are thus transformed. The notion of general equilibrium also assumes that the nature of the functions and of the social institutions—in particular the markets—are such that any given constellation of such exogenous variables will inevitably lead the system, possibly through a succession of steps, to a state of rest characterised by unchanging prices and production patterns over time: in other words that whatever the initial situation, the system will converge on a *unique point* the exact nature of which, both as regards the price system and the output system, can be deduced from the "data". Continuous economic change on these assumptions can only be conceived as some kind of "moving equilibrium" through the postulate of an autonomous (and unexplained) time-rate of change in the exogenous variables of a kind that is consistent with "continuous equilibrium" through time—such as a given rate of shift per unit of time in the production function of the so-called "Harrod-neutral" type or in the supply or resources: an exogenous rate of growth in the labour force and/or in the rate of increase in "capital"—though the very meaning of the latter concept has given rise to insoluble problems.

IV. THE THEOREM OF ENDOGENOUS AND CUMULATIVE CHANGE

Once, however, we allow for increasing returns, the forces making for continuous changes are *endogenous*—"they are engendered from within the economic system"[1]—and the actual state of the economy during any one "period" cannot be predicted except as a.result of the sequence of events in previous periods which led up to it. As Young put it, with increasing returns "change becomes progressive and propagates itself in a cumulative way".[2] Further, "no analysis of the forces making for economic equilibrium, forces which you might say are tangential at any moment of time, will serve to illumine this field, for movements away from equilibrium, departures from previous trends, are characteristic of it".[3]

The basic consideration underlying Young's analysis is surprisingly the same as that underlying Say's Law. If one takes an all-inclusive view of the economic process, economic activity ultimately consists of the exchange of goods against goods; this means that every increase in the supply of commodities enlarges, *at least potentially*, the market for other commodities. (The qualification "potentially", as we shall see, is very important and distinguishes Young's views from that of Say or Mill.) Hence the "extent of the market" depends on the division of labour almost as much, according to Young, as the division of labour depends on the extent of the market; and [quoting Young again] "modified . . . in the light of this broader conception of the market, Adam Smith's dictum amounts to the theorem that the division of labour depends in large part upon the division

[1] Young, *op. cit.*, p. 530.
[2] *Op. cit.*, p. 533.
[3] *Op. cit.*, p. 528.

of labour. *This is more than mere tautology.* It means that the counter forces which are continually defeating the forces which make for economic equilibrium are more pervasive and more deeply rooted than we commonly realise."[1]

Myrdal, writing twenty-five years later, called this the "principle of circular and cumulative causation".[2] But neither Young nor Myrdal expressed the consequences in the radical form stated by Hicks[3] who said that "unless we can suppose . . . that marginal costs generally increase with output at the point of equilibrium" . . . "the basis on which economic laws can be constructed is shorn away". The words "economic laws" and "at the point of equilibrium" are of course question-begging. The issue is whether such laws (and "economic equilibrium") exist or not. In the scientific sense, the postulate of the existence of such "laws" is refuted if they can be logically shown to be valid only under assumptions that are contrary to observed phenomena.

The whole issue, as Young said, is whether an "equilibrium of costs and advantages" is a meaningful notion in the presence of increasing returns.[4] When every change in the use of resources —every reorganisation of productive activities—creates the opportunity for a further change *which would not have existed otherwise,* the notion of an "optimum" allocation of resources— when every particular resource makes as great or greater contribution to output in its actual use as in any alternative use— becomes a meaningless and contradictory notion: the pattern of the use of resources at any one time can be no more than a link in the chain of an unending sequence and the very distinction, vital to equilibrium economics, between resource-creation and resource-allocation loses its validity. The whole view of the economic process as a medium for the "allocation of scarce means between alternative uses" falls apart—except perhaps for the consideration of short-run problems, where the framework of social organisation and the distribution of the major part of available "resources", such as durable equipment and trained or educated labour, can be treated as given as a heritage of the

---

[1] *Ibid.*, p. 533. My italics.
[2] *Economic Theory and Underdeveloped Regions,* London, Duckworth, 1957.
[3] *Value and Capital,* Oxford, 1939, pp, p. 88–9.
[4] *Op. cit.,* p. 535.

past, and the effects of current decisions on future development are ignored.[1]

Young saw clearly that the combination of Say's Law with Adam Smith's theorem is not enough in itself to ensure that change is progressive and "propagates itself in a cumulative way". Something more is needed linking the effects of changes of production to demand: something that would ensure that an increase in supply emanating from any particular part of the economy has a stimulating effect, and not a depressing effect, on production in other parts. Given that factor, the process of economic development can be looked upon as the resultant of a continued process of interaction—one could almost say, of a chain-reaction—between demand increases which have been induced by increases in supply, and increases in supply which have been evoked by increases in demand. Lacking a theory of income generation such as was supplied by Keynes in the General Theory eight years later, he thought that the necessary additional condition to ensure a continued chain reaction is to be found in the nature of reciprocal demand and supply functions—in other words, in the elasticity of Marshallian "offer curves", when the "commodities exchanged are produced competitively, under conditions of increasing returns". According to Young, when the demand for each commodity is elastic, "in the special sense that a small increase in its supply will be attended by an increase in the amounts of other commodities which can be had in exchange for it" progress is bound to be cumulative for "under such conditions an increase in the supply of one commodity *is* an increase in the demand for other commodities, and it must be supposed that every increase in demand will evoke an increase in supply. The rate at which any one industry grows is conditioned by the rate at which other industries grow, but since the elasticity of demand and supply will differ for different products, some industries will grow faster than others. *Even with a stationary population and in the absence of new discoveries in pure and applied*

---

[1] The only respect in which market prices have an indispensable "allocative" function to fulfil is that involved in the distribution over time of the use of *exhaustible* natural resources (i.e., in the decision how far the current use of such resources should be restricted for the sake of the future) and it is notorious that it is in this respect that the price mechanism fails completely in making any allowance for the probable higher scarcity of such resources in the future.

science (as contrasted with such new ways of organising production and such new 'inventions' as are merely adaptations of known ways of doing things, made practicable and economical by an enlarged scale of production) *there are no limits to the process of expansion except the limits beyond which demand is not elastic and returns do not increase.*"[1]

V. THE ROLE OF DEMAND AND THE TWO KINDS OF "INDUCED INVESTMENT"

If the above passage has not received the attention which it deserved, it was, I believe, mainly because of the obscurity surrounding the meaning of "elasticity of demand" in the particular context. Clearly what Young intuitively perceived was that the pre-condition of cumulative change is that the rise in production of any one commodity *a*, should be associated with an increase in demand for all other commodities. He thought that this condition will be satisfied when the elasticity of demand for commodity *a* is greater than unity, since in that case the sales-receipts (or income) of the producers of *a* will be the greater the larger the production.

A little reflection will show however that if by "elasticity of demand" we mean something which is a reflection of the elasticity of substitution of consumers—in other words, of the elasticity of "flow" demand, as defined below—the increase in purchasing power of the producers of commodity *a* following upon the rise in the production of *a* must have been the result of a *diversion* of expenditure in favour of *a* and against other commodities. The rise in incomes of the *a* producers must therefore be offset by reduced incomes of the producers of some other commodities. It is possible that if the elasticities of substitution are high, and income elasticities are all positive, the elasticities of demand for all commodities, *taken individually*, should be greater

---

[1] Young, op. cit., p. 534, italics mine. In a footnote attached to the beginning of the above passage, Young also says that "if the circumstance that commodity *a* is produced under conditions of increasing return is taken into account as a factor in the elasticity of demand for *b* in terms of *a*, elasticity of demand and elasticity of supply may be looked upon as different ways of expressing a single functional relation". This almost suggests the view that the elasticity of demand for some commodities is a reflection of the elasticity of supply of other commodities.

than unity. But this is not enough to produce a chain reaction of rising demand followed by rising production, followed by rising demand, and so on, unless *total income* measured in terms of money is rising as well, which in turn presupposes that *total* expenditure, and not just the expenditure on a particular commodity, rises in response to a rise in production.

In order to show how an increase in the production of a commodity may involve the generation of additional incomes which in turn generates additional demand for other commodities and thereby becomes a "chain" in a continuous sequence, we must first of all take into account the fact that there are two kinds of demand (and supply) in a market: a "flow" demand and a "stock" demand: the former is the demand and supply of "outsiders" (i.e., producers and consumers), whereas the latter represents the demand (or supply) originating from *inside* the market.

In pure theory the existence of this "stock" demand or "inside demand" is ignored. In a state of equilibrium, production and consumption, or "flow"-demand and "flow"-supply, are necessarily equal in each market, and in the rarefied world of Walrasian perfection where markets are *continually* in equilibrium, the question of how the market responds to "disequilibria" does not arise because all such "disequilibria" are ruled out—all equilibrating adjustments are assumed to be instantaneous, either because changes are timeless or because all changes have been perfectly foreseen.

However, the markets of the real world are not in continuous equilibrium in this sense; there are, or can be, persistent differences between production and consumption which are reflected in increments or decrements in stocks. The impact effect of any undesigned or unexpected rise in production (due to a bumper harvest, for example) must be a rise in stocks; any subsequent adjustment in flow-demand or supply due to consequential price-changes requires time to materialise. For that reason, competitive markets are inconceivable without intermediaries—merchants or "dealers"—who are both buyers and sellers at the same time (at different prices) and who carry stocks so as to make "a market" that enables producers to sell and consumers to buy.

The size of the difference between their buying and selling prices (normally called the "dealer's margin") depends both on the degree of perfection of the market in which they operate and on the amount of "processing" or "transformation" performed by them. This may consist of pure merchanting activities—such as transportation, breaking bulk, packaging, etc.—and could also include varying degrees of physical transformation through manufacture. But what differentiates a merchant from other economic agents (such as a "producer") is that his natural response to "outside" influences is to vary the size of his stock—to absorb stocks in the face of excess supplies and to release stocks in the face of excess demand. The merchants' function in other words is to create and preserve an "orderly" market which they can only do through their willingness to act as a shock-absorber: through their readiness to enlarge their commitments when prices are sagging, and to curtail commitments when they are rising. The very notion of "merchanting" or "commercial" activities involves therefore the assumption that there is a certain elasticity of demand for *holding* stocks by the traders: an elasticity which is ultimately governed by the traders' expectations concerning prices and selling opportunities in the future. In a paper published many years ago I called this factor the "elasticity of speculative stocks" in a market[1] though the term "speculative" was perhaps a misnomer. It is true of course that traders only carry stocks in the expectation of making a profit, and therefore any inter-temporal transfer of goods could be called a form of "speculation," though it is fundamentally no different from any geographical transfer; and since the transportation of goods takes time, merchanting activities normally involve transfers of both kinds.[2]

---

[1] "Speculation and Economic Stability", *Review of Economic Studies*, October, 1939, p. 7 (reprinted in *Essays on Economic Stability and Growth*, London, Duckworth, 1960, p. 30).
[2] Any kind of merchanting activity—buying things with a view to their subsequent re-sale—is "speculative" in the sense that it involves the assumption of risks: by carrying stocks, traders *deliberately* take an "open position". Hence an increase in investment in stocks which occurs in response to an increase in supplies, though "induced", is a form of "voluntary" investment and not "involuntary". On the other hand, an increase in stocks which occurs as a result of a disappointment in sales-expectations—failure to *close* a position at the time and to the extent expected—may be regarded as "involuntary investment", in the sense that the addition to

It is a hen-and-egg question whether historically it was the growth of commerce which continually enlarged "the size of the market" and thereby enabled increasing returns to be realised, or whether it was the improvement of techniques of production and the improvement in communication which led to the growth of commerce. In the process of the development of capitalism the two operated side by side. And it involved a tendency for a continual rise in the *value* (and not just the volume) of stock carried by traders in the markets, which meant in turn that the growth of production resulting from any favourable change on the supply side led to a growth in incomes which in turn generated an increase in effective demand for commodities.

The essential element missing from Young's presentation, and which can only be supplied on the basis of Keynesian economics, is the addition to incomes resulting from the accumulation of capital (in other words, from investment expenditure) combined with the induced character of such investment which arises more or less as a by-product of changes in the organisation of production.[1] It operates moreover in two different ways. In the really "competitive" markets, such as those for most primary products, which approximate the economist's notion of perfect competition (where individual buyers and sellers are faced with infinitely elastic demand and supply curves, and where increasing returns *cannot* be operative, at any rate at the level of the individual producer) the stocks which are essential for the functioning of the market are carried by merchants who are independent both from the producers and the consumers; it is their ability to act as a buffer—to absorb stocks in the face of a short-term excess of supply and vice versa—which will lead to induced

stocks *ex-post* must have been greater than that planned *ex ante*. However, any step which implies an increase in commitments—the "opening" of a position—may be assumed to be deliberate, even when in response to events which may have been unforeseen.

[1] On re-reading Young in the light of Keynes, one is tempted to quote Keynes' account of Marshall's view that " . . . those individuals who are endowed with a special genius for the subject and have a powerful economic intuition will often be more right in their conclusions and implicit presumptions than in their explanation and explicit statements. That is to say, their intuitions will be in advance of their analysis and their terminology. Great respect, therefore, is due to their general scheme of thought, and it is a poor thing to pester their memories with criticism which is really verbal." (*Economic Journal*, September 1924, p. 235, note, reprinted in *Essays in Biography*, p. 232.)

investment in the face of a rise in production: provided that the merchants' expectation of future prices makes it appear profitable for them to increase the *value* of their stocks (and not only their volume) when prices sag in the face of excess supply.[1] In the markets for commodities in which increasing returns are important, and which, for that very reason, are only "imperfectly" competitive—as is the case with manufactures—the producers carry their *own* stocks and adjust the rate of their production in response to changes in their sales (or in the state of their "order book") and there will be "induced investment" in response to an *increase* in demand and the associated depletion of stocks. Such induced investment will partly take the form of circulating capital—that is to say, of an increase in the value of goods in process that is inevitably associated with the rise in production—and partly of fixed capital, in so far as the rise in current sales causes a revision of expectation of future sales.

It may seem paradoxical that "induced investment" should result from both increases in supply and increases in demand, but there is nothing necessarily inconsistent in this, provided there is asymmetry in market organisation between the two kinds of commodities, primary products and manufactures, an asymmetry which is imposed on the system by the differing incidence of the theorem of the "division of labour" between industry and agriculture—a feature of life which was already noted by Adam Smith. If, in the first approximation, one regards the essential division in economic activities as that between manufacturing activities and land-based activities (agriculture and mining) which provide the inputs (the food and raw materials) for manufacturing activities, and if we suppose that the quasi-automatic process of growing diversification and technological improvement resulting from the growth of activities—in other words increasing returns in the broad sense—is mainly a feature of the latter

---

[1] Strictly speaking, there should be a net demand effect in real terms whenever there is an increase in the volume of stocks carried in relation to turnover (and not only when there is a rise in the total value of stocks) since any such increment implies a rise in investment (in real terms) in relation to output. However, when the merchants' elasticity of demand for increasing the stock-turnover ratio is less than unity—so that a 1 per cent increase in the volume of stocks carried requires more than a 1 per cent reduction in price—the purchasing power of producers will diminish in consequence of a rise in production, while the (theoretically) more-than-offsetting rise in the real purchasing power of consumers will be slow to percolate through the system.

rather than the former, then the process of endogenous self-sustained growth requires both a certain *inelasticity* of expectations concerning *prices* (in regard to primary products) and also a certain *elasticity* of expectations concerning the *volume* of sales (in regard to manufactures). Induced investment reflecting the "acceleration principle" is a property of the latter; induced investment reflecting the price-stabilising effect of the operation of traders is a property of the former.[1]

And it requires, above all, a monetary and banking system that enables capital investment to increase in response to inducements, so as to generate the savings required to finance additional investment out of the *addition* to production and incomes. This is the real significance of the invention of paper money and of credit creation through the banking system. It provided the precondition of self-sustained growth. With a purely metallic currency, where the supply of money is given irrespective of the demand for credit, the ability of the system to expand in response to profit opportunities is far more narrowly confined.

VI. SOME CONCLUSIONS

To end, we can do little more than to sketch some of the main consequences of this marriage of the Smith-Young doctrine on increasing returns with the Keynesian doctrine of effective demand. I should like to make three observations.

First, the sharp distinction made by Keynes between a "full employment" situation where real income is confined by resource-endowment, and an unemployment situation where it is limited by effective demand, disappears in the presence of increasing returns. Except in a purely short-term sense, total output can never be *confined* by resources. At any one time, there is, or there may be, a maximum potential output for the world as a whole resulting from past history which has determined the existing network of institutions and organisations, the different kinds of plant and equipment available and their geographical distribu-

---

[1] In post-Keynesian models of cycles and growth (such as, for example, Hicks, *A Theory of the Trade Cycle,* Oxford, 1950) the only kind of "induced investment" considered was the demand-induced kind—the kind relevant to the manufacturing sector. The other, induced by excess supply, was completely neglected.

tion, as well as the distribution of the available labour in all the different areas and their educational endowments and skills. Over a period, there may be a maximum *rate of growth* of output determined by the maximum rate of growth of production in some key sectors of the economy (such as the food-producing sectors) which limits the sustainable rates of growth of the other sectors. If that happens, it must be on account of the scarcity of natural resources, and the impossibility of substituting capital goods for natural resources at more than a certain speed, on account of an insufficiency of land-saving innovations. But if we take an inclusive view, neither labour nor capital can limit either the level, or the rate of growth, of production over a longer period. Capital accumulation can always be speeded up— or rather it automatically *gets* speeded up, with a faster growth of production. In the case of labour, there is no such thing as an "optimal" distribution of the labour force—with each man making a greater contribution to output in his existing employment than in any alternative employment—since every re-organisation of production resulting from overall expansion or new investment will mean the transfer of some of the labour force to new employments where its contribution to production will be greater than before. Just as Young emphasised that the adoption of more roundabout methods of production, due to an increase in the size of the market, and the adoption of more capital-intensive processes, are different facets of the same thing, so in the case of labour, no valid distinction can be made between an increase in the effective labour supply due to a rise in numbers employed and that due to a rise in productivity secured by a re-deployment of labour.

Second, it is evident that the co-existence of increasing returns and competition—emphasised by Young and also by Marx, but wholly excluded by the axiomatic framework of Walrasian economics—is a very prominent feature of de-centralised economic systems but the manner of functioning of which is still a largely uncharted territory for the economist. We have no clear idea of *how* competition works in circumstances where each producer faces a limited market as regards *sales* and yet a highly competitive market as regards *price*.

H

Third, it is evident from our analysis that the "self-sustained growth" of decentralised economic systems, largely directed not by exogenous factors, but by the growth and the constellation of demand, is a fragile thing which will only proceed in a satisfactory manner if a number of favourable factors are present simultaneously: such as merchants who are ready to absorb stocks in the short run rather than allow prices to fall too far—because experience has taught them that market prices have some long-run stability—and manufacturers who respond to the stimulus of growing sales with an expansion of productive capacity, because experience has taught them that over a period markets are growing and not stable. It also requires a "passive" monetary and banking system which allows the money supply to grow in automatic response to an increased demand for credit.

In the nineteenth century, with the background of rapid technological change, particularly in transport and communications, all these factors seem to have been present. In the present century, continued growth seems to have owed more to active government intervention—in the primary producing areas, through government-operated buffer stocks for commodities; in the industrialised countries, through "Keynesian" fiscal policies; both of which secured the continued growth of *real* purchasing power (i.e., of effective demand in real terms and not just in money terms) without which economic growth would quickly grind to a halt.

APPENDIX

ON INDIVISIBILITIES AND INCREASING RETURNS

In an article published in the *Economic Journal* in 1934 I wrote that

" . . . it appears methodologically convenient to treat all cases of large-scale economies under the heading 'indivisibility'. This introduces a certain unity into analysis and makes possible at the same time a clarification of the relationships between the different kinds of economies. Even the cases of increasing returns where a more-than-proportionate increase in output occurs merely on account of an increase in the amounts of the factors used, without any change in the proportions of the factors, are due to indivisibilities; only in this case it is not so much the 'original factors,' but the specialised functions of those factors, which are indivisible."[1]

This proposition was later criticised in some detail by E. H. Chamberlin[2] while my own view was subsequently defended by Tjalling C. Koopmans.[3] I did not participate in this subsequent controversy since the question of whether increasing returns are "fundamentally" due to indivisibilities or not, did not then appear to me a matter of great moment. Recently, however, on reading Professor Koopmans' defence of my 1934 views, I have come to the conclusion that I ought to make a belated apology to the memory of the late Professor Chamberlin and acknowledge that he was basically right in his main contention—even though I was not persuaded by his arguments at the time.

The point is of more than semantic interest since if indivisibilities were the sole cause of increasing returns, there would always be some level of production at which such scale economies were exhausted and "optimum scale" production reached. Moreover, the prevalence of competition could itself be taken as an indication that the effects of "indivisibilities" are not such as to prevent optimum-scale production prevailing for a sufficiently small fraction of total output to be consistent with a reasonable approximation to perfect competition.

As was shown above, not all causes of increasing returns can be attributed to indivisibility of one kind or another and there is no reason to suppose that "economies of scale" become inoperative above certain levels of production. There is first of all the steady and step-wise improvement in knowledge gained from experience—the so-called "dynamic economies of scale" which

---

[1] "The Equilibrium of the Firm", *Economic Journal*, March 1934, p. 65, reprinted in *Essays on Value and Distribution*, p. 39.
[2] "Proportionality, Divisibility and Economies of Scale", *Quarterly Journal of Economics*, February 1948, reprinted as Appendix B to the sixth edition of *The Theory of Monopolistic Competition*, Cambridge, Mass., 1948.
[3] *Three Essays on the State of Economic Science*, New York, McGraw-Hill, 1957, pp. 150–2.

have nothing to do with indivisibilities. But even in the field of "static" or "reversible" economies, there is the important group of cases which I described above as being due to the three-dimensional nature of space—i.e., the fact that the capacity of, say, a pipeline can be quadrupled by doubling its diameter while the costs (in terms of labour and materials) are more nearly related to the diameter than to its capacity. There is nothing "indivisible" about tubes or pipelines as such: technically, it may be just as easy to make tubes of a relatively small or a relatively large dimension and there can be a continuous range of sizes in between; the existence of a non-linear relationship between costs and capacity is inherent in the nature of *space*, and there is nothing "indivisible" about space as such. Moreover, this "space principle" applies equally to non-durable items (like plastic containers or paper bags) no less than to durable equipment (like steel pipes).

Professor Koopmans mentions the case of the pipeline explicitly but misses the point of the example:

"I have not found one example of increasing returns to scale in which there is not some indivisible commodity in the surrounding circumstances. The oft-quoted case of a pipeline *whose diameter is continuously variable* can be seen as a case of choice between alternative pieces of capital equipment, differing in diameter, used to carry oil from Tulsa to Chicago, say. *No matter what diameter is selected, one entire pipeline of the requisite length is needed to render this service. Half the length* of the line does not carry half the flow of oil from Tulsa to Chicago."[1]

There is a clear misunderstanding here as to the relevance of the indivisibilities involved to the existence of increasing returns. This has nothing to do with the *length* of the pipeline but only with the *width* of the pipeline: the "indivisibility" on the other hand (as Koopmans says) relates to the length and not the width. Increasing returns arise because the capacity of a pipeline of *unit length* to carry oil—i.e., the maximum volume of throughput

[1] *Op. cit.*, p. 152, n. 3. Italics mine.

per unit of time—increases with the square of diameter, whereas the cost of production is a linear function of it. If a pipe of 5 feet diameter can transmit 5,000 tons per hour, a pipe with 10 feet diameter will transmit 20,000 tons per hour, and so on.

Professor Koopmans' method, if I understand him correctly, is to treat pipelines of differing diameters as different "commodities", so that the choice of a pipeline with a particular diameter comes to the same as the choice of a particular "linear activity", or process of production. He regards every produced commodity which has the characteristic that "the ratios of inputs into their manufacture to outputs from their use cannot be reproduced at a smaller scale" as undergoing a "qualitative change" with every change in the ratio of inputs to outputs.[1]

However, each of these "linear processes" would only be relevant for a *particular* output,[2] and there is also an underlying functional relationship between outputs and inputs which may show perfect continuity but which is basically non-linear. This underlying relationship links the quantity of oil transmitted per hour as the "output" and the labour, materials, etc., involved in constructing the pipeline and all other associated outlays as the "inputs".

Professor Koopmans agrees with Chamberlin that his definition of "commodities" makes the whole issue a tautological one[3] but he believes that nevertheless the indivisibility has the right "intuitive connotations":

" . . . the reproach of tautology has been levelled against many propositions of economic theory. What matters is that a model which differs from the linear activity analysis model in that it omits the proportionality postulate or at least excepts from it all activities involving certain commodities seems to express those aspects of reality that have been recognised as responsible for increasing returns to scale. Such a model

---

[1] *Op. cit.*, pp. 151–2.
[2] Defined in this case as the *throughput* of oil (at any particular point) per unit of time.
[3] Although the statement, quoted earlier, that he has not "found a single case in which there is not some indivisible commodity in the surrounding circumstances" would suggest that he regarded the proposition as a factual one, and not as a logical (tautological) one.

may therefore be a suitable vehicle for a first exploration of this phenomenon, and on the suitability of prices as guides to allocation. So far, mathematical difficulties have been the main obstacle to such an exploration."[1]

The significance of all this depends on what is meant by the "suppression of the proportionality postulate". At one end, it may mean nothing more than the introduction of discontinuities which may rob the analysis of some of its elegance and simplicity, but without destroying the existence of a convex "Pareto-frontier" of some kind. At the other end, it may mean that the whole notion of a Pareto-optimal equilibrium and of the price mechanism as a means of bringing about an "optimal" resource-allocation becomes illegitimate.

Allowance for indivisibilities means that for activities involving certain commodities there is a minimum scale of output, and the activity can only be "attained" at integral multiples of that minimum scale. If in an actual economy the level of output of any one final commodity is some multiple of the minimum output of the "best" available technique for producing it, the existence of indivisibilities will simply mean that the "efficiency frontier" becomes a "jagged surface" instead of a smooth one, but yet remains convex in the large.

However, if at any actual level of output the "best" available technique for that output is less efficient than that available for a somewhat larger output—if, in other words, there is a whole hierarchy of activities not all of which are feasible or attainable at any point of time—the choice among "activities" becomes primarily a matter not of prices but of the scale of production. With every enlargement of production new "activities" become profitable which could not have been employed earlier, whilst the introduction of such new "activities" leads to the invention of further "activities" which have not been "known" earlier.

Since (as was argued above) the demand for any particular product or group of products is a reflection of the level of production of other products, this means that any re-allocation of resources which enlarges the range of feasible activities comes

[1] *Ibid.*, p. 152.

to the same as an "outward shift" in the production frontier. The problem then becomes not just one of "solving the mathematical difficulties" resulting from discontinuities but the much broader one of replacing the "equilibrium approach" with some, as yet unexplored, alternative that makes use of a different conceptual framework.

8

WHAT IS WRONG WITH ECONOMIC THEORY[1]

There is a widespread and growing dissatisfaction with prevailing economic theory in numerous quarters in England. It has even reached such respectable pillars of the economic establishment as the President of the Royal Economic Society and the British Association, as shown by their recent (1971) Presidential addresses. I do not believe that this wave has yet reached America in its proper dimensions—except perhaps at the graduate student level, and among a few rather isolated critics or heretics—but I have little doubt that some day it will. For primarily because the logical system of general equilibrium theory has been more thoroughly explored by American economists of the mathematical school of the post-war generation than anywhere else— clarifying in detail the number and kind of postulates required to establish its conclusions and their precise implications—they (or rather their pupils) should also be the first to perceive that the result of that great exercise has ended in a "cul-de-sac": it made the theory a less usable tool than it was thought to have been in its early and crude state before the full implications of general equilibrium had been so thoroughly explored.

My basic objection to the theory of general equilibrium is not that it is abstract—all theory is abstract and must necessarily be so since there can be no analysis without abstraction—but that it starts from the wrong kind of abstraction, and therefore gives a misleading "paradigm" (or scenario?—the now fashionable word in America) of the world as it is: it gives a misleading impression of the nature and the manner of operation of economic forces.

[1] A Political Economy lecture given at Harvard University, April 29, 1974 and published in the *Quarterly Journal of Economics*, August 1975.

In this connection there is not, in my view, a single, over-whelming objection to orthodox economic theory: there are a number of different points which are distinct though inter-related. Some of my Cambridge colleagues are "monists" in this respect: they believe that there is a single basic, logical objection to the theory of marginal productivity which is alone sufficient to pull the rug out from under the neo-classical value theory. I am referring to the difficulty of isolating or measuring the change in the quantity of capital when the inventory of capital goods changes—which makes it impossible to regard capital as a quantity, *per se*, irrespective of the actual forms in which it is embodied at any one time, and makes it impossible to attribute to capital a marginal productivity of its own. But there are other things to object to that in some ways are even more misleading than the application of marginal productivity theory to the division between wages and profits, which has been the main subject of discussion.

I

The first of these is that economic theory regards the essence of economic activities as an *allocation problem*—"the allocation of scarce resources among alternative uses"—to use Lord Robbins' famous definition of the subject matter of economics. This means that attention is focused on what are subsidiary aspects, rather than the major aspects, of the forces in operation. The principle of substitution (as Marshall called it) or the "law of variable proportions" or of "limited substitutability" is elevated to the central principle on the basis of which both the price system and the production system are explained; and it is implied that the world is one where elasticities of substitution are all-important. This approach ignores the essential complementarity between different factors of production (such as capital and labour) or different types of activities (such as that between primary, secondary and tertiary sectors of the economy) which is far more important for an understanding of the laws of change and development of the economy than the substitution aspect. Indeed, it is, I think, the concentration on the substitution

I

aspect which makes "pure" equilibrium theory so lifeless and motionless: it purports to "explain" a system of market-clearing prices which are the resultant of various interactions: it cannot therefore deal with the problem of prices as signals or incentives to change. Attempts have been made to graft growth and development to equilibrium theory, but they have not succeeded in transforming it into a seqence analysis in which the course of development is dependent on the path of evolution.

Perhaps the best way I can illustrate this point is by asking the question: *Is Say's Law valid, and if not, just what is wrong with it?* This is a very old question, hotly debated already in the early 19th century, if not earlier, and ever since then (until Keynes came along) it was the hallmark of all true economists to have understood the reasons why competitive markets necessarily bring about a situation in which all scarce resources are fully utilised.

The reason, in essence, is a very simple one. The laws of supply and demand state that in any competitive market, say, for the *j*th commodity, there is a "market clearing" price, characterised by

$$d_j = s_j,$$

where d_j and s_j respectively are the *maximum* quantities that buyers are willing to buy or sellers to sell, at those prices (not just sales $\equiv$ purchases).

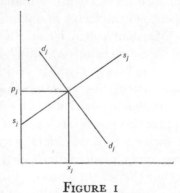

FIGURE I

At p_j buyers are ready to buy and sellers to sell x_j or **any** quantity *less than* x_j.

If this is true of any one market, it must be true for all, $j = 1 \ldots n$ $(0 < n < \infty)$, in the markets for resources, as well as commodities. Hence if all markets are in equilibrium, all resources must be utilised, and production in total must be supply-constrained, or resource-constrained; it cannot be *demand*-constrained.

Or, put in other words, since taking all markets together it is commodities which are exchanged against commodities, there is no sense in saying that the production of commodities can be limited by demand. As Ricardo said, "there is no amount of capital which may not be employed in a country, because demand is only limited by production".[1] Or, John Stuart Mill made the point more forcibly—"All sellers are inevitably and *ex vi termini* buyers. Could we suddenly double the productive powers of the country, we should double the supply of commodities in every market, but we should, by the same stroke, double the purchasing power." Hence, "production can be ill-assorted, but it can not be excessive".[2]

Keynes thought he found the answer to this compelling bit of logic by postulating, in effect, that in one particular market, the market for savings, the price is not, or need not be, "market clearing" (owing to liquidity preference) and if it is not, there is another mechanism, that of the multiplier, to bring about equality in that market—equality between savings and investment (or the supply and demand for savings). But that mechanism operates by varying the amount of production in *general*. It leads to a situation which is *not* resource-constrained.

However, there is a more basic reason why Say's Law is wrong: a reason that might apply equally in a barter economy, and not just a money economy, or in an economy where there is no capital market because people save directly in "real terms" by accumulating stocks of their own produce—e.g., the farmer who accumulates corn so as to increase further corn output, or the steel producer who saves by ploughing back steel into the business so as to increase steel capacity. All we need to assume is the

[1] Ricardo, *Principles* (Sraffa ed.) Cambridge University Press, 1951, p. 290.
[2] J. S. Mill, *Principles of Political Economy*, London, 1849, vol. II Book III, ch. XIV, §2–§4.

absence of constant returns to scale in terms of transferable resources as a general or universal rule (applicable to *all* productive activity).

Suppose we take a simple two-sector model, consisting of *A* and *B* sectors, of agriculture and industry. And let us assume that *land* exists as a specific factor in agriculture—i.e. land is required for agricultural production but not (or not in significant amounts) for industrial production. Industrial production consists of the *processing* of basic materials produced by agriculture, for example, transforming raw cotton or wool into finished textiles, shirts or suits (or for that matter, iron ore extracted from the soil into steel and machinery) with the aid of Labour, which also requires food, which is the wage-good par excellence. Hence agriculture (and mining) produces both direct and indirect inputs for industry—basic materials and food.

If agriculture is subject to the Law of Diminishing Returns, agricultural output may be constrained by land and the available technology which limit the number of workers who may be effectively employed in agriculture.[1] The rest could only be effectively employed in industry.

Supposing that the employment of all the available labour in industry (and assuming adequate capital for their employment in the form of physical equipment at the prevailing technology) would lead to a relative "over-production" of industrial goods (and services)—relative to the available supply of *agricultural* goods—Mill would have said that this is a case of production becoming, or threatening to become, "ill-assorted". But the movement of prices that would accompany this event would bring its own remedy. Agricultural prices would rise in terms of industrial prices, and this process will go on until the excess supply of

---

[1] Though the classical economists (and of course, the neo-classical economists) reasoned as if agricultural production were simultaneously constrained by the supply of both land and labour, it is in fact unlikely that in any given situation (i.e in a given state of technology) the land/labour ratio will be such as to permit effective "full employment" for both labour and land. Since there is only a limited range within which these two factors are substitutes for one another at the margin, the likelihood is that either the land constraint or the labour constraint will be operative, i.e. that there will be too much labour (relative to land) or too much land (relative to labour) though for reasons given below, it would be vain to look for evidence for this by asking which of these two resources has a zero price.

industrial goods—which is the same as the excess demand for agricultural goods—is eliminated. Even if agricultural output were wholly inelastic owing to the shortage of land, the very rise in prices would be sufficient: for it would transfer purchasing power from industry to agriculture, and this transfer will go on until the agriculturists are willing and able to buy all the goods which industry is capable of producing (in excess of industry's own requirements for investment and consumption).

There must be *some* price, therefore, at which the excess supply of B (or excess demand for A) disappears: to suppose otherwise is to assume that industrial goods would remain in excess supply even at a zero price. And this formal conclusion (as I already said) is not dependent on the supply of agricultural products being elastic, which would be the case if the land shortage did not impose a constraint on output.

Now the error in this reasoning is that it ignores the peculiar character of labour as a commodity or resource, the price of which cannot be regarded as being determined by supply and demand in the same way as the price of other resources, such as land, for example.

Whatever the supply of labour (or the potential supply of labour) in relation to demand, the *price* of labour in terms of food cannot fall below a certain minimum determined by the cost of subsistence, whether that cost is determined by custom or convention or by sheer biological needs. (The food-value of wages tends to be very rigid downward in all communities at some *attained* level.) Ricardo and Mill (just as Adam Smith and Marx) were fully aware of this point, but they had not thought out its consequences in terms of Say's Law.[1]

---

[1] Or rather they assumed that the dependence of population on capital (through a Malthusian process) will ensure that the labour supply in existence will be no greater than can be employed at a positive profit. Mill in particular argued that as capital accumulates, and population grows in consequence of it, profits would fall on account of the operation of the Law of Diminishing Returns in agriculture and this would cause "all further accumulation of capital to cease"—implying (without putting the point explicitly) that this itself will limit the size of the labour force to the numbers that can be effectively employed in the given natural and technological environment. It was for this reason, I presume, that Mill made the statement that "low profits, however, are a different thing from deficiency of demand; and the production and accumulation which merely reduce profits, cannot be called excess of supply or of production." But what if the absorption of the unemployed involved a negative profit? This latter possibility as far as I know was never considered. Yet there is no reason

If wages (or minimum wages) can be taken as given in terms of food, the prices of manufactured goods (or rather the "value added" by manufacturing activities) are equally constrained, and this constraint may prevent both markets from being in equilibrium simultaneously.

The supply price of industrial goods is given by the equation

$$p = (1 + \pi)\bar{w}l,$$

where p = prices of industrial goods per unit, in terms of agricultural prices

$\bar{w}$ = wages per man, ditto

l = labour required per unit of output (inverse of productivity)

π = profits as a share of output

and this will *not* be a "market-clearing" price, so long as the supply of labour exceeds the demand; or so long as there is a low-earnings "subsistence" sector of the economy which enables people to survive without being effectively employed or effectively contributing to output.

This has important consequences.

(1) First, the level of $\bar{w}$, cannot be less than earnings in the subsistence sector; but otherwise it is by no means tied to it: the *optimal* wage to a capitalist employer may be a great deal higher owing to the dependence of the efficiency of work-performance on food intake. The poorer the country, the higher $\bar{w}$ is in relation to earnings in the subsistence sector. (A. Smith, Ricardo, Mill and all classical economists assume a *constant* food wage—i.e., an infinitely elastic supply curve of labour to industry.) Hence one cannot say that the relative price of industrial and agricultural goods is determined by marginal rates of substitution between the two sectors. There is no such thing as a

---

why the density of population resulting from the Malthusian Law (and which operates so as to keep income per head at a bare subsistence level) should coincide with the highest population density at which the whole of the labour force can still be effectively employed—i.e. which is consistent with a positive marginal product of labour in agriculture. (See Mill, *op. cit.*, Book III, ch. XIV, §4, and Book IV, ch. IV, *passim.*)

"production frontier" showing output combinations, a maximum A for any given B, or vice versa, reflecting the allocation of resources between sectors. For each sector accumulates its own capital as it expands its own output; and labour which is common to both has a positive marginal product only in industry, not in agriculture.[1]

(2) Secondly, the fact that the price of "value-added" by manufacture cannot be reduced or compressed in terms of basic products (if basic products rise in money prices, as they do now, it results in general inflation rather than in a fall in industrial prices in terms of primary products) is the equivalent of a "fixed price" situation (as Hicks called it)[2] where production is determined by demand, or rather by the exogenous components of demand which in turn determine, through the usual multiplier and accelerator effects, the endogenous components of demand. (Hicks called the relationship of endogenous to exogenous demand the "super-multiplier"—to allow for induced investment as well as induced consumption.)[3] Hence it is the income of the agricultural sector (given the "terms of trade") which really determines the level and the rate of growth of industrial production, according to the formula:

$$O_I = \frac{1}{m} D_A,$$

where O_I = industrial output

D_A = demand for industrial products coming from agriculture

m = share of expenditure on agricultural products in total industrial income.

---

[1] It will be readily seen that this conclusion is critically dependent on the existence of diminishing returns (in terms of capital and labour) in agriculture. For assuming that agriculture were subject to constant returns to scale, the excess supply of industrial goods at a given price-relationship would cause a transfer of labour and capital into agriculture until the excess demand for agricultural goods is eliminated and "full-employment output" would cease to be "ill assorted". Hence the postulate of constant returns to scale (in terms of transferable resources) as a universal rule applicable to all "processes" or "activities" (which is a common axiom of the general equilibrium theory) is sufficient to ensure a Walrasian equilibrium which is truly resource-constrained.

[2] *Capital and Growth*, Oxford, 1965, chs. VII–XI (pp. 76–127).

[3] *A Contribution to the Theory of the Trade Cycle*, Oxford, 1950, p. 62.

This is really the doctrine of the foreign trade multiplier, as against the Keynesian savings/investment multiplier. In both cases multipliers arise on account of a "fixed-price" situation: the liquidity preference rate of interest in the one case, and the fixed real wage giving a cost-determined supply price for industrial products in the other case. In some ways I think it may have been unfortunate that the very success of Keynes' ideas in explaining unemployment in a depression—essentially a short period analysis—diverted attention from the "foreign trade multiplier", which, over longer periods, is a far more important principle for explaining the growth and rhythm of industrial development. For over longer periods, Ricardo's presumption that manufacturers and traders only save in order to invest, so that the amount and/or the proportion of savings would adapt to changes in the opportunities for, or profitability of, investment, seems to me more relevant than the Keynesian assumption for explaining the true constraints on the growth of production and employment in the "capitalist" industrial sector.

II

(3) Added to this is the second major point I want to make at this point—albeit only briefly—and this concerns the existence of *increasing returns to scale* or falling long-run costs, in industry. This was first emphasised by Adam Smith in the first three chapters of the *Wealth of Nations,* and subsequently emphasised by English economists of the Ricardian school and by Marshall; while in the United States (in a more isolated way) by a single great economist, Allyn Young.

Marshall's falling long-run supply curve, unlike the ordinary supply curve, is a schedule of *minimum* quantities, not *maximum* quantities: see diagram opposite. At p_j manufacturers are willing to supply x_j or any amount *larger than* x_j but not *less than* x_j.

Neither Marshall, nor anyone else, has ever succeeded in reconciling this assumption with neoclassical value theory—which is the reason perhaps why, according to Hahn and

Matthews,[1] it has received so little consideration in recent economic literature.

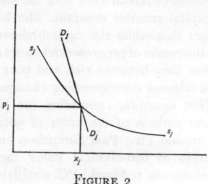

There are three important consequences that I would like to emphasise here. The first, which was emphasised by Allyn Young is that with increasing returns "change becomes progressive and propagates itself in a cumulative way".[2] There can be no such thing as an equilibrium state with optimum resource allocation, where no further advantageous reorganisation is possible, since every such re-organisation may create a fresh opportunity to a further re-organisation. There can never be full employment in the sense of "efficient" or Pareto-optimal full employment, and the very distinction between changes in the *quantity* of resources, and changes in the *efficiency* with which they are used, becomes a questionable one.

Second, the accumulation of capital becomes a by-product, rather than a cause, of the expansion of production—indeed it is only one aspect of it. Again, as Young emphasised, it is the increase in the scale of activities that makes it profitable to increase the capital/labour ratio: the larger the scale of operations the more varied and more specialised the machinery which can be profitably used to aid labour. As Young said, "It would be wasteful to make a hammer just to drive a single nail; it would

[1] "The Theory of Economic Growth: A Survey", *Economic Journal*, Vol. LXXIV, December 1964, p. 833.

[2] Allyn A. Young, "Increasing Returns and Economic Progress", *Economic Journal*, December, 1928, p. 533.

be better to use whatever awkward implement lies conveniently at hand".[1] The form which increasing returns normally takes is that the productivity of labour rises with the scale of production while that of capital remains constant. The best proof of this resides in the fact that while the capital/labour ratio increases dramatically in the course of progress (and varies equally dramatically at any given time between rich and poor countries) these differences arise without corresponding changes in the capital/output ratio. (For example, comparing the U.S. with India, the capital/labour ratio is of the order of 30:1, while capital/output ratio is around 1:1.) Paul Samuelson emphasised as the central proposition of neo-classical value theory (placed in italics in his well-known textbook) "Capital/labour up: interest or profit rate down: wage rate up: capital/output up".[2] These propositions are *only* true in a world of homogeneous and linear production functions, where an increase in capital relative to labour increases output less than proportionately. In reality this is not so—higher wages rates in terms of product are associated with higher capital/labour ratios but are *not* associated with higher capital/output ratios. (This is to my mind an even more important "pull on the rug" than the discovery of the possibility of "double-switching" of techniques.)

Third, for the same kind of reason for which increasing returns lead to a monopoly in terms of microeconomics, industrial development tends to get polarised in certain "growth points" or in "success areas" which become areas of vast immigration from surrounding centres or from more distant areas—unless this is prevented by political obstacles. As the post-war experience of European countries (e.g. Germany, France, Switzerland) has shown, the emergence of a labour shortage need not hold up the further fast development of a successful industrial area, since such political obstacles tend to be removed when it becomes profitable to import foreign labour.

But this process of polarisation—what Myrdal called "circular and cumulative causation"—is largely responsible for the growing

---

[1] *Ibid.*, p. 530.
[2] P. A. Samuelson, *Economics—an Introductory Analysis*, Seventh ed., New York, 1967, p. 715.

division of the world between rich and poor areas which, in per capita terms at any rate, still appears to be widening. It would be foolish to pretend that we understand *all* the causative influences which make the industrialisation of *some* parts of the world so much more successful than that of others. But I am sure that a better understanding of the nature and mode of operation of market forces making for change and development will increase our powers of control for counteracting inherent trends toward greater inequality as between the different regions of the globe.

9

INFLATION AND RECESSION IN THE WORLD ECONOMY[1]

The first twenty-five years after the end of the Second World War were an exceptional period of economic growth and prosperity in the leading industrial countries, marked by fast-rising living standards, very low levels of unemployment and—omitting the Korean War period, the effects of which were over by 1953—by the absence of instabilities of the pre-war kind, whether of production or prices. I think I can safely say that almost no one *expected* this to happen, since it was in such marked contrast to the course of events after World War I. This time there was no post-war slump.

True, during the whole of this period there was a continued increase in prices—the ideal of *complete* price stability (as measured, say, in terms of an index of consumer prices) was, as far as one can tell, not attained anywhere. But for a long time the rate of inflation (as measured by consumer prices) remained moderate, and until the closing years of the 1960s it showed no clear tendency to acceleration. In the fourteen years 1953–67 it averaged in 11 leading industrial countries just over 2 per cent a year.[2] And it was confined to, or at least originated in, the industrial sectors of the advanced countries: the world price of foodstuffs and basic

[1] Presidential address to the Royal Economic Society, delivered on 22 July, 1976, and printed in the *Economic Journal*, vol. 86, December 1976.
[2] The 11 countries comprise the United Kingdom, United States, France, Germany, Italy, Netherlands, Belgium, Sweden, Switzerland, Canada and Japan. The rate of increase in consumer prices tended to be rather higher (between 3 and 4 per cent a year) in some of the fast-growing countries—like Japan, Italy, France and Sweden—and rather less (between 1 and 2 per cent) in the United States and Canada. (In Germany, Belgium and Switzerland it was around 2 per cent; in the United Kingdom and the Netherlands around 2¾ per cent.)

materials (again omitting the Korean episode) remained, on the average, remarkably stable.[1]

But from about 1968 things began to change. The rise in labour costs per unit of industrial output began to accelerate in all the main industrial countries, though at differing rates. There was an increasing strain on the international payments system which led to the general abandonment of the system of fixed exchange rates in 1971. This was followed by rapidly rising commodity prices in the course of 1972 and 1973,[2] which preceded the sudden fourfold rise in oil prices following the Arab–Israeli war. The rise in commodity prices was followed in turn by an inflation in wage settlements which served to augment the general rate of increase of prices. There resulted an unprecedented inflation in consumer prices in all countries. In the two years 1973–5 it averaged 26 per cent for *all* O.E.C.D. countries, ranging (for the two-year period) from 44 per cent for the United Kingdom and 39 per cent for Japan to 13 per cent for Germany and 17 per cent in Switzerland.

Nothing of this kind has ever occurred before in peace-time—I mean an inflation of that magnitude encompassing not just one or two countries, but *all* the leading industrial countries of the world. The other unique feature of this inflation was that it was accompanied by a marked recession in industrial production. World industrial production, which rose at a fairly steady rate of 6–7 per cent a year throughout the sixties and by 8 per cent a year in 1971–3, was stagnant in 1974 and *fell* by 10 per cent in 1975, accompanied by unemployment levels which had not been encountered since the 1930s.

This combination of inflation and economic recession is a new phenomenon, the explanation of which presents an intellectual challenge to economists.

In my view it would be futile to look for a single basic cause— such as the increase in the money supply in all countries, or

---

[1] The U.N. index of the export prices of primary commodities in terms of U.S. dollars was virtually the same in 1970 as in 1950. In the intervening period (again, abstracting from Korea) it had a gently falling trend up to about 1962, and first a stationary, then a gently rising trend thereafter.

[2] The U.N. index of primary commodities excluding fuels rose (in dollar terms) by 58 per cent in the two years 1971–3 and a further 26 per cent in 1974, so that the index doubled in three years.

universal cost-push resulting from collective bargaining—and it would be wrong to suppose that the great acceleration of inflation of the last few years was the inevitable sequel of the long creeping inflation which preceded it.

THE PRIMARY SECTOR AND THE INDUSTRIAL SECTOR

In order to show this I think it is necessary to disaggregate economic activities more than is generally done in macro-economic analyses (whether of the Keynesian or the monetarist variety) by distinguishing between the "primary sector" of the world economy on the one hand and the "secondary" and "tertiary" sectors on the other hand. These sectors are largely complementary to each other—the primary sector provides the indispensable basic supplies for industrial activities in the form of food, fuel and basic materials; the secondary sector processes the materials into finished goods for investment or consumption, while the tertiary sector provides a variety of services which are ancillary to the other sectors (such as transport or distribution, or professional expertise of various kinds) as well as services which are an independent source of enjoyment (such as theatrical performances).

While no great problems are likely to arise on account of the tertiary sector, both the industrial sector and the primary sector can become sources of inflation, but of a different character—differing both in the nature of the causal mechanism and in the general economic consequences.

Continued and stable economic progress requires that the growth of output in these two sectors should be at the required relationship with each other—that is to say, the growth of the saleable output of agriculture and mining should be in line with the growth of demand, which in turn reflects the growth of the secondary (and tertiary) sectors.

However, from a technical standpoint there can be no guarantee that the rate of growth of primary production, propelled by land-saving innovations, proceeds at the precise rate warranted by growth of production and incomes in the secondary and tertiary sectors. To ensure that it does is the function of the price mechanism, more particularly of relative prices, or the "terms of trade" between primary commodities and manufactured goods. The more favourable are the terms of trade to agriculture and mining, the more current technological advance will be exploited through new investment, and the faster the growth of output. If the growth of primary production runs ahead of the growth of industrial demand, the terms of trade will move in favour of industry: this, in theory, should stimulate industrial growth and thereby the demand for primary commodities, whilst retarding the growth of production of primary commodities.

Since the "terms of trade" is the *ratio* of two kinds of prices, of primary commodities and manufactured goods, we must look at the nature of the markets for commodities and for industrial products respectively more closely before we can say how efficiently this mechanism works. In the field of primary production the market price is given to the individual producer or consumer, and prices move in direct response to market pressures in the classical manner described by Adam Smith. Changes in prices act as "signals" for the adjustment of production and consumption in the future. In industry, on the other hand—at least in a modern industrial society where the greater part of production is concentrated in the hands of large corporations—prices are "administered", i.e. fixed by the producers themselves, and the adjustment of production to changes of demand takes place independently of price changes, through a stock-adjustment mechanism: production is reduced in response to an accumulation of unsold goods, and raised in the face of a depletion. Industrial prices (in contrast to the prices of primary products) are not "market clearing", since normally the typical producer operates at less than full capacity; he can increase production without incurring higher costs per unit, and indeed, frequently benefits from reduced costs resulting from a greater volume of production. Such "administered prices" are cost-determined, not "market determined"; they are arrived at by applying various percentage additions to direct labour and material costs on account of overheads and profits. Neither profit margins nor labour costs in the industrial sector are particularly responsive to changes in demand.

This means that the burden of any maladjustment between the growth of primary production and the growth of manufacturing activities is thrown almost entirely on the commodity markets, the behaviour of which is erratic owing to the large influence of speculative expectations on the holding of stocks, as well as on account of the price-inelasticity of demand, and of the time-lags involved in the adjustment of supply to price changes. When the growth of production exceeds the growth of consumption (as was the case in the 1920s) the immediate effect is an accumulation of stocks, which, with favourable expectations concerning the growth of future demand, may go on for years with only moderate changes in prices. This happened in the years 1925–9, during which, according to the League of Nations index, end-year stocks of primary products rose by no less than a third with only a moderate fall in prices.[1] When the boom did break, prices fell catastrophically—by more than 50 per cent in three years—and this, so far from stimulating the absorption of commodities by the industrial sector, had the very opposite effect: the fall in demand for industrial products coming from the primary producers, and the fall in investment by the industrial countries in primary production—in opening up new areas, etc.—more than offset any stimulus to industrial demand on account of the rise in real incomes of the urban workers resulting from the fall in food prices; the rapid fall in commodity prices ushered in the greatest industrial depression in history.

The above is an illustration of a more fundamental proposition that *any* large change in commodity prices—irrespective of whether it is in favour or against the primary producers—tends to have a dampening effect on industrial activity; it retards industrial growth in both cases, instead of retarding it in the one case and stimulating it in the other. There are, as I shall now show, two reasons for this. It is partly a consequence of the fact that whilst a *fall* in commodity prices tends to be an effective instrument in moving the terms of trade against the primary producers, a *rise* in commodity prices is not likely to be nearly as effective in moving the terms of trade in their favour. It is partly

[1] Quoted by Lewis in "World Production and Trade, 1870–1960", *The Manchester School*, 1952, p. 128.

also a consequence of an asymmetry in the behavioural consequences as between a gain and a loss of real income, the result of
which is that any sudden shift in the distribution of world income,
caused by a change in the terms of trade, is likely to have an
adverse effect on industrial demand (in real terms).

The important cause of the first asymmetry is that while commodity prices are demand-determined, industrial prices are cost-
determined, and because of that the rise in commodity prices has
a very powerful inflationary effect operating on the *cost* side. The
rise in the price of basic materials and fuels is passed through the
various stages of production into the final price with an exagger-
ated effect—it gets "blown up" on the way by a succession of
percentage additions to prime costs which mean, in effect, an
increase in cash margins at each stage. This causes (initially) a
rise in the share of profits in the value added by manufacturing
which in itself is a powerful factor (in countries where trade union
power is strong) in causing pressure for wage increases. Added to
this is the price-induced rise in wages caused by what Sir John
Hicks called "Real Wage Resistance"—the reluctance of workers
to accept a cut in their standard of living[1] (which is not paralleled
by similar reluctance to accept a rise). For these reasons a swing
in the terms of trade in favour of the primary producers is not
likely to last for long. The industrial sector with its superior
market power, resists any compression of its real income by
countering the rise in commodity prices through a cost-induced
inflation of industrial prices.

Moreover—and here we come to the second reason mentioned

---

[1] *Lloyd's Bank Review*, October 1975, p. 5. According to Professor Milton Friedman
and his followers, this "real wage resistance" is in itself evidence of an excessive demand
for labour—of unemployment being less then some "natural rate"—because at a
higher level of unemployment the desired real wage—the real wage *ex-ante*—would
have been less and the *ex-post* real wage (owing to higher "marginal productivity")
would have been greater. I am sure, however, that in all this the monetarists are
barking up the wrong tree. The *ex-post* real wage is smaller, not greater, at higher levels
of unemployment—both because of short-term increasing returns ("Okun's Law")
and of social overheads which cause a disproportionate part of any increase in output
to be available for wage-earners' consumption, whereas the "desired real wage" is
mainly governed by the attained standards of living of the working population and is
not much affected if at all by the level of unemployment. The inflation in industrial
countries was not the result of excess demand, either for labour or for the products of
labour: if anything, it was the result of an excess demand for primary products
(food and raw materials), which is quite a different thing (cf. Hicks, *op. cit.*; H. G.
Johnson, *Lloyd's Bank Review*, April 1976, p. 14).

above—the inflation itself has a deflationary effect on the effective demand for industrial goods in real terms, partly because the rise in the profits of producers in the primary sector is not matched by a rise in their expenditure—this was particularly marked on the present occasion through the vast accumulation of financial assets by the oil producers—and partly because the governments of most, if not all, of the industrial countries are likely to react to their domestic inflation by fiscal and monetary measures which reduce consumer demand and put a brake on industrial investment. Thus the rise in commodity prices may well result in a wage/price-spiral type of inflation in the industrial sectors which in turn causes industrial activity to be restricted. The latter tends to eliminate the shortages and thereby reverse the trend in commodity prices. A good example of this has been the U.S. inflation of 1972–3, which was clearly cost-induced but not wage-induced; it was caused by the rise in commodity prices (with wage rises trailing behind the rise in living costs) and which led to strongly restrictionist monetary policies in order to counter the inflation, which in turn brought about a considerable economic recession. (Somewhat later similar restrictionist policies were adopted by governments of other leading countries, such as Germany and Japan.)

If the above analysis is correct, the market mechanism is a highly inefficient regulator for securing continuing adjustment between the growth of availabilities and the growth in requirements for primary products in a manner conducive to the harmonious development of the world economy.

The emergence of commodity surpluses which should, in principle, lead to accelerated industrialisation may have a perverse effect by diminishing effective demand for industrial products. Similarly the emergence of shortages which should accelerate the growth of availabilities of primary products through improvements in the terms of trade may lead instead to an inflation of manufacturers' prices which tends to offset the improvement in the terms of trade, and by its dampening effect on industrial activity, worsens the climate for new investment in both the primary sector and the industrial sector.

In retrospect, the remarkable thing was that the great post-war boom in the industrial countries could go on for so long with so few interruptions and with a background of stable commodity prices (ignoring the sharp but short-lived commodity boom during the Korean War) right up to the early 1970s. The main reason for this was that the progress of land-saving agricultural technology proceeded much faster than in any previous period of history.[1] This led to large surpluses in the main grain producing and exporting countries, the normal price effects of which, however, were obviated by government price-support policies in all the main producing countries, combined with stock-piling policies for strategic purposes. These price-support policies secured a steady growth of agricultural incomes and provided an important primary source for the growth of demand for manufactured goods.

REASONS FOR THE "CREEPING INFLATION"

However, while export prices of primary products were stable (or rather fluctuated around a stationary trend) the export prices of manufactures were slowly rising, due to the "creeping inflation" of the industrial countries to which I have already referred. On looking back at this period—say the period extending from 1953 to 1967—I do not think that either of the two standard theories of a wage-induced inflation, the "cost-push" due to the collective bargaining process or the "demand pull" due to excessive tightness in the labour market, provides the key to an explanation.

The explanation which I think is much nearer the mark is to be found in the powerful social forces which make for constancy in relative earnings in different trades and occupations[2] as a result of which the increase in wages obtained in certain "leading" or

[1] Sir Arthur Lewis, writing in 1952 (*op. cit.* p. 13) predicted that the growth in world food production in the decade 1950–60 was likely to be in range 1·3–2 per cent per annum; though he held that owing to various adverse circumstances the lower figure was more likely. He put the possible growth of world manufacturing production as 3·9–5 per cent, depending on the availabilities of raw materials and the success of economic management in avoiding slumps. As it turned out, world manufacturing production (according to U.N. estimates) increased by 6⅔ per cent a year (on the average) in the decade 1950–60 and also in 1960–70, while world food production increased by 2·7 per cent a year in both decades. (In the three years 1970–3, however, it fell to 1·6 per cent a year.)

[2] For evidence, see in particular *Problems of Pay Relativities*, Advisory Report No. 2 of the Pay Board (Cmnd. 5535, 1974).

"key" sectors tends to set the pace for the *general* rate of wage increases in the economy combined with the tendency for wages in the so-called "dynamic sectors"—where the rate of productivity growth is appreciably *above* the average—to rise at the rate which tends to be *less* than the rate of productivity growth in those industries, but appreciably *more* than the rate of productivity growth in other sectors.[1]

In an economy dominated by large corporations price competition is not so prompt or effective as to compel firms which experience exceptional reductions in costs (owing to the introduction of new products, or new processes, or a fast increase in selling volume, or both) to pass on the full benefit to the consumer in the form of lower prices *pari passu* with the reduction of costs. The very existence of this situation leads to wage increases that are, in a sense, unnecessarily large—i.e. they are governed by what the employer can *afford* to pay (without compromising his competitive position) and not by what he *needs* to pay, in order to obtain the necessary work force.[2]

---

[1] For empirical support for this proposition see Eatwell, Llewellyn and Tarling, "Money Wage Inflation in Industrial Countries", *Review of Economic Studies*, October 1974, pp. 515–23, particularly Table III, p. 520.

[2] The above account of what causes wage increases to exceed productivity increases in capitalist economies is one particular version of the "leading-sector" hypothesis which I personally favour but which cannot be regarded as firmly established to the exclusion of others. Another version, more in accord with traditional thinking, attributes this rôle to the particular firms or sectors which show a fast rate of expansion in the number of their employees either because it is a case of a new firm which has to recruit its labour force, or of firms the demand for the products of which has shown a sudden rise (as a result, for example, of the abolition of HP restrictions) and which therefore are anxious to recruit additional labour by the offer of higher pay. Yet another version asserts, contrariwise, that the "leading sectors" are found in those industries where the workers have been compelled to allow a deterioration of relative earnings because (owing to falling demand for their products, or exceptional productivity gains, or both) there was a prolonged shrinkage in the labour force; when this comes to an end, their bargaining position improves, enabling them to "catch up" so as to regain their previous position. (This version is tailor-made to fit the British case where coal miners set the standard for wage increases for several years in succession.) Yet another variant of this theory is the so-called "Swedish theory of inflation" according to which the prices in the export and import competing industries (broadly the manufacturing industry) are set by world prices, and the rate of wage increases in these sectors—which are also the "dynamic sectors" with a high rate of productivity growth—are then applied to the so-called "sheltered" industries whose rate of productivity growth is much smaller. It is doubtful, however, whether the Swedish theory is applicable to an economy like the United Kingdom where the domestic prices of industrial products are much less under the influence of world prices, and still less to the United States, whose foreign trade is small in relation to domestic trade. (For an account of the "Swedish" theory see Edgren, Faxen and Odhner, *Wage Formation and the Economy*, London, Allen & Unwin, 1973.)

This explanation is heavily dependent on the hypothesis that the percentage rate of wage increase demanded and obtained in the great majority of settlements in any particular period are imitative in character: they are motivated by the desire to maintain the position of any particular group of workers relative to other groups, rather than to secure some given absolute improvement in the standard of living. There have been a number of studies tending to show that custom and tradition form a strong element in pay differentials between groups of workers who are in close contact with one another; and since any particular group is closely related to some other group which in turn is more closely related to a third, there is a kind of chain reaction by means of which any particular standard for wage increases communicates itself through the influence of the principle of "fairness" or "comparability" which is the great social force behind the (long-term) constancy of such differentials. Lacking any objective and universally accepted criteria of "fairness", this attribute attaches itself to differentials which have been hallowed by custom and therefore the mere passage of time tends to reinforce them.[1]

YEARS OF THE WORLD-WIDE WAGE EXPLOSION, 1968–71

An analysis on the above lines of the long creeping inflation of 1953–67 clearly cannot account for the sudden acceleration of the rate of increase in wages and prices in the years 1968–71—years during which the movement of commodity prices, though upward, was still relatively moderate. For reasons which are still in dispute the rate of increase in wages took a sudden spurt in a large number of industrial countries more or less simultaneously; it happened in the course either of 1968–9 (as in Japan, France, Belgium and

[1] The fact that in 1975–6 the voluntary incomes policy of a uniform increase of £6 a week, without any regard to differences in earnings, has so largely succeeded, does not necessarily weaken the above argument. An incomes policy, provided it is *believed* to be generally observed, sets a new criterion of "fairness" which temporarily displaces the traditional criteria—in much the same way as equality of consumption achieved through comprehensive rationing is the most promising way of gaining approval to austerity in war-time. If the incomes policy is maintained for a limited period only, the old differentials will re-assert themselves on its termination; if, however, the policy could be maintained (possibly in a relaxed form) for a whole series of years, this might exert a permanent effect on the scale of pay differentials which are considered "fair".

the Netherlands) or of 1969–70 (as in Germany, Italy, Switzerland and the United Kingdom). In the United States the process began earlier but was far more moderate, the annual rise of hourly earnings in manufacturing having reached a peak rate of 6 per cent between 1967 and 1968; whilst the annual increase in earnings reached double figures in all Western European countries and Japan by 1970.

There is a school of thought which attributes all this to a demand-inflation in the United States caused by the Vietnam War which communicated itself, through international prices or else through the demand pressures induced by unrequited balance of payments surpluses (the counterpart of growing U.S. deficits) to other countries,[1] but this explanation seems to me implausible for several reasons. First, since the rate of wage and price inflation in the United States was more moderate than that of Europe or Japan it is difficult to attribute the rise in international prices to the internal inflation in the United States. Second, to assume that the American balance of payments deficit created additional demand pressures in other industrial countries implies that the pressure of demand in those countries did increase in those years and the wage explosion could be regarded as a consequence of increased demand pressure on the labour market. While this may have been the case in some countries, it was clearly not the case in others. For example, it would be very difficult to explain the British wage explosion in late 1969/1970 by additional pressure of demand—since it occurred at a time when unemployment was relatively high and, as became evident in the course of 1970, the economy was moving into a recession.[2]

I find the alternative explanation put forward by the O.E.C.D. and others[3]—which regards the basic cause as increased trade-union militancy mainly attributable to the sharply rising deductions from the pay packet for payment of income tax and

[1] See William Nordhaus, *The Worldwide Wage Explosion*, Brookings Papers on Economic Activity, no. 3, 1972.

[2] For a detailed analysis see John Williamson and Geoffrey Wood, "The British Inflation: Indigenous or Imported?" *American Economic Review*, September 1976, pp. 520–31.

[3] See for example, Jackson, Turner and Wilkinson, *Do Trade Unions Cause Inflation?*, D.A.E. Occasional Paper, Cambridge, 1972.

insurance contributions—more plausible.[1] This hypothesis still leaves unexplained why the wage explosion occurred at that particular time and not earlier—since the trend of an increasing share of income being deducted at source for tax and insurance contributions has proceeded for more than a decade—or why the explosion should have occurred more or less simultaneously in so many different countries. For this there is no fully satisfactory explanation on present evidence—any more than for the social forces which caused simultaneous outbreaks of student revolts in America and all over Europe in 1968—or the wave of revolutions which swept Europe in February and March 1848. In all these cases there had been long-smouldering resentment and dissatisfaction which, when matters came to a head in one country, caused the rapid spread of the eruption to others.

THE EXPLOSION OF COMMODITY PRICES

The acceleration of wage inflation was associated with a far more rapid increase in the price level of manufactured goods in international trade. Thus the U.N. index of prices in world trade of manufactures in dollar terms rose by 1 per cent a year between 1953 and 1968, and by 5 per cent a year during 1968–71.

The slow and steady rise in the price of manufactured goods involved a corresponding deterioration in the terms of trade of primary producers; the cumulative deterioration amounted to 24 per cent between 1953 and 1971, all but 3 per cent of which occurred in the period 1953–68. This was because during the three years when the price of manufactured goods increased fast, the prices of primary products also rose, though at a lesser rate.[2]

[1] As the O.E.C.D. has shown, there has been a steady fall in the proportion of privately financed consumption to total private consumption in all the main O.E.C.D. countries throughout the period 1955–69 with an accelerating trend from 1966–7 onwards. (See *Expenditure Trends in O.E.C.D. Countries 1960–80*, O.E.C.D., July 1972, charts B and E and table 12.) This was partly to be accounted for by higher public expenditure on goods and services, but mainly by increased social transfers reflecting an increased scale of social service benefits and welfare services.
[2] The above figures are derived from the U.N. index of primary commodities excluding fuels, divided by the U.N. index of export prices of manufacturers in world trade (all in dollar terms). It is arguable, however, that the slow deterioration in the primary producers' terms of trade over the 18-year period was more apparent than real, since the price-indices take no account of the increase in real purchasing power

The real explosion of commodity prices began in the latter half of 1972 and there can be little doubt that much of it was in anticipation of shortages, since the end-of-season stocks of the main agricultural commodities did not show a big fall until 1973. World wheat stocks fell to less than half their normal level in 1973 (with no significant improvement in 1974 and 1975). This was mainly the result of unexpected purchases by the U.S.S.R. following the failure of their 1972–3 harvest and in later years; and the slowness of the Americans in realising that, after so many years of burdensome surpluses, they were now entering an era of prolonged shortages. Though food presents a special case, the sharp rise in the prices of fibres, and later of metals, in 1973 and early 1974 does seem to indicate that the rate of absorption of commodities threatened to outrun the growth of availabilities at the rate of growth of world industrial activity of over 10 per cent a year experienced in the latter half of 1972 and the first half of 1973.

But this was not the only factor at work. To an unknown extent the currency upheavals following the formal suspension of the gold convertibility of the dollar, together with general inflationary expectations, must have induced a great deal of commodity buying as an inflation-hedge—in the same way as the outbreak of the Korean War 25 years earlier led to the rapid rise in commodity prices in anticipation of shortages which in the event did not materialise. That boom (which increased commodity prices by some 50 per cent) collapsed within a year or so. In the present instance there was a remarkable correlation between movements in the price of gold and of *The Economist*'s index of commodity prices which followed much the same time-path.[1]

After commodity prices had thus doubled or trebled came the big rise in the price of oil with consequences that are well known. The subsequent world-wide industrial recession caused some commodities—metals and industrial materials—to fall back in price with almost equal rapidity, only to rise again, since

---

resulting from the appearance of innumerable "new" industrial goods (like new types of tractors or fertilisers, washing machines or television sets) which greatly enlarged the range of goods available for purposes of consumption or investment.
[1] Cf. the diagram on page 106 of the O.E.C.D. *Economic Outlook*, December, 1973.

February 1976, with even greater rapidity—with the first signs of renewed industrial expansion.[1]

The price of food had fallen only moderately from its 1974 level and is now rising again. Yet the level of employment in the industrialised countries is still far from restored to pre-recession levels; production is also lower, at least in relation to trend. And the terms of trade of commodity producers *other than* oil appear to be not much better in terms of manufactures than in 1970; if their need to purchase oil is taken into account, they are probably worse.

The danger now is that the rise in commodity prices will bring in its train a new inflationary wave in the industrial countries, causing the repetition of the same kind of process as we experienced in 1974 and 1975, but starting from much higher levels of unemployment. The very jumpiness of commodity prices shows that they are increasingly under the influence of inflationary expectations.[2] The absence of any stable monetary medium which would serve as a hedge against inflation may well come to mean that any revival of demand will lead to spectacular increases in commodity prices, fed by speculation; and the problem of keeping inflation at bay will increasingly be at the centre of preoccupations of *all* industrialised countries, with untoward consequences in terms of waste of resources and unemployment.

It would be premature to conclude, however, that the terms of trade required to secure an adequate rate of growth in the supply of primary products will prove to be incompatible with the maintenance of price stability in the industrial world. For all past experience has tended to show that when prices in commodity markets are stabilised (by means of official market intervention of some kind) the very stability of prices thus created, by reducing the subjective risks of producers and investors, is likely to call forth greatly enhanced supplies. Hence under a regime of stable

---

[1] *The Economist* index of commodity prices in dollar terms has risen by nearly 30 per cent since February 1976 and is now (July 1976) above its previous peak in May 1974.

[2] Without being a "monetarist" I do believe in the importance of inflationary expectations; but unlike the monetarists, I believe they are mainly of importance in markets where speculation is important—i.e. in commodity markets, and not in the labour market or the market for goods with cost-determined prices.

commodity prices the terms of trade adjustment that may be required for securing adequate supplies in the long run, when brought about slowly and gradually, is likely to be one that the industrial sectors of the world are well capable of accommodating.

THE MONETARY SOLUTION TO WORLD ECONOMIC GROWTH

The primary need is to strengthen the adjustment mechanism between the growth of supply and demand for primary products. This requries that governments (or international bodies) acting singly or in concert should be prepared to carry much larger stocks than private traders are willing to carry on their own; and be ready to intervene in markets in a price-stabilising manner.

For reasons given earlier the duration and stability of the post-war economic boom owed a great deal to the policies of the United States and other governments in absorbing and carrying stocks of grain and other basic commodities both for price stabilisation and for strategic purposes. Many people are also convinced that if the United States had shown greater readiness to carry stocks of grain (instead of trying by all means throughout the 1960s to eliminate its huge surpluses by giving away wheat under PL 480 provisions and by reducing output through acreage restrictions) the sharp rise of food prices following upon the large grain purchases by the U.S.S.R., which unhinged the stability of the world price level far more than anything else, could have been avoided.

I remain convinced—as I have been for a long time—that the most promising line of action for introducing greater stability into the world economy would be to create international buffer stocks for all the main commodities, and to link the finance of these stocks directly to the issue of international currency, such as the S.D.R.s, which could thus be backed by, and directly convertible into, major commodities comprising foodstuffs, fibres and metals. Assuming these buffer stocks cover a sufficiently wide range of commodities, their very existence could provide a powerful self-regulating mechanism for promoting growth and stability in the world economy.

Assuming the system starts off in the right circumstances when commodity surpluses are about to develop, and the intervention of the buffer stock authorities serves to prevent a recession in commodities by accumulating stocks, they would have a far-reaching effect in influencing the rhythm of development. The value of the commodities bought by the authorities would represent a net addition, in terms of international currency, to the incomes of the producers. The addition to world investment would have a powerful multiplier effect—it would increase the export demand for industrial goods which in turn would stimulate industrial investment; the process thereby set in train would tend to increase the rate of absorption of commodities until it comes into balance with the rate of production. If it went beyond this point, the mechanism would go into reverse—the sale of commodities by the buffer stock authorities would cause a contraction of demand for industrial goods (for the incomes of primary producers would now fall short of consumers' outlay, and hence there would develop a net adverse balance on current account of the industrial countries); it would thereby again operate in the direction of restoring balance—through a downward adjustment of the rate of absorption of commodities by the industrial countries to limits set by the availabilities of primary products. The system of buffer stocks would thus substitute the mechanism of income-stabilising variations in stock accumulation for the crude mechanism of rising and falling commodity prices—which latter, as we have seen, operates slowly and wastefully, and tends to set up perverse and unnecessary cycles in world industrial activity.[1]

Moreover, it is yet to be demonstrated that a monetary system consisting of paper currencies convertible only into each other can ever succeed in keeping their value stable in terms of commodities. Though the role of gold has been purely ephemeral ever since the 1920s, the formal though distant link embodied in the Bretton Woods system sufficed to maintain the illusion that dollars were as good as gold, and that commodities have a (long-run) *normal* dollar price, around which their market prices

[1] Looking at the matter from another angle, a system of this kind would enormously enhance the effectiveness of monetary policy. For the international monetary authority would then come to regulate the supply of basic money (or "very high powered money") through open market operations in commodity markets (and thereby ensure that such operations have a direct and powerful effect on demand and on incomes) and not in the market for high-grade substitutes for money (such as Treasury bills) the income effects of which are both slow and highly uncertain.

fluctuate. The formal demonetisation of gold, as subsequent events have shown, has greatly weakened this stabilising force in the markets, and I do not believe that the regulation to the money supply, when "money supply" means current account deposits and other forms of liquid financial assets, could ever be an adequate substitute for direct convertibility of money into commodities or that without such convertibility we could, in an unregulated market economy, create a monetary medium that is adequate for maintaining stability whilst giving a free rein to the forces of economic expansion.

INDEX TO AUTHORS